THE HOLY SPIRIT

Amazing Power for Everyday People

"Everyone who gets their hands on this book should be prepared. This book is careful, respectful and bold. Anyone who reads '*THE HOLY SPIRIT: Amazing Power for Everyday People*' will walk away humbled, grateful and hungry for more of the Spirit's work in their lives and more effect of the Spirit's work through them. After reading this book, I was taken back to the sense of being a new believer, full of excitement about what God can do through me."

—William J. Powis, II
President, Barnabas Consulting, Inc.

"As I read, my walls of wariness tumbled and my relationship with God deepened. Susan Rohrer's common-sense approach uses Scripture and her own experiences to unlock the mysteries of the Holy Spirit. This book is a life-changing 'must read' for every Christian."

—Catherine Palmer
Missionary, award-winning and bestselling Author

"This book is a challenge to the common man to really live by faith, not by dogma. For those of us who seek higher ground, this is a delightful roadmap, a '*PILGRIM'S PROGRESS*' for the modern age!"

—Carter Adams
Principal, Lighting Virginia, Bible Study Teacher of 25 years

D1377838

"This book is not for the faint of heart Christian. Are you ready to dig deep? This book will take you on a journey to learn about the Holy Spirit, the gifts, and about hearing and discerning God's voice."

—Cheryl McKay
Screenwriter of *The Ultimate Gift,* and *Never the Bride;*
Author of *Finally the Bride: Finding Hope While Waiting*

"While a Christian since my youth, and familiar with the Church's 'traditional' teaching about the Holy Spirit, this biblically-sound, well-researched book was instrumental in unleashing the true Person and Power of the Holy Spirit in my own 'everyday' life. He has not only transformed me inwardly, but has equipped me to utilize my spiritual gifts far more effectively and fruitfully within the Church. I highly recommend this book for any follower of Jesus who yearns to experience a greater sense of His life-changing freedom, power, and purpose in 'everyday' life."

—Wendy Caskey
Wife, Mother of two, Women's Ministries Leader

"Whether you are Jesus on the road to the Cross, the Apostles witnessing in the first century, or a contemporary Christian participating in God's mission to redeem this world, you need the Holy Spirit to power your mission. This book is a 'must read' for any Christian, young or mature, who wants to understand how the Holy Spirit can completely change your life as a disciple of Jesus. In her compelling analysis of Ezekiel 47:1–12, readers are enticed to dive into the life-giving river of the Holy Spirit. You'll be glad you did."

—Julie Leib
Small Group Leader, Women's Bible Study Coach

"In His loving kindness, God miraculously placed this inspirational and instructive book into my hands. As an everyday believer with a lifelong passion for seeking the presence of God, 'The Holy Spirit: Amazing Power for Everyday People' played a profound role in my relationship with the Holy Spirit. I encourage the reader to study the Scriptures and Rohrer's text with an open mind—setting aside preconceptions, theological constructs and denominational tradition—while asking the Holy Spirit to teach, counsel and guide. It is humbling to realize the gift we have been promised is not only a personal blessing, but empowers us to impact the world for God's glory."

—Barbara Quillen Egbert
Wife & Mother,
Women's Ministry Leader,
Author of *Portrait of a Woman and Jesus*

THE HOLY SPIRIT

Amazing Power for Everyday People

SUSAN ROHRER

Infinite Arts Media

THE HOLY SPIRIT:
AMAZING POWER
FOR EVERYDAY PEOPLE

Written by Susan Rohrer

Kindly direct all professional inquiries via Infinite Arts Media at:
InfiniteArtsMgmt@gmail.com

Readers may contact author at:
shelfari.com/susanrohrer

Except as otherwise noted, all
Scripture quotations taken from the
New American Standard Bible®,
Copyright © 1960, 1962, 1963, 1968, 1971, 1972, 1973,
1975, 1977, 1995 by The Lockman Foundation
Used by permission." (www.Lockman.org)

Scripture quotations noted as ASV are from:
THE HOLY BIBLE, American Standard Version,
which is in the public domain.

Author photograph by Jean-Louis Darville, used by permission.

Published in the United States of America

First Edition 2011

Acknowledgments

My heartfelt gratitude goes out to the many people who have so generously encouraged, exhorted, and helped me along the way to publishing this book, including those who are mentioned in brief anecdotes throughout these pages. To those special friends and family members: though I may have described you in general ways or changed names mentioned for the protection of your privacy, know that you are dearly loved by this author and even more so by the merciful God who has graced me to take this journey of faith with you.

To my Teacher

"But the Helper, the Holy Spirit, whom the Father will send in
My name, He will teach you all things, and bring to your
remembrance all that I have said to you."

John 14:26

Table of Contents

Preface

Ever wonder what you're not hearing about the supernatural power of the Holy Spirit? What happened to the greater works Jesus said His followers would do in His name?

Granted, in all of Christendom, it's tough to find thornier issues than those swirling around the least known person of the Godhead—The Holy Spirit—tougher still to navigate these waters with grace. Politics abound, denominations have split, leaders agree to disagree, and often table the delights of God's River as taboo. Fear and control dominate as many opt out of addressing key passages of Scripture, bereaving countless congregations of much-needed instruction on this vital subject. Willful ignorance is epidemic, while the continuing wonders of the Holy Spirit remain hidden in plain sight.

The tragic result: much of the Church of our miracle-working God is reduced to operating predominantly on natural effort, denying the supernatural power needed by and promised to every believer.

Make no mistake. This book is decidedly pro-church. It is written out of enormous affection and respect for the faithful Bride of Christ, as well as a desire to see all of her members set aside man-made traditions and seriously consider what the Bible really has to say about what might just be Christianity's best-kept secret: the all too often marginalized Third Person of the Trinity.

Peppered with contemporary anecdotes, this book tracks an in-depth, Bible-based exploration of the Person and supernatural gifts of the Holy Spirit, the majority of which were never presented to the author in traditional Christian teaching. Therein lies the need for everyone who claims the name of Jesus to bravely and personally investigate the significant body of Scripture so many avoid, to allow the Holy Spirit to equip and mobilize us to truly experience God's uncommon graces, and to serve in the fullness of His amazing power.

CHAPTER ONE

Father, Son, and Holy Who?

While making small talk at a party, a man I'd just met arrested me with an honest question. He put it something like this: "I don't mean this to sound rude, but...who are you to write a book about the Holy Spirit?" I could feel God encouraging my uncelebrated heart as I answered, "I'm nobody; I'm just an everyday believer—a girl with a Bible—who found out something that her church never told her, that God can move in supernatural power through every believer, even through nobodies like me."

Seriously. If this were a book on resume writing or even listing in the Personals, anyone with an ounce of business savvy would advise, "Lead with your strong suit. Flash those credentials." So, this is the part where one would think any respectable author would do just that. I'd tout years in seminary, ordination, and official affiliations—only, oops! I have none of those traditional qualifications.

Right from the start, I'm going to be straight with you. As of this writing, I am not lettered in theology. I'm not ordained. I hold no church title or position. My knowledge of Greek and Hebrew is limited to what I look up—a word, phrase, or verse at a time. I am just a flawed, forgiven, garden-variety believer with a college education, a rank and file member of the body of Christ.

You may have read any number of books on this subject, written by giants of the faith. I am not one of them. But though I'm a contented nobody within theological circles, perhaps my very lack of stature there will help you relate to this take on how everyday people can move in the amazing power of the Holy Spirit, especially if you're a Jane or John Doe believer like me.

Some might say that working in the entertainment industry isn't an altogether ordinary career path. But I see the opportunities I've been given there as all the more evidence of what can happen in an ordinary life left open to the extraordinary graces of the Holy Spirit. I'll take credit for all my mistakes along the way—trust me, I've made plenty—but when it comes to the truly good stuff, let me go on record here. Anything of note about me is an unmerited gift from the God who changed my life decades ago, and who still astonishes me with His wonder-working power through commonplace believers to this day.

From my earliest recollections, I believed in God. I was raised by wonderfully functional, loving Christian parents. We had family devotions, grace before meals. I went to Sunday School and church virtually every week of my life. There was choir, youth group, Christian summer camp, Bible Studies—you name it, I went—collecting a broad working knowledge of traditional Christian theology along the way. It was in my mind as I grew and (predictably for a middle child) rebelled as a teen, but it was not in my heart, certainly in no way the passion it became for me after I made a full-on commitment to God at almost seventeen.

So, what turned the head-knowledge of a rebellious teenaged girl toward a vital relationship with God? A teenaged boy, of course! Michael was unlike any Christian I had ever encountered. He was a championship surfer and effortlessly cool. God had used Michael's magnetic personality to lead countless teenagers to redemption, some who would have been considered very tough cases. He was at the center of a revival that touched off at his high school, and then spread to mine as well as other schools in the area. The more I watched Michael, I knew he had something I didn't have, something I wanted.

On March 12, 1972, I prayed with Michael to receive Jesus, outside of a church, in the back seat of a car. In one glorious moment, my sins were washed away and I was brought into relationship with God. After all my grimy rebellion, I felt refreshingly clean. There was an indescribable dousing of love, joy and peace. I didn't know that the Holy Spirit had come to live in me. I just knew I was an entirely new person after I gave my life to Jesus.

The change in me was as radical as it was apparent to my secular friends. A former boyfriend taunted that I'd never make it as a believer.

He bet I'd be back to my old ways within a month. My closest friend distanced herself, saying I was just going through a phase. But the rejection of my peers didn't matter anymore, because I was truly in love, for the first time in my life. I ate, drank and breathed Jesus, the lover of my soul.

The seed of faith took root inside me as Michael and I developed a very pure, close relationship. He discipled me intensely, through Bible studies and impromptu prayer meetings, as I eagerly explored the faith to which I'd once only given intellectual assent.

Now, for a rookie among the rank and file of the redeemed, I thought I had a pretty good handle on the basics when I made my commitment to Jesus. Ballpark estimate—I figured I'd heard maybe a thousand or so sermons by then. (Take fifty-two Sundays over almost seventeen years; throw in tons of sermonettes at Vacation Bible School, plus Christian summer camp, an evangelical crusade or two, and you pretty much get the picture.) So, as you might imagine, I grew like a pre-schooled weed after making my commitment, much to the delight of those who had prayed for me before I'd met Michael. But before long, I remember being sincerely cautioned about the Holy Spirit by a trusted older woman.

I must confess that though I already knew a respectable amount about the Father and about Jesus, when it came to the Spirit, it really was more like *Father, Son, and Holy Who?* Don't get me wrong. I'd heard of the Holy Spirit by name. My mainline denominational upbringing was replete with vague references to Him in blessings, hymns and benedictions, let alone all those sermons. I'd even heard quite a bit about the fruits of the Spirit. But I knew virtually nothing about who the Holy Spirit is as a person, or about the manifest power of the Spirit Jesus said believers would need to equip them as His witnesses. What's more, I was clueless about this miraculous power being available in the here and now. Sure, the pastor led us in prayer for the sick from the pulpit, but I'd never heard of anyone actually getting healed, much less in answer to the prayers of everyday believers like me.

Naturally, when this older woman warned me about what was a taboo subject in my traditional church, I listened attentively. Not wanting the joy of my new birth to be spoiled by the controversy that had surfaced amongst her peers, she urged me to be very wary of anyone who might try to tell me about being *"baptized with the Holy Spirit."* She reasoned that it was an experience that had happened once and for all at Pentecost. She pleaded with me not to listen to anyone on the subject of speaking in tongues, a phenomenon she accepted as only for the first century and that she specifically cautioned was *"of the devil"* in contemporary practice.

You must understand. This woman loves God with all her heart and is still genuinely devoted to Him as of this writing. She is every bit as saved as I am. She was in leadership. She was much more mature in the Lord, and exemplary in the fruits of the Spirit. I had no reason to resist her admonition. I was happy, comfortable, and blossoming in my relationship with Jesus. So, I put her fears to rest, saying that I hadn't even heard of these things anyway. Her traditional theology fit neatly into the foundation I was building. It dovetailed with everything I'd ever heard from the pulpit. It wasn't scary or weird. I embraced it.

Freakishly soon, Michael and I were at a gathering of new believers when, lo and behold, the subjects of baptism with the Holy Spirit and power gifts were raised. With the best of intentions, I parroted the dire warning I had been given, saying that I'd been told those things were only for the heroes of the faith in Bible times, that they weren't from God now, much less for everyday Christians like me.

Imagine my unmitigated horror when, later that night, Michael privately confided in me that he had been baptized with the Holy Spirit and that, worse, he spoke in tongues! Seeing how rattled I was, he didn't push me, but he did ask me to pray about it.

You bet I prayed! I remember hitting my knees as soon as Michael left, praying desperately that God would reveal the truth to him and save him from the terrible error he was practicing. That's when it came to me. Suddenly, I knew what to do. I decided that it would not be enough to simply tell Michael he was wrong. I needed to show him all the correction I was convinced I'd find in the Bible, something I knew he'd never refute. So, I set about scouring the Scriptures about this subject, deeply concerned to rescue my dear friend.

Funny thing, though—the more I dug into the Bible to prove Michael wrong, the more the Scriptures themselves convinced me that Michael was right, and that it was I who had wrongly adopted a doctrine based on errant human traditions, rather than on the Word of

God. Sure, I found exhortations about proper use of the Holy Spirit's gifts and the rightful priority of the fruits; however, I was surprised to be persuaded that my supernatural God had much more in store for me in the Spirit than I had ever anticipated in the natural.

I discovered that the wonder-working power of Jesus was poured out to supercharge the testimony of every believer, and their children, and their children's children, and as many as ever called on Jesus throughout every earthly generation. I saw in the Bible where young and old, sons and daughters alike could experience this. Shocking, huh? I was astonished to see that this power wasn't reserved just for leadership, but that it was also not only available, but encouraged for commonplace believers, even wet behind the ears teenagers like I was at the time. I found out that if I really wanted to be like my Lord Jesus, that meant that, in addition to walking in His grace and truth, even I could walk in His miraculous power, available through the Holy Spirit.

Now, one would think that this kind of epiphany would have sent me excitedly diving into the river of God's empowering Spirit. But like a child who hesitates, yet hopes her father will catch her when she leaps off the edge into the deeps for the first time, I still wrestled big-time with fear. Sure, it made sense that our supernatural God could operate through His people in supernatural ways, but faced with that moment of jumping off truth, I confess that my prayer went something like this:

> *"Okay, Lord, I can see in your Word that this is of You, and You have this for people like me, and I'll do it if You want me to, but right now, I'm just really, really scared. But if I have to, okay. Go ahead."*

Surprise! Nothing happened. This came as a spectacular relief. It also taught me an early lesson about the Holy Spirit: *He is a great gentleman.* He did not push me to go deeper in Him when, clearly, I wasn't ready. Rather, He waited patiently for me to not only be just okay with Him manifesting Himself in me. He waited till I desired Him to do so. I trust that He will be that same understanding guide with you, taking things at your individual pace.

Personally, I was reassured when the Bible confirmed that the timing of this process is different for different people. Like Michael, there are those who gleefully cannonball into the Spirit's river while others, like me, stick a toe in, then wade a bit, acclimating as they go progressively deeper, till they're finally ready to let Jesus fully immerse them in the Spirit's waters. As you might guess from that prayer I prayed, it wasn't being baptized with the Holy Spirit I feared so much. I was already enjoying the company of His indwelling presence. It was the possibility of those powerful gifts that freaked me out, especially the terrifying prospect of speaking in tongues.

Just past that month my former boyfriend gave me to renege on my commitment to Jesus, I was on the beach, taking Jesus' hand, asking Him to baptize me with the Holy Spirit. Michael and I went out with a couple of other teenagers on a cloudy night—no moon, no stars. Only the light of God illuminated our hearts as we prayed a simple prayer that the indwelling Spirit would overflow the confines of my being. I surrendered myself to the movement of His current, trusting wherever He would take me.

The Holy Spirit responded to my invitation with a gentle effervescence. I exuded faith as I discerned that the He was no longer only indwelling me, He was also falling on me, enveloping me in a deeper way, baptizing me with power. I didn't speak in tongues that night, but somehow I knew that when I was ready, I would. I just opened myself to receive whatever gifts the Spirit wanted me to have, not even knowing what they all were. My heart was set ablaze with the fire of God and His glow shone on my face.

Michael jubilantly ran to the edge of the Atlantic. He called out toward the hazy heavens, thanking God for answering our prayer. Instantly, one radiant star broke through the pervasive cloud cover to the east, glimmering in bright confirmation. The four of us celebrated with abandon.

After that night on the beach, I began to see more evidences of the power I'd received by faith. There was no still unknown language of prayer, but I enjoyed a continual shower of God's comforting presence. That's why the contrast was so distinct when I first discerned an enemy intruder. I didn't know anything about the distinguishing of spirits as a gift yet, but I'd read in the Bible that God could protect me during any enemy attack. Just like Jesus in the wilderness following His baptism, I believed I could prevail in the power of the Holy Spirit.

As I walked into my room that night, instead of the warmth and light I had come to know, a chilling darkness assaulted me. Oddly, it was settled on a psychedelic poster that still hung on my wall, a symbolic remnant of my rebellion against God and my parents. There I was, still feeding on the milk of the Gospel, and yet I quickly found myself in a very meaty situation. How was I, an everyday baby believer, to deal with this all by myself?

Well, I wasn't all by myself anymore. The ever-present Holy Spirit brought reinforcing Scripture to mind. I firmly rebuked that demonic spirit and ordered it to leave in the name of Jesus. I didn't stomp, flail or get near that poster, but the moment I spoke Jesus' name, the poster spontaneously fell off the wall and crashed to the floor. No kidding. The evil presence abruptly vanished and the Holy Spirit flooded me with peace. It was a striking reminder that it's not about the stature or maturity of the believer; it's about the power of God.

During my late teens, the Holy Spirit began to introduce me to more supernatural gifts, empowering my testimony. I had read where Jesus said that His sheep would know His voice, but I started to learn what that meant on an experiential level.

One night, I remember leading a young woman to Jesus. Afterward, I sensed God's pleasure over this rebirth, accompanied by a confidence that the Holy Spirit wasn't finished moving. When we parted, I followed a subtle prompting to visit a friend.

My sweet friend had been hobbling around on crutches with a badly sprained ankle. It was swollen to the size of a grapefruit, with lots of ugly black and blue bruising curving under the anklebone. Everyone on my friend's hall knew about her condition.

When I entered my friend's room, I found her sitting on her bed with that bulging, discolored ankle propped up. Suddenly, as I looked at her, a quiet surge of faith welled up in me. Ever so gently, the Holy Spirit compelled me to pray for her. I just looked at my injured friend and spontaneously heard Him whisper: *It doesn't have to be this way.*

Though I'd never prayed for an instantaneous healing by myself before, I suddenly knew that was what I was sent there to do. Still in pain, my friend welcomed the prayer.

It was nothing fancy. I didn't beg God or get worked up. Honestly, the prayer was extremely short. I simply put my hand on her ankle and asked God to heal her in the name of Jesus, overflowing with the gift of faith I'd been given.

Within moments my friend, her roommate and I watched in amazement as all of the swelling quickly went down. (I have to say: God is so *very* cool.) It was as if a balloon suddenly deflated within her ankle until every bit of that grapefruit-shaped puffiness was gone. Next, we watched as all the bruising faded away completely, right before our astounded eyes. The whole healing process lasted about thirty seconds, after which my friend's ankle looked and felt back to normal.

Whereas she'd been unable to walk without pain or crutches, my friend leapt from her bed. She began to run through the outer hall ecstatically, jumping up and down on her ankle to show her secular hall-mates that she had been healed. As you can imagine, it caused quite a stir and opened a significant opportunity for witnessing. No one could deny that a miracle had occurred.

Remember, now, I'm only Little Miss Nobody. I was just an imperfect teenaged tree rooted by God's River, completely unworthy to drink of His wonders. This healing had nothing whatsoever to do with me, and everything to do with the power of God.

Over the decades that followed, I have been graced to experience many of the Holy Spirit's power gifts, tools that have equipped me for service, ministry, and harvest. It wasn't that I was seeking the gifts themselves or the attention they can draw. I was seeking the Giver, and the gifts were a supernatural by-product.

Along the way, the Holy Spirit tutored me about each of His manifest gifts, as the teachings of the Bible were brought to life in me and in the lives of my believing family and friends. I was healed, myself. I've seen storms calmed, blind eyes opened. Food has been multiplied, tormented souls have been delivered, and the dead have been raised—all amongst the ranks of everyday believers.

Understandably, I left the traditional church and I gravitated to fellowships that actively walked in the Spirit's power. In like-minded company, I grew from spiritual childhood, through adolescence, toward maturity. Not that I've arrived—I'm still growing every day. But eventually, I became like an overgrown bird in that comfortable nest.

In time, God urged me out of that nest and put me back into a more traditional church. Next, He moved me from a women's group that freely flowed in His power to another small group of believing women, many who had never been taught about the Holy Spirit's power, just like I hadn't, so many years ago.

After my first day there, I scanned the study materials for the coming months, since they said each woman would eventually be called upon to lead and share her personal testimony. When I saw a unit touching on spiritual gifts, I heard the still, small voice of the Lord, telling me that particular unit would be my assignment. I was not to volunteer or ask for it. I was just to wait patiently and it would simply fall to me. Indeed, a couple of months later, it did.

Reactions to my testimony were mixed. Many were amazed, intrigued to learn more. One woman looked as freaked out as I had once been. A couple of women retreated from me, having been burned by past experiences. Most hadn't had an ounce of teaching about the Holy Spirit, who He is or anything about His manifest power today, though they'd been committed believers for years. Even one of the leaders had never heard teaching on the subject. I offered to teach a Bible-based series from a detailed scriptural outline that I submitted to the leadership of the church for approval. That outline, and the resulting series I taught, became the springboard for this book.

These pages do not track the exploits of spiritual superstars. The many stories I include are about everyday sheep like me, who have become living proof that our amazing God still does wonders through all believers, even those of the most humble station within the body of Christ.

This book does not draw upon the doctrines of any particular denomination; rather, it is simply based on the actual text of the Bible, significant passages I had never been taught in my traditional church upbringing. This book charts the scriptural road map I found waiting when I searched out what might just be the best-kept secret in Christendom. It details the amazing adventure God took me on as He schooled me about the least known Person of our Triune Godhead: His Majesty, the Holy Spirit.

For whom is this book intended? It's for every believer who would press in to know God and to serve Him in the power Jesus said we'd need to reach the lost. It's for the newly born again as well as those more established in the faith, for both sheep and the shepherds who feed them. It's for those who've never heard or considered these things, for those hungering for further study, as well as for those who might utilize it as a framework for teaching the rank and file, especially in small group settings.

Whether you're studying this with a group, or all by yourself, know that it's okay to have questions. I've had and heard plenty along the way, many of which are fielded verbatim in this book. Don't worry that your sincere questions may offend God. He knows our hearts anyway, so why not be honest about our concerns and fears? He stands, lovingly waiting to counsel us and to confirm answers through His Word.

Before we get started, I'll make two requests of you, Dear Reader:

First, please take the time to look up and consider each of the many Bible references you'll find in this book. That way, you'll build a solid foundation of Scripture for what you believe, rather than simply relying on what I have to say or what other human beings may have told you. You'll see with your own eyes what the Bible really has to say about the Holy Spirit's ministry in the life of every believer, which will help you to separate the nourishing wheat of truth from the chaff of human tradition.

Second, and I believe of great importance, I'd ask—before you turn this page—will you take the time to pray and ask the Holy Spirit to reveal the truth about Himself to you? That's right. Resist the temptation to read on until you've asked God to help you understand everything He would have to say to you. Know that even the most unsung sheep of His flock are very welcome to this kind of direct, individualized tutoring.

So, please, stop right now and open your heart to what God can show you through His Word. Tell the Father you're inviting the Holy Spirit to be your personal Teacher as you set out on this adventure in the name of Jesus—our Savior, Baptizer and Friend.

CHAPTER TWO

Why I Hadn't Heard This in a Thousand Sermons

What I have heard more than once from the pulpit is: We don't talk about the Holy Spirit much here. Years ago, I asked my church leadership why. "Too controversial," was the reply. I was told that the denomination was split on the subject. Some were certain that the manifest gifts ceased at the end of the first century, and others believed that they continue to this day. Rather than risk upsetting either group, their solution was to withhold teaching either persuasion, tacitly tucking the Third Person of the Trinity into a "we don't go there" closet.

Since the Holy Spirit fell at Pentecost, He has created quite a buzz. Two thousand years later, there's still enough disagreement over His supernatural work to make Him a virtually taboo subject in major Christian circles. Churches have split, whole new denominations have formed, and significant portions of Scripture aren't preached or taught, much less openly practiced. Family and friends become polarized on the subject, giving rise to the widespread misconception that God's powerful River is far more foreboding than delightful, way too treacherous for the rank and file believer.

It's odd, really. Who wouldn't like to distribute miraculously multiplied food to the hungry or to still a raging hurricane in the name of Jesus? Who wouldn't like to be an instrument in seeing a suffering loved-one healed? Who wouldn't want to hear God's voice? Who wouldn't think it could be useful to speak in an unlearned language? There's that flashing red hot button. But I'm getting ahead of myself.

Suffice it to say, that though even the most cautious of believers pray for healing, when it comes to certain of the Spirit's wonders, particularly those that involve the concept of two-way communication with God, people get nervous, even downright testy. One-way communication to God through prayer is encouraged, but when it comes to God communicating back to us, that gets dicey. After all, how are we to know it really is God? How do we know it's not just us, attributing our own desires to the Almighty? How do we know we're not crazy or deceived?

"But I've had a bad experience with this."

It's easy to see why, over the centuries, walking in the supernatural power of the Holy Spirit began to seem way too messy to many in church leadership. Rather than follow the apostle Paul's admonitions about prioritizing the fruits and maintaining proper order in the use of gifts, many have gone beyond maintaining order to restricting, from restricting to quenching, and from quenching to actually forbidding the scriptural flow of God's power.

It's not that we don't trust God per se. It's that we don't trust people to truly manifest His Spirit. But what's interesting is, that's exactly what God is willing to do, even with the least of His flock. Without respect of persons, He says we know His voice. He entrusts us with His power.

It's understandable that people are wary. Face it. Many have been burned. There has been error. Countless believers have been ambushed by over anxious proponents of the gifts. And since it seems wildly inappropriate to fight about a Spirit who is all about love, we drop back. We get sensible. We relax into what is comfortable, readily understood and natural to us. We accept a historical view of the miraculous work of Jesus. For all practical purposes, we confine the Holy Spirit to producing character fruits. We embrace a natural God, even if, in the exercise of our free will, it means stripping the Almighty of His contemporary privilege to move in supernatural power, power that was freely offered to all children of all generations who believe.

"Yeah...but it's nice here and I so hate conflict."

So do I. Particularly within the church, we make nice. Discord feels inappropriate, despite the fact that our exemplary Savior raised conflict at every turn. But before we jettison the power of the Third Person of the Trinity in the interest of accord, let's remember: Each person of the Godhead is controversial by nature, *because each challenges our human desire to control.*

Admittedly, the Holy Spirit causes a stir. He disrupts the flesh and creates controversy. This is a good thing. It's one of the ways He gets unbelievers' attention and compels believers to act upon what they believe. Even though we claim to have turned control of our lives over to God, when it comes to His Spirit, we tend to either: a) take control back for ourselves, or b) divert control to our spiritual leaders, abdicating personal responsibility to seek God about this. We neglect to study the Bible ourselves to learn about what we don't know or understand.

Don't get me wrong. I am strongly pro-church. Submission to leadership can be a very good thing. It is biblically advised, but it is meant to foster one-on-one relationship with the whole Godhead, not replace, derail, or quench that. While we respect our leaders, while we look to them for guidance, we should remember that, as when Jesus walked the earth in the flesh, human leadership can be mistaken, even radically so.

Since so many churches are split on this subject, that can mean at least half of these dear souls are sincerely mistaken, and I include those who fail to act on what they rightly believe in that number (John 12:42–43). I am so grateful to God for the move of the Holy Spirit that has begun as our local church leaders have bravely invited Him to move in power. But sadly, as many leaders avoid over-emphasizing the gifts, the pendulum often swings to the other extreme, eliminating their operation altogether.

So, how can we, as the rank and file, gauge if our church is guiding us correctly or in error, especially if even our highly educated leadership can't agree? I find no substitute for the regular, personal reading of God's Word. Godly leaders wisely encourage private study of Scripture, unthreatened by what we will discover.

My goal is neither to draw you away from the covering of your leadership nor into my way of thinking. (In fact, I welcome you to ignore my interpretations and experiences, and just read through the Scriptures I cite in this book.) My goal is simply to provoke you to honestly examine exactly what the Bible has to say about the power of the Holy Spirit, and to consider the impact He might have on your testimony to the lost. It's not just about a chapter or phrase here or there. I'm not suggesting that your theology should be built on a stray verse, taken out of context. We are talking about a major body of Scripture, a clear pattern of confirmed instruction on dynamic life in the Holy Spirit, personally given for every believer.

"Isn't preserving unity the most important thing?"

Often, when questions are raised about the Holy Spirit's wonders, leaders take a cautionary stance, avoiding discussion in the interest of preserving unity. We're most comfy when we're in agreement. Conflict is messy and—didn't even Jesus pray that we'd be one?

Read John 17:11, 20–23, Jesus' earnest prayer that we would be one. It follows three chapters containing explanations about how the Holy Spirit would preserve unity through continuing communication. Notice that Jesus didn't just pray that we would simply be *one*. He prayed that we'd be one *in the same way Jesus and the Father are one*. It's not a matter of being randomly one with other people, even other believers. Yes, preserving church unity with God, through Christ, in the Spirit is vital. That's what Jesus was praying, knowing how the world, even the church itself, would threaten that holy and complete unity.

Whereas holy unity with our brethren can be a very good thing, a place where God commands blessing (Psalm 133), misplaced unity can be a wolf in sheep's clothing, a detriment to our relationship with God, depending on the cause around which that brand of unity rallies (James 4:4). Consider Genesis 11:1–8, an ancient instance of human unity that was counter to the purposes of God. God deliberately divided them, knowing their misguided unity would vault human ingenuity against the knowledge of God (II Corinthians 10:5).

Check out the prophets, one after another, challenging those within Israel who united in wandering away from God. Jeremiah was appointed to speak the words God put into his mouth, prophetic words purposed to pluck out and overthrow human error before building and planting anew (Jeremiah 1:9–10).

Unified rebellion within Israel manifested in overt forms such as worshiping idols; however, the enemy's more subversive work of "unity" was to get the religious leaders to unify around man-made religious traditions, so much so that they resisted the God they were supposed to be worshiping, as well as the promised Messiah God sent (Mark 7:6–9).

Yes, Jesus was all about unity with God, but He was also big into breaking up the fallow ground of religious tradition that we so easily fall into and idolize. That's right. Unity can actually become an idol if we're more concerned with preserving unity with people than in being one with our Triune God.

Absolutely, interact with grace. Seek unity within the body, but only if that unity preserves solidarity with all of God's purposes. Quenching the Holy Spirit may preserve accord with people, but it cuts us off from union with God. So, carefully examine God's Word concerning the Holy Spirit and stand in unity with what Scripture deems to be good (I Thessalonians 5:19–21).

"But this causes division. That can't be good. Can it?"

Indeed, division can be a destructive thing, but it can also be a vehicle of growth. Check out Jesus' words in Matthew 12:25–32, where Jesus preached that a kingdom divided against itself can't stand. We need unity within the kingdom, no doubt. But what do we need to rally around? God's Word. As much as we may respect church doctrine, leadership, and tradition, the final authority that should unite us is an adherence to God's Word as recorded in the Old and New Testaments. In accordance with Hebrews 4:12, there is everything right about dividing the truth of the Bible from the error of human traditions.

Jesus' teachings and actions were revolutionary, even offensive to many. He motivated people to take a stand that could separate them from those of contrary persuasions, even religious leadership.

Think about this as it applies today. Are we more concerned with standing with religious people or standing with God? Are we willing to water down or essentially omit Scripture in the interest of getting along?

Jesus said we're either for Him or against Him, preparing us to make a decision that may potentially divide us, even from the well-meaning leadership of our day, in order to unite us with Him. Then, He punctuated that point with a sobering warning about speaking against the Holy Spirit, a subject that has remained chronically controversial all the way to the contemporary age.

"Aren't we cautioned to turn away from those who cause division?"

Definitely, but look up Romans 16:17. We are only instructed to *turn from those who cause division by teaching what is contrary to the Word of God!* Conversely, if a believer is teaching the truth about the Holy Spirit from a firm foundation of Scripture, even if it naturally divides us from those who resist what the Bible says, we should stand on God's side of the dividing line.

I am not advocating Christian anarchy. I will be forever grateful for the spiritual leaders God has placed in my life. But as we mature in the Lord, it's important to prayerfully consider what sort of teaching is fashioning our faith, including this substantial arena.

If there had been no danger of false teaching within the church, there would have been no need for the caution of Colossians 2:8, warning us not to be spoiled by following the traditions of men, rather than following Christ.

Know that there are many devoted believers who mean well, but who have mistakenly embraced the traditions of men at the expense of following the instructions of the Bible concerning the operation of the Holy Spirit. That is why it's so vital that we go directly to the source and study God's Word for ourselves. If you find everything tracks with what you're being taught, then hallelujah! If not, then reject the traditions of men and embrace the truth of the Bible.

"But my church says the supernatural gifts of the Spirit ceased after the first century."

Since Christendom's leaders are split about whether or not the manifestations of the Holy Spirit are for today, how do we know what to believe? We simply read the Bible. We find God's specific words to inform us about if and when the gifts of the Holy Spirit will cease.

I challenge each of you to dig in, find out if there's any place in Scripture that says the supernatural power of the Spirit should or would die off with the original apostles. To the contrary, Scripture confirms Peter's declaration of Acts 2:38–39, that this promise is for every believer of every generation now or to come who calls on the name of the Lord. But don't just believe it because I say it. Find out for yourself. Or, if you disagree with what I'm saying, prove me wrong! Make sure any verse you use to evidence your point doesn't require you to ignore other Scripture. That means we need to carefully study the Bible, all of it.

A common argument that the supernatural gifts ceased after the first century asserts that these gifts must have ceased because we don't see them practiced in the church today. It's a conclusion based upon human behavior rather than the Word of God. What's more, it requires its proponents to essentially negate major points of Scripture that are contrary to the cessationist position (cessationists believe that the supernatural gifts of the Holy Spirit ceased after the first century).

Can you see what a slippery slope this could be? Imagine if other major directives of the New Testament were dismissed simply because fallible leaders failed to adhere to them or no longer found them to be relevant once the original apostles died. This flawed logic smacks of following after the "traditions of men" Scripture clearly exhorts against, yet all too many have unknowingly assimilated into a long-standing culture of man-made traditionalism.

Hear me when I stress that I am a huge fan of biblical leadership. Whereas traditionalists mix in fallible doctrines devised by man, biblical leaders rightly reject man's traditions and focus on the comprehensive counsel of God's authoritative Word.

"How can I tell man-made traditions from biblical practices?"

Do what I did. Search the actual Scriptures, cover to cover. Some commentaries can be helpful, but since men wrote them, they may also be laced with the human author's erroneous traditional thought. You may even find that there are "study Bibles" that, in addition to the Scriptures, include cessationist commentary in the margins, printed right on the same page as God's inspired Word. So, be careful about what you accept beyond the actual biblical text.

For the purpose of this study, I urge you to back-burner commentaries (even mine!) and resolve to purely search God's Word. Test everything I say by the authoritative standard of Scripture. Allow the Holy Spirit to teach you about Himself and His amazing power. The more clearly you see the truth of God's Word, the more readily you'll recognize the counterfeits of human tradition.

Take a look at II Corinthians 10:3–5. (*Really. Stop and look it up.*)

As we get to know the Holy Spirit, we want to destroy every stronghold and imagination of man that has been exalted above the knowledge of God. We should make sure that the relationship we're building with the Spirit is firmly based on God's Word. Dig in and find scriptural support for every aspect of the Spirit you embrace. Bravely tear down old experiences or mind-sets that have no foundation in Scripture. Reject any teaching that has raised itself up above the knowledge of God as revealed in His Word.

"What if I realize I've been following man-made traditions?"

No matter how much you love your church traditions, your pastor, your leaders, your family, and friends, I exhort you to set your heart to love God's Word more. Every doctrine you embrace should mesh with the whole Bible, including the many passages cited in this book.

Over the course of many years, since I first set off on this journey, I have read the entire Bible countless times. I still devour it daily. The more I read it, the more I see that the whole of Scripture supports the continuation of the Holy Spirit's powerful supernatural work. I have yet to find any verse or passage in the Bible to support the contention that His wonders have ceased, except as tragically quenched by man today. And yes, the results of quenching really can be tragic.

"Doesn't this seem like we're getting off track?"

Do you know how to use a compass? Contrary to popular assumption, if you're hiking through a forest due north to a spring at a particular location, you don't just walk with the compass and follow the direction of the arrow. If you do, you might head generally in the right direction, but you'll gradually drift off track. What seems like just a step or two off track will incrementally lead you far off course and leave you very thirsty, maybe even perilously so.

Compasses are correctly followed by use of a leapfrogging system. One charts a sure course by finding successive new markers, confirmed by the compass before leaving the prior marker. The parched hiker can then be assured of successfully reaching the sustaining spring.

The Bible is our compass. If we head off in what appears to be the right general direction without confirming our course, we, like the hiker, will invariably get off track, perhaps only a little at first, but before long, we can be miles from the life-giving waters of the Holy Spirit.

The Bible itself demonstrates the tendency of human beings to get off track with God. Over and over, God directs His people. They nod their heads and set off. Life happens. After a little while, it seems too much bother to observe every point of God's direction. The conscientious are mocked and overruled as the crowd follows what they're starting to forget of God's specifically outlined path, gradually getting off course. Pretty soon, the skewed trail they've blazed in the flesh becomes familiar. It begins to feel comfortable, like it's the track. They camp and procreate in this place. As time goes on and generation teaches generation about where they're headed, they make a practice of following this skewed trail, convinced that this now time-honored tradition is on track with God's original directions.

So, yes. Let's acknowledge that there is something that can feel off track about exploring the supernatural power of the Holy Spirit in the here and now; however, it only feels off track to us because we've been on that skewed trail so long. We have developed such a stronghold of human tradition that we no longer know what the real track is. Sadly, we allow this man-made doctrine to trump Scripture.

How do we get back to the real track? We set aside our traditions. Even if it means we have to go it alone, we get out our compass: the Bible.

In fact, pick up your Bible right now. Seriously. Look at it and say: *"This is the track!"* Say it out loud if it helps to break you free of doubt or fear about taking this revolutionary path along God's Holy River. Then, continue with me as we follow Scripture's compass, point to point, carefully lining up each directive, faithfully staying on course, till we reach the wellspring of power Jesus told us we'd need to equip us for service, ministry, and harvest.

"My church already teaches that this is for today."

That's great. I hope they do. I've just written this book because my churches didn't. With relatively few exceptions, this book explores scriptural passages I didn't hear about from the pulpit. There are, however, many churches that are diligent to teach the Bible on this subject, many pastors who bravely preach the uncompromised Word about the Holy Spirit, and who regularly meet the challenges of godly correction as their congregations operate in His power.

But Friends—even those who sit under what is called *"charismatic"* teaching—you would do well to study the Bible carefully for yourself to make sure what you're embracing is based on Scripture itself rather than something man has amplified beyond the actual text to support a man-made point. Please don't assume that because this subject is being preached that you are receiving a balanced view. Whatever you're hearing should readily stand under the close scrutiny of Scripture. Shine God's light on it and see what's really there.

II Timothy 2:15 urges us to diligently study to show ourselves approved as workers who needn't be ashamed because we're handling the pure Word of Truth in the right way. So, roll up your cuffs and wade into the water! Examine the Bible for yourself. You can even look at the Greek and Hebrew like I do. (There are great Bible programs available for free on the Internet that allow you to compare Bible translations with the original language.)

I Timothy 4:14–16 exhorts those who are already gifted to not only persist in using our gifts, but also to pay close attention to what we teach concerning them, to diligently continue in them, for the sake of others as well as ourselves. We don't want to be numbered among the overzealous souls who are responsible for turning off, burning, or leading others off God's track concerning His Spirit. We should want to teach the whole truth and nothing but the truth, even if that means admitting that some things are open to legitimate interpretation.

"Aren't the meanings of many Scriptures debatable?"

Indeed, many things are clear in Scripture, while others leave some room for interpretation of meaning. While we should graciously stand on what is clear, we should resist the human impulse to push others into our own views, especially in these interpretable areas. Over and over, I've found that if I gently direct others to Scripture, I can trust the Holy Spirit to counsel those who are sincere seekers.

As demonstrated in Scripture, God moves upon different people in different ways. Let's let go of the fleshy need to affirm our experiences by insisting that it happen to everyone the same way it happened to us. Remember the Holy Spirit is gentle. He didn't push us and we shouldn't push Him on others. Rather, we should treat those who differ with love, patience, and humility.

"What should I do about my relationship with the Holy Spirit?"

First, pray. Below is a simple pneumonic device, based on the word **PRAY**. In distilled terms, it contains the essential directives of this book:

Pray that the Spirit will teach you.
Research the Bible about the Spirit.
Abandon what is contrary to the Bible.
Yield to what the Bible teaches.

Ask yourself: *Am I willing to step out in these ways?*
If not, why not? If so—let's go!

CHAPTER THREE

The Holy Spirit for Newbies

My parents closely monitored our TV and movie watching when we were kids. There was no sci-fi allowed, no violence, and there were definitely no ghosts. When I finally braved my first ghost movie, it just about scared me to running, screaming pieces. (And it was just a mild family comedy!) Ghosts were dark, spooky, dangerous spirits, ready to yank you into the underworld. Even at Christian summer camp, we sat on the ground, the campfire casting eerie shadows about, as the counselor (flashlight under chin) terrified us with tales of malevolent spirits still wandering those woods. No wonder I had an apprehensive association when it came to the Holy Spirit. Weren't ghosts and spirits the same thing?

Maybe I'm not the only one who was afraid of the Holy Spirit at first. I'm not talking about the reverential kind of fear, the respectful awe we're supposed to have. It was more like the willies we get around really powerful people we don't know yet. Getting to know and love the Holy Spirit was like exposure therapy for me. It taught me that I was safe with Him. It also helped me to prioritize my relationship with the Giver over the gifts. So, as we embark on this journey together, getting acquainted seems like a good place to start. Just who is the Holy Spirit? Let's go back to the beginning.

The Holy Spirit was present, a full participant in our creation. Turn to Genesis 1:1. The word for God in this verse is Elohiym. Did you know that this word for God is plural, evidencing the active involvement of more than one member of the Godhead from our beginnings? Scan down to verse twenty-six, where God says: "Let US make man in OUR image." The Spirit was there as God formed us from the dust (Genesis 2:7). He, the Breath of God, breathed life into us, causing us to become living souls. Job 33:4 and John 6:63 confirm that it is the Spirit (*pneuma*, meaning breath) who gives life.

You'll notice that I refer to the Holy Spirit using the pronoun *He* rather than *it*. I do this because the Holy Spirit is a person, not a thing. (As in most Bible translations, I use *He* collectively, encompassing all the masculine, feminine, and gender-neutral qualities the original language denotes.)

The Holy Spirit is living and active. He has a discernable personality. As we get to know Him as a person, it feels inappropriate to refer to Him as an *it*, don't you think? Things are called *it*. Things are inanimate objects, incapable of breathing life into anyone. So, as I mention the Holy Spirit, I'll use that collective personal pronoun, respectfully recognizing the person that He is.

"So, He's a person. What is He like?"

Okay, take a moment for an exercise. Picture God the Father. Got Him in your mind's eye? All right, now picture the Son, Jesus. (Got that picture, too?) Finally, try to picture the Holy Spirit. *Hmmm...* That's understandably different from picturing the Father or the Son, even if we haven't seen them either.

We have human fathers, and artists' renderings of the Father and Jesus that contribute to our impressions of who they are and what they're like. But how do we picture the Spirit, when we have no natural reference? We turn to the Bible. Just as surely as the Scriptures inform us about the persons of God the Father, and God the Son, they paint a vivid picture of the distinct Third Person of the Trinity: the Holy Spirit.

"How does the Bible describe Him?"

Jesus said the Holy Spirit would be our Comforter, Teacher and Helper (John 14:16, 26; 16:7). He later describes Him as the Spirit of Truth (John 15:26). Paul says that if we walk in Him, we're not under the Law and we won't fulfill the lusts of the flesh (Galatians 5:14–18). That's because the Holy Spirit is that reassuring voice of God within us, who tells us what is true, right, and good, and then helps us to fulfill the Law of love in practice.

In fact, the Holy Spirit is so gracious with us that we sometimes forget He's also incredibly powerful. Did you know that the word for *power* Jesus used when He said we'd receive power (when the Holy Spirit comes upon us) is also the root word for *dynamite*? *Dunamis* literally means miraculous, violent force. That's the kind of explosive power we're promised in the dynamic personality of the Holy Spirit.

Isn't it amazing that the Spirit—who is capable of such great force—is simultaneously characterized by gentleness? This powerful Spirit is the embodiment of all of the fruits listed in Galatians 5:22–23, fruits that Scripture prioritizes above all of the marvelous gifts He distributes. The Holy Spirit is powerfully loving, commandingly joyful, actively peaceful, compellingly patient, emphatically kind, intensely good, infallibly faithful, potently gentle, and vigorously self-controlled. Who wouldn't want to know a person like this?

"Yeah, but what exactly does He do?"

With humans, we can tell a lot about a person by observing his or her actions. This is also true of the Holy Spirit.

Genesis 1:2 records our first introduction to the Spirit: *He moves* over the waters, intimately involved with what is being created. Similarly, He moves upon human hearts, convicting them of sin and drawing them to repentance and regeneration. This is Job One for the Holy Spirit.

As Jesus explained to Nicodemus in John 3:5–10, *the Spirit is the agent of being born again.* When a person receives Jesus as Savior and Lord, that person is borne of the Spirit. Paul repeatedly emphasizes the inseparable association between being "in Christ" and the presence of the indwelling Holy Spirit (Romans 8:9–15).

Once the Holy Spirit takes up residence, He tackles a substantial to-do list in the life of the yielded believer. First, let's look at exactly what Jesus says the Holy Spirit will do in our lives (John 14:26, 15:26, 16:13–15):

- *He teaches us all things.*
- *He reminds us of what Jesus said.*
- *He testifies about Jesus.*
- *He guides us into all truth.*
- *He speaks what He hears from God.*
- *He discloses to us what is to come.*
- *He glorifies Jesus.*

While many are comfortable with most of Jesus' list of the Holy Spirit's functions, there is a lot of consternation within Christendom about two aspects of His fire-power: that the Spirit will *speak* to us and that He will *disclose to us what is to come.* Many try to mute the Holy Spirit unless He is reminding us of a direct quote from Scripture, but Jesus imposed no such limitation to the Spirit's speech. There's even more anxiety about the prospect that the Holy Spirit would show us things that are to come, but that is exactly what Jesus said He would do.

I have found that the Holy Spirit speaks in ways that are not only consistent with Scripture, but also very practical to my life today. Sure, there are times when God addresses more monumental issues and speaks like the voice of thunder, from a burning bush or mountain. But many times, He speaks in that still, small voice, guiding us about everyday concerns (Proverbs 1:23).

During a business trip, I remember leaving a prayer group with a strong sense of God's presence. When I got to my rental car and put my favorite coat and business bag in the trunk, I distinctly heard that quiet voice of the Holy Spirit ask: *Are you prepared to lose everything in your trunk today?* I would like to say that I listened, that I removed my coat and bag, but no. I just thought: *Hmm.* Then, I closed the trunk with my valuables inside, and drove to a shopping district for lunch. I don't think I was away from my car for thirty minutes, but when I returned, the trunk lock had been broken, and my coat and bag were gone! Believe me, I kicked myself for not being more attentive to the Holy Spirit.

Was this huge in the scope of eternity? No. Was this a direct quotation of Scripture? No, but the warning didn't conflict with Scripture, and it turned out to be valid. It was the Holy Spirit, whispering to me, as in John 16:13, about what was to come, that I would be vulnerable to robbery that day. God knew it would cost me to replace my coat and fix the trunk lock. He knew the bag had sentimental value. He knew I'd have to go through the hassle of reconstructing my address book and business materials, that I'd lose all the tax-deductible receipts I'd gathered that trip, that I'd have to cancel my credit card and replace it while on the road. He was trying to guide me; however, in this instance, I heard but didn't heed the warning. I did learn a valuable lesson, taught when the stakes were only material things.

Since then, there have been instances when the stakes have been higher, when the Holy Spirit has spoken to me about matters of spiritual import, and remembering the subtlety of His voice concerning this robbery, I try to be more sensitive to listen and respond when the Spirit speaks to me today.

Helping us with the practical concerns of living is only the tip of the iceberg. (I have to remember it's not all about me.) We can stay on the surface if we choose, or we can let the Holy Spirit draw us deeper into relationship with God.

Check out I Corinthians 2:9–14. It's a gold mine for relationship-building activities of the Holy Spirit, available to everyone who is borne of Him:

- *He reveals what God has for us.*
- *He searches the depths of God.*
- *He knows and tells us God's thoughts.*
- *He tells us what God freely gives to us.*
- *He teaches us to speak spiritual words.*
- *He helps us to spiritually discern Him.*

As if all of these wonderful functions weren't enough, Scripture goes on to describe many other activities of the Holy Spirit. He also leads, gathers, reminds, renews, generates fruit, seals, consoles, counsels, inspires, ministers, anoints, cautions, gives life, touches, distributes gifts, demonstrates God's power, intercedes, prompts, advises, abides with us, and falls upon us. He is God's supernatural presence with every believer.

"Sounds great. So, why do we tend to quench Him?"

The word *quench* means *to extinguish like a fire, to suppress, to cause to cease.* So, can a human being limit the operation of the powerful Holy Spirit? Sadly, yes. That's why Scripture urges us not to quench Him. We're not supposed to restrict or stop the Holy Spirit's flow.

Though I Thessalonians 5:19 exhorts us not to quench the Spirit, though Hebrews 10:38 reminds that God takes no pleasure in one who shrinks back from Him, and though we can see that Jesus didn't do many miracles in his hometown because of their unbelief (a form of quenching), still there is the tendency in all of us to become spiritual beavers, instinctively constructing dams along God's River.

Consider two primary reasons that human beings quench the Spirit of God:

- *Fear of the unknown*
- *The desire to maintain control*

Isn't it ironic that we fear that sweet Spirit who is there to help us? Maybe it's because we're scared He won't really be there in our time of need, that He'll embarrass us, or that He won't offer the kind of help we want. As much as the supernatural work of God fascinates, when push comes to shove, we'd rather be in the boat watching with the rest of the disciples than to be like Peter, stepping out onto the water toward Jesus.

Let's be real. We all have control issues. Even our protests that we don't have control issues are a telltale sign that we do, especially in front of other people. We like to be in charge of the way things go, but that is the way of the flesh, not of the Spirit.

In Revelation 2:6, 15, the Spirit says that He hates the *works* and *teachings* of the Nicolaitans. Ever wonder exactly what it was about the Nicolaitans, what it was that they did and taught? While evidence is not conclusive, they may have been followers of a man named Nikolaos, known as a teacher of heresies, advocating the traditions of man rather than the counsel of God.

When it comes to the Nicolaitans' deeds, it's also compelling to consider that the root Greek words *nikos* (to conquer or control) and *laos* (people) are combined roots of the Greek word *Nikolaites*. That means the *Nicolaitan* moniker can be literally translated as: *control people*. This could suggest that, like the Pharisees, Nicolaitan leadership may have been characterized by lording authority over their laity, likely out of fear things would escape their control.

Both fear and control have their fleshly offspring. Go over the following list of reasons we quench the Spirit and ask yourself which, if any, have ever pertained to you. I know that I have been guilty of quenching the Spirit because of nearly every reason here:

- *Pride*
- *Self-consciousness*
- *To avoid loss of dignity*
- *Unbelief*
- *Laziness*
- *Desire to indulge the flesh*
- *Intimidation*
- *Rejection of man*
- *Disapproval of others*
- *Because we've been burned by an impostor or a believer acting in error*

Most devastatingly of all, I think the main reason we quench the Spirit of God is simply because *we don't know Him*. He is a stranger to us.

Perhaps we're predisposed to shy away because we were raised to be wary of strangers. Our parents rightly cautioned us not to talk to strangers and definitely not to get in their cars. That's why it's so important to get to know the Holy Spirit, to realize He is to be trusted. He is family. Once we truly know Him, we will eagerly take His hand and go wherever He leads.

"What does it mean to 'grieve' the Holy Spirit?"

Think of any grief you've weathered. We grieve lost loved ones, lost jobs, lost money, lost relationships, and lost hopes. Anyone who has truly experienced grief knows that it evokes deep emotional distress, particularly if betrayal was involved. The Holy Spirit mourns, too. He suffers very real grief when we betray Him by preferring our fleshly desires to His leading.

Ephesians 4:30 exhorts us not to grieve the Holy Spirit who has sealed us for redemption. It's as if we're engaged as the bride of Christ, to the lover of our souls. Any godly bride-to-be would want to honor her betrothed. Any godly man would be grieved if his fiancé violated his trust by giving herself to another. The Holy Spirit indwells us for many purposes. One of them is to help us remain faithful as we await the marriage supper of the Lamb.

He's not spying on us from some celestial observatory. We are, in fact, housing the Holy Spirit (I Corinthians 6:19). Think of your body as a house that the Spirit of God occupies, a house that has been washed whiter than snow and filled with the fragrant aroma of Christ. Imagine how He feels when we wander back into the mud of the flesh, when we entertain the enemy, displacing His holiness, tromping the filth of sin into our houses, His temple. Let's face it. The Holy Spirit and the enemy just aren't compatible housemates. There's no way to satisfy both, and you, Mr. or Ms. Free Will, determine who stays and who gets evicted with every choice you make.

When we love people, we avoid doing things that hurt them. How much more should we honor our relationship with the resident Holy Spirit? How much more should we want Him to feel welcome, comfortable and adored while living in us? Don't you prefer the love, joy, and peace of the Holy Spirit to the destruction of the enemy anyway?

What is simple on paper is all-out war in practical living. If you don't want to grieve the Holy Spirit, don't give into the flesh. Track the surrounding verses in Ephesians 4:17–32 to identify some unwanted fleshy houseguests. In the name of Jesus, evict hardness of heart, ignorance, sensuality, impurity, greed, falsehood, theft, coarse words, bitterness, festering anger, slander, and malice. Sure, they'll pester, prod, and provoke. They're sleazy that way. They'll knock on your door all hours of the day and night, tempting you to invite them to move back in and bereave the Holy Spirit of His full and rightful occupancy in your heart.

We find a cautionary example of grieving the Holy Spirit in King Saul (Isaiah 63:10). Though Samuel had anointed Saul as king, and the

Spirit had come upon Saul mightily, speaking to him and blessing his early reign, later, Saul lapsed into the flesh, grieving the Holy Spirit. After the Lord spoke to Samuel about Saul's disobedience, Samuel confronted Saul saying:

> *"For rebellion is as the sin of witchcraft, and stubbornness is as idolatry and teraphim. Because thou hast rejected the word of Jehovah, He hath also rejected thee from being king."*
>
> *I Samuel 15:23 ASV*

Why is rebellion equated to witchcraft? Why are stubbornness and iniquity linked to idolatry? Because, when the Holy Spirit speaks and we reject His words, we grieve the Spirit by following after a false god: the enemy (Exodus 20:3). Every time we give into the flesh, we rebel against the Holy Spirit within us. In addition to the times we fall into overt sin, this includes the times when we stubbornly resist the Spirit's prompting and do nothing, taking control of our lives back for ourselves, playing right into the enemy's passive-aggressive hands.

Choice by choice, we're either putting God or the flesh on the throne. We must know that there are ramifications to such choices, but it does remain our option whether to serve the flesh or to serve God. Serving the flesh grieves the Spirit, whereas cheerful obedience to the Holy Spirit delights the heart of God.

"What about blasphemy against the Holy Spirit?"

Would it surprise you, dear Reader, if I say I'm not sure? You may have heard as many unsatisfying explanations about this as I have, some of which speculate beyond the actual text of Scripture. Frankly, I hesitated to delve into this question at first; however, it seems wrong to dodge even the toughest questions about the Holy Spirit, especially concerning how we might offend Him. So, here goes.

My first step was to pray and ask the Holy Spirit to teach me about this sin. (Though we may be confused about it, I'm sure God knows the answer.) Instead of telling you what people have had to say about this, I will simply point you to what came to me when studying what the Bible says.

Let's start by reading what three Gospels have to say on this subject. Mark 3:22–30 closely parallels Matthew 12:22–32. Luke 12:10 echoes the warning. Notice the context. Mark records that the religious leaders were saying that Jesus was possessed by Beelzebub, and that Jesus was casting out demons by the power of the devil. In effect, they attributed the work of the Holy Spirit to Satan. Jesus' caution about blasphemy against the Holy Spirit rose directly out of this wrongful attribution. It's a chilling admonition that we should all take very seriously.

Questions abound. Is there really something a human being can do that God will never forgive? What exactly is that *unforgivable sin* and is it literally unforgivable? Is there any room for interpretation in the original language? Wasn't Saul/Paul forgiven, despite the fact that he had viciously persecuted the Church, probably under the false presumption that Jesus and His Spirit-empowered followers were of the devil (I Timothy 1:12-14)? Can we be doomed forever because of a single disrespectful comment? Will we be held accountable if we didn't even know it was an unforgivable sin? Weighty questions, indeed. The original Greek sheds a little light on the subject.

Though I have much to learn about Greek, one thing I know is that there is more than one way to interpret a single word. Especially since the consequences of this sin appear to be so severe, it helps to examine some of the key words and concepts in the original language. While there is no escaping the seriousness of offending the Holy Spirit, there are nuances in key words that may offer comfort to sincere believers who fear they may have committed this sin.

First, let's look at the Greek word for *blasphemy*. The word *blasphemia* means to vilify, to speak of as vile or evil, to defame, degrade, slander, or rail against. We should never attribute the work of the Holy Spirit to the enemy, or speak anything about Him that disparages His sacred position in the Godhead. He is the antithesis of evil, so to speak of His works as evil is a dangerous offense, tantamount to asserting that the Spirit of God is subject to His vastly inferior enemy.

Think twice if you're tempted to credit the works of the Holy Spirit to Satan. We are advised to discern the spirits, but we tread on perilous ground when we mock the works of the Spirit of God, which can be deemed a form of taking the name of God the Holy Spirit in vain (Exodus 20:7).

Jesus repeatedly held the scribes and Pharisees accountable because they knew the Scriptures. They were familiar with Isaiah's messianic prophecy that the Spirit of God would empower the Christ, not the evil spirit of the enemy (Isaiah 61:1), yet they accused Jesus of blasphemy not long before they committed that act themselves (Matthew 9:3, 34). Just like the scribes and the Pharisees, modern church leaders will be held to an account when it comes to what they say about the Holy Spirit and His powerful works, especially in light of known Scripture.

What about the concept that this sin is unforgivable? The key Greek words *aphiemi* and *aphesis*, commonly translated to mean *forgive/forgiveness*, hold additional meanings. Whereas *aphiemi* can mean that this sin is unforgivable, it might also be interpreted to mean that speaking against the Holy Spirit *is not to be permitted*, that we should never allow such speech to go unhindered. Mark recorded how Jesus set the responsive example. When the religious leaders wrongly identified the Holy Spirit in Jesus as evil, Jesus didn't let it go unanswered. He immediately rose to the defense of the Holy Spirit, corrected their error, and hindered them from speaking further by means of a forceful warning.

The lack of *aphesis* (forgiveness) can also speak of lack of freedom, continuing bondage, imprisonment, or penalty. Surely, whenever we elevate Satan by attributing God's power to him, we are in bondage, imprisoning ourselves by believing the devil's abominable lie.

As to the state of one who has blasphemed the Holy Spirit, Mark recorded that Jesus used the Greek word *enochos*, meaning that person is considered as being *in danger of* eternal judgment before the high court of heaven. While this warning is extremely foreboding, to say a person is in danger of condemnation isn't the same thing as to say that the final condemning judgment has been rendered. Though disaster looms, the original language allows for the possibility of grace, when God, in His infinite wisdom and justice, renders His final decision.

God's grace accepted, I know that, for my part, when I speak of the Holy Spirit and His works, I want it to be with reverence, respect, and a heart filled with gratitude for His wonderful presence in my life.

"If to know the Holy Spirit is to love Him, how can we get to know Him better?"

A devout younger woman I know confessed that though she'd be born again for a number of years, though she was diligent about church work and was even leading a small group, she felt little intimacy with God. She felt that she knew about Him. She believed in Him intellectually and demonstrated her commitment by service, but she couldn't honestly relate to the idea of actually feeling love for God. After that, we both prayed that God would draw her into a new intimacy with Him in the Holy Spirit. Soon, as she studied the Scriptures and sat under the teaching that has become this book, that heavenly romance started to blossom.

Getting to know the Holy Spirit means becoming involved with Him as opposed to just observing from afar. It's the significant difference between being a *spectator* and a *participant*. Just as in human relationships, we go beyond knowing *about* a person to *knowing* that person by investing in the relationship.

Remember: Spectators aren't intimates. Spectators stay at arms' length. Spectators watch as others engage. Spectators can develop a critical, judgmental, religious spirit. But in contrast, if we act on the Word and yield to the Holy Spirit, we're *participants*. Participants quickly become intimates. Participants walk arm in arm with what God is doing. Participants personally engage. Participants radiate the fruits of the Spirit.

"How do I go from being a spectator to a participant?"

Come Clean

Intimacy with God was first compromised when Adam and Eve succumbed to sin (Genesis 3:1–13). Before then, they were naked and unashamed. They dialogued with God openly. Once they'd sinned, though, what did they do? They hid from God. They covered their nakedness with fig leaves.

Notice that it wasn't that God ceased to communicate with His people, even though they were in sin. Rather, it was Adam and Eve who first quenched the Spirit. When we're in unconfessed sin, like

Adam and Eve, we often try to hide in shame from God. We may continue to fellowship with other believers, but when it comes to real closeness to God, we hold back.

God is waiting patiently to cleanse and restore if we will just drop our fig leaves and repent, setting the stage for intimacy in the Spirit.

Communicate with Him

As in I Thessalonians 5:17, let prayer become like breathing, a continuous part of your life. It's nice to have dedicated time to sit and pray, but it's also good to find ways talk with God while you go about your day. Talk to Him while you shower or as you dry your hair. Chat with Him as you head down the hall for a meeting or on your way back from lunch. Pray as you cook, clean, or any other of the many tasks we do that don't require heavy concentration.

The more you come to think of the Holy Spirit as a Companion, the more you converse with Him, the more you'll enjoy spending time with Him (I Timothy 4:15). Allow yourself to become absorbed in your divine relationship. Remember: you're not putting in time just to check off an obligation. You are getting together with a welcomed Friend.

Learn of Him

Study God's Word (II Timothy 2:15). Pore over the Scriptures like the Spirit-penned love letters that they are. Each time you pick up your Bible, invite the Holy Spirit to tutor you as you read. That way, instead of merely going through an intellectual exercise, Bible study becomes interactive. As this happens, you'll get to know your Teacher better and better.

Recognize Him

See Him, no matter how He chooses to come to you (Luke 24:13–32). As Jesus walked with His grieved disciples on the road to Emmaus, they were kept from recognizing Him in the natural way. It's not that they went physically blind. They just couldn't see that it was Jesus. Perhaps the Lord wanted them to sense His presence in another way, without depending on their natural eyes. Indeed, when Jesus vanished from their sight, they recognized Him. They remembered how their hearts had burned within them as He talked with them. We can invite the Holy Spirit to burn in our hearts the same way, helping us to recognize His presence.

Allow Him to Manifest Jesus in You

Manifesting Jesus means being like Jesus (II Corinthians 4:7–13). Being like Jesus means more than exhibiting the fruits of the Spirit. It also means flowing in His miraculous power. Jesus regularly performed wonders in the Spirit, and He said those who followed Him would, too—not just the leaders—but all those who believe.

Let Him RAIN on You:

Relate to the Holy Spirit.
Allow Him to take control.
Invite Him to fall on you.
Notice what He says and does.

As we allow Him to fall on us, we fall in love with Him. It is just that simple.

"But it's outside my comfort zone."

Does it help to know that we all hesitate for this reason? Let's recognize that comfort zone for what it truly is: *Our comfort zone is really our control zone.*

It's taken some practice for me, but the more I yield control to Him, the more comfortable I become with my Comforter, the Holy Spirit. Think about it. We find comfort with those with whom we've become familiar, with those we've grown to trust. We relax as experience bears out what we can expect. As we invest in our relationship with the Spirit, as we get to know Him, as we experience what it's like for Him to manifest Himself in us, He becomes our comfort zone. The gentle rain of heaven falls on us and our little parched seeds begin to sprout and grow.

CHAPTER FOUR

Sensing the Spirit without Getting Weird

A man returned from a trip to testify about what he believed to be a new wave of the Holy Spirit. Ordered services had been totally eclipsed as sincere, intelligent believers began to laugh or cry uncontrollably, roll around on the floor, bark like dogs, or squawk and flap around like chickens. Busloads of believers were flocking to this place to get in on the experience. This man had gone in a skeptic, but had come out convinced that this was a genuine move of the Spirit. He explained that even though he resisted at first, even though there was no biblical precedent for most of it, he ended up joining the cacophony. With leaders riding this wave in agreement, I was left, an everyday layperson, to ask: Was this really the Holy Spirit?

Is this getting a little too bizarre for you? Are you starting to worry about swimming in emotionalism instead of staying in the legitimate current of the Holy Spirit? These are valid concerns. So, let's talk about some distinctions between SENSES vs. FEELINGS.

Though senses and feelings are often confused, flowing in the power of the Holy Spirit involves heightening our *spiritual senses*, so we aren't misled or overwhelmed by our *natural feelings*, even if others around us are. Feelings can be fleeting or overblown. Feelings can skew us away from spiritual realities. They're a perilously shaky foundation because they originate within our flawed human frames. However, what we truly sense in the Spirit comes from an altogether different source: the omniscient mind of God.

Sensitivity to the Holy Spirit is just one of the forms spiritual discernment takes, as God reveals the truth about our circumstances on a spiritual level. Though we'll go over the manifest gift of distinguishing of spirits in more detail later, certainly all believers should seek this aspect of discernment, that is the ability to distinguish the movement of the Holy Spirit from the storm-tossed seas of our own human nature.

Feelings are our natural emotional reactions to what is happening on a human level; whereas, the Holy Spirit wants to help us to sense, process, and willingly partner with what God is actually doing on a comprehensive spiritual level, even when our emotions threaten to derail us. If we yield in sensitivity to the Spirit, He will take our feet out of the miry clay of emotions and set our feet on the sturdy Rock of His Word (Psalms 40:2–3).

The Bible tells us that the flow of the Holy Spirit can be sensed in the following ways, each of which goes far beyond our five natural capabilities:

- **See:** Look for what He is doing *(Ezekiel 47:6)*.
- **Hear:** Listen for what He is saying *(Revelation 3:22)*.
- **Taste:** Savor the goodness of God *(Psalm 34:8, Ezekiel 3:3)*.
- **Touch:** Feel His dynamic power *(Matthew 9:21)*.
- **Smell:** Breathe the aroma of Christ *(II Corinthians 2:14–15)*.

Always remember: the works of the Holy Spirit are spiritually discerned (I Corinthians 2:14). We need to go beyond our natural senses and become sensitive to the Spirit, because the two can be diametrically opposed. In the flesh, Lazarus looked, felt, and smelled dead to Mary and Martha. They were overcome by emotion based on what they experienced in the natural. However, in the Spirit, Jesus sensed quite the opposite was to happen, that Lazarus would be miraculously raised from the dead.

"How do I tell my natural feelings from Spirit-led senses?"

Though seeking godly counsel and confirmation can help, we should always start with our ultimate authority, God's written Word. The more familiar you are with what the Bible actually says, the more readily you can use it for verification. If what you're sensing is contrary to something in the Bible, then you can know right off that it's not from the Holy Spirit, who will never contradict or countermand God's already spoken Word of Scripture.

On the other hand, have you ever been reading the Bible and suddenly sensed the Holy Spirit flood you with fresh understanding or application, something that is fully consistent with the truth of Scripture? I like to refer to that as *rhema* word. The Greek word *rhema* has an immediate, active connotation. It refers to words spoken by a living voice.

Job 37:2 joins in the exhortation that we should be attentive to *hear the noise of His voice, and the sound that goes out of His mouth.* Though we may be reading God's written Word utilizing our natural sense of sight, we may also hear what God is saying to us about His Word in that specific moment through the *rhema* of the Holy Spirit. Just like the children of Israel needed fresh manna every day, we should seek the fresh *rhema* of God to sustain us, as the Spirit helps us to digest and apply God's already spoken Word to our present circumstances.

If you'll turn to Matthew 4:4, you'll find a New Testament translation of the word *rhema*, as Jesus answers temptation from the devil using Scripture:

> *"Man does not live by bread alone, but man lives by everything that proceeds out of the mouth of the Lord."*
>
> *Deuteronomy 8:3b*

Isn't it interesting that Jesus affirmed that we need spoken words from God's mouth to live? Though Jesus had gone forty days and nights without physical food, even as He was being tempted to snack on the suggestion of Satan, Jesus sensed the Holy Spirit's provision. Despite the natural feeling of extreme physical hunger, Jesus turned to the table that was set for Him in the very presence of His enemy, preferring the nourishing application of God's Word (Psalm 23:5).

"Does God still speak other than by Scripture quotes?"

Early in our relationship, my friend, Michael, told me that he had clearly heard God speak on two separate occasions. The first was God

saying that I belonged to Him and that Michael was to always treat me with godly respect and complete purity. This was a contemporary revelation, wholly counterintuitive for a teenaged boy, but very much in keeping with the counsel of God's word. It's also the reason that, since we both grew up and eventually married other people, we've been able to remain friends. As Michael faithfully obeyed that first directive, God spoke again, this time with a word-for-word quote of Scripture.

In His capacity as our teacher, helper, and guide, the Holy Spirit not only reminds us of Scripture, but He may also expound upon how a verse or passage applies. Further, though everything the Holy Spirit speaks is always fully consistent with the comprehensive counsel of Scripture, the Bible itself tells us that He may show us things we don't yet know, even including things that are to come (John 16:13).

Consider the way God engaged Jeremiah's senses of sight and hearing with this invitation of Jeremiah 33:3, a modern translation of which was the second instruction Michael heard in the Spirit: *"Call to me, and I will answer you, and I will tell you great and mighty things, which you do not know."*

God promised not only to answer Jeremiah, to speak so he could hear, but also to utilize his sense of sight as He showed Jeremiah things that Jeremiah hadn't already known in the natural. Now, many might say, *that was just for Jeremiah*; however, Jeremiah's sensory experience in the Holy Spirit is akin to countless biblical examples throughout the Old and New Testaments. As we read through the Bible, we see account after account of God intimately communicating with His people in sensory ways.

Isn't it wonderful to see that the delight of receiving messages from God is not just reserved for earthly kings, priests, and men of high regard? We learn in Amos 1:1 that Amos was an everyday herdsman. Yes, God speaks to shepherds, and women, and those of humble station, too—even children! Clearly, we serve an extremely communicative God who is no respecter of persons. The pronounced pattern of Scripture is that God wants to speak to all of us, to be in vital, personal contact.

Admittedly, this is where some clergy get concerned. It's easy to see why many such as the Nicolaitan leadership may have discouraged the very interactions with lay believers that God initiates.

Certainly, there can be human error. However, at the same time as I want to rightly discern mistakes, I don't want to fall prey to the error of closing my eyes to the great and mighty things God might want to show me, or to the error of stopping my ears from hearing His wonderful, living voice. If God wants to show something to me, I want to see it. If He wants to say something, I want to hear it, all of it. Don't you?

Family: God isn't calling us to control or ration His flow. He's not calling us to sip of His River of delights; He wants us to drink deep, saturating our parched souls with the sustaining refreshment of the Holy Spirit (Psalm 36:8).

"Why didn't God just plainly say everything once and for all?"

There's a clue to this answer in Proverbs 25:2, where we learn that it is God's glory to conceal a matter, and an honor even for kings to search it out.

Isn't it glorious that God deliberately keeps his message close, drawing us deeper into intimacy to hear what He's saying, whispering information that may pass unnoticed by the casual observer? We, as children of the King, are royalty. We have the privilege to press in, to draw near, and seek out His meaning.

The fact is, God doesn't always reveal everything for common consumption. He wants to engage us to actively seek Him for what we don't initially understand, and then to learn to recognize His responsive voice in the Spirit. He does this because He wants our relationship to be current, living, and interactive, not just based on intellect, tradition, or history.

Think of how Jesus sowed parables into people's lives. Consider how those who stayed close to Him were rewarded by reaping the underlying meaning. I'm convinced that God still wants to capture our attention in this way today. He wants us to hear, not only in the natural sense, but also in the Holy Spirit. Notice Revelation 2:7: *"He that has an ear, let him hear what the Spirit says..."* This indicates that there may be more for us to hear than is audible to the natural ear. There's also more to see than is visible to the natural eye.

"Is the Holy Spirit going to make me act weird?"

We've all heard of people behaving strangely, claiming to be under the unction of the Holy Spirit. Some roll, writhe, jerk or yelp sporadically, some squawk or bark. Some adopt overly emotional or unnaturally affected patterns of speech. Many of these believers seem sincere, and yet all I can say is that I don't see any of these behaviors associated with the Holy Spirit in the Bible. Some may claim that these behaviors are part of a new wave of the Spirit; however, they appear to be in conflict with the model of Scripture. These behaviors draw uncomfortable attention to the person. They're disruptive of order and interfere with worship. They're distracting during prayer. Rather than attracting unbelievers to the faith, they repel them. Fruit of the Spirit or fruit of the flesh? You make the call.

Fleshy add-ons can have a domino effect. A person may mimic what he or she has seen someone else do or what other people have come to expect as a show of true devotion. After all, if you see a row of people fall over as each forehead is touched in prayer (with catchers in the waiting), there's a not so subtle pressure to conform, even if it's not the Holy Spirit prompting you. So, unprompted falling becomes a reasoned response. You don't want the minister to feel challenged or ineffective. You don't want to seem insensitive to the Spirit. You want your prayers to be answered. You sure don't want to be the only one left standing (or vice versa).

I get it. Believe me. But be sure, Friends: showmanship, fakery, and spiritual peer pressure have nothing do with the suggestion of God's Spirit. He does not need a human to whip people up with a warm-up act. He is authentic in every way. Peer pressure is following people, not the Holy Spirit. Yes, there are instances in Scripture when people fell as dead men, overwhelmed by God's presence (Revelation 1:17). It can and does legitimately happen, and we should not resist the Holy Spirit's touch. But let's make sure that all of our responses to the Spirit are completely genuine and divinely initiated, regardless of what others do or don't do.

It's possible, in some instances, that a person is, in fact, being ministered to by the Holy Spirit, but fleshy add-ons are muddying the waters. Perhaps, with pure intent, they've relaxed to such a degree that their natural inhibitions are down. Being open to the Lord is a very good thing; however, we still have the ability to curtail the adding on of any voluntary human response that compromises the Spirit's flow. When this happens in a church or group setting, it's incumbent upon someone in leadership to offer loving correction, embracing the brother or sister's devotion, while guiding toward more scriptural responses to the Spirit.

Know this: the person of the Holy Spirit is characterized by truth, grace, and love. People are attracted by a believer who is under the anointing, because the fruits of the Spirit overflow when in His presence. He is altogether lovely. Nothing whatsoever about the Spirit of God is weird, bizarre, repulsive, or off-putting. He does nothing to draw attention to Himself or the believer upon whom He falls. Rather, He calls attention to Jesus, and so will you when under the Spirit's anointing. He is gentle. He's not out to embarrass you. You may humble yourself, but He will not humiliate you. That wouldn't be kind, and the Holy Spirit is the epitome of kindness. If you're worried about losing control, take heart, because Holy Spirit is all about self-control.

That said, I have witnessed other reactions to the Spirit that seem more consistent with the Bible. Some are moved to tears. Some tremble inconspicuously in awe. Some are washed with joy or peace.

Many years ago, I remember the Holy Spirit falling on a young woman I didn't know who came to me, crying hysterically. I did almost nothing. I simply touched her and said the words that the Spirit gave me for her in that moment: *"I speak peace to you in the name of Jesus."* Instantly, she slumped onto my bed, sound asleep. She went from frantic sobbing to tranquil slumber, literally in a moment. When she awoke twenty minutes or so later, she was completely serene, though I never even counseled her.

Maybe you've never seen anything like this. I know I hadn't. Though it was a new experience for me, one I'd never heard of before, there was nothing weird about it. The peace of the Holy Spirit was palpable. Later, in Psalm 127:2, I was able to find confirmation that the Lord gives sleep to His beloved. In Isaiah 63:14 I saw: *the Spirit of Lord gave them rest.* There are other references, but you get the idea. If you're unsure about whether a reaction is biblical or not, just search on a pertinent word or phrase. Refer regularly to the fruits of the Spirit and see if the reaction dovetails with the expressed character of the Holy Spirit.

Remember, though the Spirit may do a new thing, that activity will always be constructive toward the spread of the Gospel of Christ and it will always be in keeping with God's written Word. There is no need to fear His amazing presence and every reason to draw near.

"What does it mean to be under the anointing of the Holy Spirit?"

Good question. Don't ever be afraid to ask what something means, especially if someone throws out unfamiliar terminology like I just did. And again, don't hesitate to search on words like *anointing* in the Bible and let the Holy Spirit teach you about it.

In the Old Testament, we find that those who ministered as priests to the Lord were anointed with holy oil as a sign of their everlasting priesthood (Exodus 40:15). Back then, this holy anointing oil was meant for priests, but isn't it great that the New Testament proclaims the priesthood of even everyday believers (I Peter 2:9)?

There is a type of anointing all believers can take part in using actual oil, but Isaiah also spoke about another type of anointing, one that's more spiritual in nature. He prophesied that the yoke of bondage would be destroyed through the Lord's *fatness* [anointing] on His people (Isaiah 10:27). The word for *anointing* Isaiah used has a figurative definition of *richness*, like an aromatic olive oil. For this reason, many associate the Holy Spirit with fresh oil and use olive oil when anointing others in prayer.

Keep in mind that whether or not there is any actual oil present, there are times when the spiritual anointing prophesied by Isaiah falls upon modern day believers. This anointing may come as they minister to the Lord, and He, in return, ministers to them. He breaks the yoke of bondage, and lifts heavy burdens off their shoulders.

When the Holy Spirit pours Himself out on believers in this way, some sense warmth or a gentle effervescence. Others say it's like being washed with refreshing water, or a fountain bubbling up from within. I've heard it said that it can be as if holy oil is running down a person's face, like it was when the holy anointing oil ran down Aaron's beard

(Psalm 133:2). But even those who feel no physical sensation are promised yet another type of anointing: the ongoing inner anointing of the indwelling Spirit, an anointing that both sanctifies and teaches us all things as we abide in Him (I John 2:27).

So, there are different types of anointings, both physical and spiritual. It's biblical to anoint those who minister to the Lord, and those who need healing or ministry with oil (James 5:14). However, when a person is said to be under the anointing of the Holy Spirit, it often means that there is an unusually discernable sense of the presence of the Holy Spirit moving upon or through a believer.

Here's the thing about spiritual anointings: even though we invite the anointing by sincerely ministering to the Lord, He turns around and gives the gift of that ministry back to us, setting the example to use the anointing to serve other people. Even though it's a wonderful personal sensation, even though it relieves personal burdens, and even though you may sense the anointing of the Holy Spirit when you're alone, remember that the anointing is a gift God may want you to re-gift. We give ministry to God; He gives the anointing to us, and often, we are purposed to give of the anointing to others as the Holy Spirit overflows in power.

If you feel the anointing of the Holy Spirit, simply open yourself to any ministry the Lord might ask you to do. Whether it's to speak, teach, pray, or take some action under that anointing, humbly step out and allow Him to demonstrate His power through you.

"Isn't this getting a little, you know...out there?"

Actually, it is. It's getting out of our comfort zones, out of the dulling error of human traditions, out of the way of natural restrictions, out of the boat with Peter, and stepping out onto the waters of God's Spirit.

Sadly—as when Jesus walked on this earth—much of the church has largely confined God to a natural, comfortable box ashore. But we, as everyday believers, have a choice. We can quench the Holy Spirit's call. We can shrink back to what's generally considered sane, sensible, and usual. We can stay "in there."

The spiritual reality is that God is, by nature, supernatural. If we're close to Him, if we're truly like Jesus, then supernatural sensory manifestations go with the territory, just like they did with Jesus. Granted, moving toward greater intimacy with God in the Spirit calls for a massive step of faith. Like children, we're unsure, wary of the unknown, fearful of failure, disappointment, or of what others might think. But despite all of our reluctance, the Holy Spirit still beckons, ever so patiently, drawing us deeper into the flow of our astonishingly sensory God.

CHAPTER FIVE

Getting Our Feet Wet in God's Powerful River

As a preschooler, I stood at the edge of a swimming pool while my father coaxed me to jump in, promising to catch me. An Air Force doctor, my dad went with teams that fished astronauts out of the sea after their capsules splashed down, so it would have been reasonable to assume that he could save a little girl like me. Nonetheless, I hesitated. I knew he loved me. I knew he would not let me drown. But I still wrestled with taking that giant leap of faith for the very first time.

Are you ready to move beyond your natural feelings and sense what God could want to show you? We'll start by looking at a vision received by Ezekiel, one that helps me see where I am in my journey with the Spirit. This vision was imparted thousands of years ago, but I believe it still speaks volumes about the role of the Holy Spirit in the life of all believers to this day.

"Interpretations make me nervous."

Interpretation of symbolic Scriptures does necessitate a step of faith. It requires us to venture out beyond the natural in the here and now. It's not for the spiritually faint of heart, but it does come with great rewards.

Yes, there's the possibility that you'll make mistakes, but God is like an adoring parent, encouraging His child to take those first steps. He knows when your heart is to move toward Him. He understands if you unintentionally wobble or stumble, and He helps you to get up and try again, knowing that ultimately, these are steps that bring you closer into intimacy with Him. Though we may feel safer just crawling, God knows that it is in our best interest to rise, mature, and step out in the Spirit.

As we consider Ezekiel's vision, I'll encourage you to see what might come to you in the Spirit first. Then, understanding that interpretations may vary, I'll offer what I believe the Spirit has revealed to me. Maybe you'll see and hear some of the same things. First, there is the rich literal text to consider, but keep in mind, this vision is also laden with symbols, pictures infused with subtext. While always consistent with the text, subtext is the complementary treasure hidden beneath the text or symbol, waiting to be discovered in the Spirit.

"How do I know if I got it right?"

As believers receive correct interpretations, the Spirit Himself bears witness within us. Sometimes there is simply a knowing, a discerning assurance that the revelation is, indeed, from Him. Those of us who only receive this simple knowing should not feel less assured or less spiritual than those who receive more physical confirmation. God treats us as individuals, and He delights in those who have the faith to trust His presence in less spectacular ways.

Sometimes, however, the Spirit manifests this knowing with a physical accompaniment. We should not simply go by our feelings (as they may mislead), but sometimes there is an actual physical sensation in the Spirit, that anointing we just mentioned.

You may feel a tingling. Your heart may "burn" inside you, just as the disciples sensed on the road to Emmaus. Some report what is almost like a current of water or electricity, moving from within. In time, you'll recognize the ways the Spirit confirms Himself to you.

Much more important than confirming interpretations by sensation, however, it is vital to confirm what you're sensing with the Bible. Think of the elements of the interpretation as clues on a treasure hunt. Look for other passages that confirm what you believe you're hearing. As an additional point of confirmation, you can also talk to another mature believer about what you believe the Lord is showing to you.

"This sounds kind of exciting. Can we try it?"

Yes! Let's walk through this step by step together.

First: take a moment to pray in Jesus' name. Ask God to open your eyes and ears in the Spirit so you can see and hear what He wants to show you and say to you through this very sensory vision. Ask Him to block out any voices other than His voice of truth. Ask Him to let you experience this as if you were being guided through this vision, just as Ezekiel was.

Now, put yourself in Ezekiel's shoes as you set this book aside and read Ezekiel 47:1–12.

"Okay, I'm knee-deep in symbols. Where do I start?"

The first thing I do is ask the Holy Spirit to speak to me. Then, I wait quietly to see what springs to mind about the passage in general or any of its symbols. I might stop to ask the Lord about a particular symbol that seems striking to me.

When we look at Ezekiel 47:1–12, what's the predominant symbol we find in this vision? The River. Let's start there.

"So, what is this river?"

I believe the river represents the Holy Spirit. Two cross-references confirm the interpretation that comes to me in the Spirit:

> *"He who believes in Me, as the Scripture said, 'From his innermost being shall flow rivers of living water.' But this He spoke of the Spirit, whom those that believed in Him were to receive..."*
>
> *John 7:38–39a*

See? There's that river again. Jesus clearly identified the river as the Spirit. Now, take a look at another vision, recorded by John, the same disciple who recorded the passage above. Notice the striking similarities between John's vision and Ezekiel's vision:

"And He showed me a river of the water of life, clear as crystal, coming from the throne of God and of the Lamb, in the middle of its street. And on either side of the river was the tree of life, bearing twelve kinds of fruit, bearing its fruit every month: and the leaves of the tree were for the healing of the nations...And the Spirit and the bride say, 'Come.' And let the one who hears say, 'Come.' And the one who is thirsty come; let the one who wishes take the water of life without cost."

Revelation 22:1–2, 17

Not only does Scripture confirm that the river symbolizes the Holy Spirit, Ezekiel's vision is also consistent with important evidences of the Spirit in believers: increasing depth, perpetual freshness, consistent fruitfulness, capacity to give life, and effect healing.

Just as it is with the River in this vision, often there is a key symbol within a vision that helps us to unlock the rest. Once we've correctly interpreted that key symbol, we find that the remainder rests comfortably within that framework. Nothing has to be forced. It just fits.

Starting with Ezekiel 47:1, we find that God is giving Ezekiel a tour of a house. In prior chapters, we see that the house is actually the house of God, the temple (I Kings 5). Ezekiel is brought back to the door (in John 10:9, Jesus identifies Himself as the door).

Ezekiel is directed to observe that there is water (the Spirit) flowing from under the threshold of the temple. So, we see that from beneath the foundation of the house of God, the eternal spring of the Holy Spirit is flowing.

As I considered my journey of faith, I saw myself in this picture, in the temple, at that time when I was being drawn into reconciliation with God through Christ, welcoming Him to make my body into the temple of the Holy Spirit.

The first sacred work of the Holy Spirit concerning us is to draw us to Jesus, to bring us through that everlasting door of salvation, to lead us to the altar of His sacrifice. So, before we're even aware of His presence, the Spirit accompanies us, patiently awaiting our response. Consider Jesus' words, spoken to the disciples before their redemption:

"And I will ask the Father, and He will give you another Comforter, that He may be with you forever, that is the Spirit of truth, whom the world cannot receive, because it does not behold Him or know Him, but you know Him because He abides with you, and will be in you."

John 14:16–17

Notice that last part, that the Spirit is WITH us (prior to salvation). The Greek word for WITH is *para*, meaning *alongside*. I find it amazing that even when I was wandering from God, even before I accepted Jesus' atoning sacrifice, the Holy Spirit—who was actively drawing me into the house of God—was faithfully accompanying me.

The second work of the Holy Spirit concerning us is regeneration. As we, in turn, give our lives to God in Christ, the Spirit goes from being WITH us to being IN us. Scripture confirms that from the moment I prayed to receive Jesus, the Holy Spirit came to live in me.

In John 3:3-8, Jesus talked to Nicodemus about this miracle of being born again, connecting it with being borne of the Spirit. Colossians 2:9–10 assures us that, in Jesus, we have the fullness of the Godhead bodily and that we are made full in Him. We become that temple of God spoken of in I Corinthians 3:16, that place where the Spirit dwells, and not just for a moment. The Greek word for IN used in John 14:17 is *en*, which denotes a fixed position, meaning the Holy Spirit comes to stay.

So, the Holy Spirit indwells us as believers; however, this vision is only beginning. Ezekiel is beckoned onward. Many believers rest at this point. I did. I was saved. I was indwelt by the Holy Spirit, but I felt more at home inside the familiar temple, so I resisted answering the Spirit's call to move beyond to more and deeper experiences with Him.

You'll notice that Ezekiel is guided out of the temple (v.2). He is shown that the waters representing the Spirit are flowing from the south side of the altar toward the outside of the temple. Whether we answer this call to walk forward in the Spirit is entirely up to us, but the invitation is open to all believers to get outside of ourselves and build on the foundation of regeneration.

Okay, take a look at verse three. Suddenly, we see there's a *Man* leading Ezekiel into the water, an extension of the same water that is flowing out of the temple.

"Who is the Man, and what's going on here?"

I asked this question and, in response, I was shown Jesus, fulfilling His promise to baptize us in the waters of the Holy Spirit (John 1:33, Luke 3:16). Having redeemed us, it is Jesus' sacred privilege to lead us into this Holy River, where we find that the Spirit's third work in us is to envelop and overflow us. So, before I knew Jesus, the Spirit was WITH me. At regeneration He came to live IN me. Then, when I asked Jesus to baptize me with the Holy Spirit, suddenly, I was also IN HIM, in an ongoing relationship where unlimited future anointings for witnessing could manifest. This is the divine purpose for baptism with the Holy Spirit: Jesus baptizes us with the Spirit's power to equip us for service, ministry, and harvest (Acts 1:8).

Notice how Jesus led Ezekiel into incrementally greater depths in the Spirit. Picture that process in your mind. At first, when we're just ankle deep, we dominate the image. The water has very limited impact on our ability to walk in the natural; whereas, when we follow Jesus into greater depths, the water (the Spirit) increasingly covers our flesh till our feet can't even touch bottom. Since walking in the natural is no longer possible, the believer is swimming, moved by the current of what is now a mighty River. It stands to reason: the more the flesh is still above water, the more control we maintain; however, the deeper we go into the river, the more we subject ourselves to the control of the Spirit.

Then, the Man (Jesus), asks Ezekiel if he has *seen* this (v. 6). Does this question seem strange to you? Ezekiel is having a vision. Of course, he sees it. This suggests Jesus' underlying question: *Do you understand what this means?* It tells us Jesus wants us to see not only in the natural, but also in the Spirit. He's implying that there's a message imbedded in the symbols He's showing Ezekiel.

Not everyone has spiritual eyes to see. Not everyone has spiritual ears to hear. Jesus wants us to be in the river, in the Spirit, as John was in Revelation 1:10, in that place where we can hear the voice of the

Lord and see what He is really showing to us. This revelatory experience is preserved in God's Word, an open invitation to all who believe.

Notice that Jesus doesn't get hung up with this baptism. Instead, He leads the regenerated, baptized believer out of the River and onward. Remember: when Jesus was baptized and the Spirit descended upon Him, it was certainly a pivotal experience, but Jesus did not linger there. Rather, Jesus went out, empowered and equipped.

"What's up with all of the trees along the River?"

Did you recognize trees as a symbol that is used elsewhere in Scripture? Check out Isaiah 60:13 where it talks about all the different trees that will beautify God's sanctuary, then verse twenty-one, which refers to God's righteous people as the branch of His planting, purposed for glorifying Him. Isaiah also calls God's people *trees of righteousness* in Isaiah 61:3. If you turn to Jeremiah 17:7–8, you'll find it also identifies the trees as believers and, what's more, it places those ever-yielding trees at the River's edge, just like Ezekiel saw in his vision.

Believers, we are those trees! Even though we're planted back in the world, we're at the edge of that River where we can sink our roots deep and continually drink of the Spirit's limitless supply. In nature, roots seek out the nearest water source. If we remain right at the bank of His River, our roots will quite naturally be inclined to drink of the Spirit (Psalm 36:8).

"No offense. But aren't trees kind of stationary and boring?"

Not these trees. I have to admit that I'd wondered: if we're supposed to move in the Spirit, to go with His flow in our lives, and since Scripture exhorts us to *walk* in the Spirit (Galatians 5:16), then why are we planted like trees? Trees can't walk. Can they? I asked the Lord this specific question, and the answer I received really surprised me, in part because I didn't wait around for a reply. I didn't try to figure it out. But my heart did burn within me a day or two later, when the Spirit reminded me to consider Mark 8:23–25, when Jesus healed a blind man.

I'll admit that I'd long been puzzled by this story. I mean Jesus is Jesus. Why did it take Jesus two tries to heal this guy? In an instant, I received the answer to these two seemingly unrelated questions. I realized I'd been looking at both the trees in Ezekiel's vision and the two-step healing of the blind man through natural eyes and not through the eyes of the Spirit. Oops.

First, I was prompted to consider the blind man. Lest I would deem Jesus' first action unsuccessful, I was compelled to take a closer look. I see Jesus take of the water from within Himself (the Spirit) and anoint the blind man's eyes. I hear Jesus ask the blind man if he sees. It hits me:

This is the same question Ezekiel has also been asked in his vision, just before he is shown the trees.

The Spirit instructed me to note the blind man's response. He says: he sees *men like trees walking*.

My heart burned within me.

Frankly, I'd always thought that to be odd before. Why didn't the blind man just say that things looked blurry or that he could see unfocused forms of people moving around? Why, of all things, did a man who'd never seen trees describe people as trees walking?

All I know is that almost 2,000 years later, the Holy Spirit used the blind man's description to explain to me that those trees planted by the River in Ezekiel are dynamic, miraculously capable of walking in the Spirit from which they drink. In the natural trees don't walk; however, in the Spirit, naturally impossible things can happen!

Though we don't know exactly what happened on a physical level in Mark 8:23–25, it's interesting to consider the possibility that Jesus opened the blind man's spiritual eyes first. He may have prioritized this as the first of two levels of healing, so the blind man could see Jesus' surrounding disciples walking like trees, before Jesus fully opened the blind man's natural eyes.

So, toss out the concept that your life in the Spirit will be sedentary, stiff or stodgy, like the planted trees you think of in the natural. Decide to be a spiritual tree, a tree that is supernaturally grounded and walking in power, all at the same time.

"Where does the River lead now?"

For years, I just read past the geographical course of the River. In a more recent study, however, I heard the Spirit prompt me to examine the places Ezekiel mentions more closely. I was not disappointed.

In verse eight, the Man (Jesus) points out that the River goes down into the desert, *the Arabah*, before flowing to the sea. So, we're baptized with the Holy Spirit then first up, we flow with that River into more than a hundred miles of dry, depressed Arabah wilderness. What's up with that? This place is arid, hot, barren, and unfruitful. We're freshly equipped and ready to go. *"Why do we start here?"* I asked.

The Holy Spirit showed me a remarkable parallel in Luke 4:1–13. After John baptized Jesus and the Holy Spirit descended upon Him, Jesus returned from the Jordan, full of the Spirit, ready to start His ministry. And where did Jesus go first? He went into the dry, barren wilderness where He was tempted by the devil. (Insert more heartburn for me, the good kind.)

Some might try to by-pass this part of the journey, saying, *"I'm not a good wilderness person."* We tend to say this kind of thing when we're in seasons of comfort or abundance, hoping that God will spare us hardship of this type. (He won't.) The Arabah is far better for us than we know, and the fact is that God loves us all too much to withhold any experience that will be for our good and for the good of His kingdom. Sure, we love those mountaintops, but our mettle is tested in the devil-prowled desert.

The desert is a proving ground. It's a place without natural water, where we must learn to rely fully on the refreshment of the Holy Spirit. Like the children of Israel, we must rehearse reliance upon God to be our source of supply. We're so used to depending on natural refreshment that we need to acclimate to the new practice of drinking from the Spirit. It can be hard to break old habits, particularly when natural water is right there. So, the River leads us into a place where our new reliance upon Him can be established, practiced, and proved.

My first taste of the Arabah came right after college. I'd just been married a couple of weeks when my new husband and I moved to another state. Instead of the tightly knit fellowship of kindred spirits we'd enjoyed, we were suddenly in an area where we knew no one.

Cessationist doctrine dominated area churches. I was outside of the classroom and into the lab of the world. I complained about this at first, thirsty for fellowship, just like the Israelites did only days into their desert. But it was in that arid place that I learned to fly solo with the Holy Spirit, to find sweet refreshment in communion with Him (Exodus 15:25).

Do not be surprised if you find yourself, newly baptized with the Spirit, plopped into your own kind of wilderness. In the natural, we resist such experiences. We assume that if we're on the right course, everything will be pleasant. God knows better for us, though.

The Arabah is spiritual boot camp. Yes, God's holy River takes us down into the dry, depressed world, training us to drink from Him, strengthening us to endure harsh conditions, to resist temptation from the enemy. In so doing, He prepares us for the battles of service to come.

This boot camp does not go on forever. (Relieved?) The Arabah starts low and runs some 112 miles to the Great Sea, the elevation gradually rising to a spectacular waterfall, 660 feet above sea level. These are the cliffs of *Engedi*, mentioned in Ezekiel's vision.

"What's the significance of Engedi?"

That's what the Holy Spirit compelled me to ask. I found that Engedi means "the *fountain* of the kid." It's a renowned place, some 400 feet over the west bank of the Dead Sea. Imagine the sight as fountains of *warm water* cascade over the limestone cliffs of Engedi, tumbling down to one of the world's most celebrated garden spots below. This is one fertile plain! Plant life abounds. The young frolic in the spray. Tree-o-rama. Fish are plentiful and diverse, as in the fresh waters of the Great Sea.

Read in Ezekiel's vision how, as the River cascades over the cliffs of Engedi and flows into the sea, the Man tells Ezekiel that the waters of the sea become fresh. In the American Standard Version, it says the waters shall be *healed*. This is a picture of the Holy Spirit, flowing in to cure the sea of humanity.

Normally, when a fresh water river flows into the sea, the river water takes on the salty makeup of the sea. Here, the opposite happens.

Humanity is miraculously refreshed and purified as the Spirit brings life and healing wherever He flows.

We see in verse ten that the river of the Spirit has brought us to this place expressly for the spreading of nets. This is the ultimate fishing spot! I've never been good at catching fish, but remember how Jesus said He was going to make us fishers of men? Just look at the bounty of fish Ezekiel is shown in verse nine! Now that the believer is drawn, redeemed, baptized, equipped, and trained, it's time to go fishing, fishing for people! This is what life in the Spirit is about, involving us as He pulls a great harvest of souls into the Kingdom.

The trees at the banks under the cliffs of Engedi thrive. Not only do they drink deeply from the River, they are also positioned near the waterfall where the warm spray of the Spirit continuously anoints and refreshes them.

Interestingly, it was in a cave in these very cliffs of Engedi that David had the opportunity to move in the flesh and kill Saul (who was trying to kill David), yet in sensitivity to the Spirit, David didn't dare to touch God's anointed. There's an important principle we can glean from David's experience: *When we're under the anointing of the Holy Spirit, we act in sensitivity to what God wants to say and do, even if it conflicts with what makes sense in the natural.*

"Isn't the anointing just for leadership?"

Notice that there are *very many trees* drinking from God's River. Remember: we are those trees, every single believer who lives alongside His River. It doesn't matter if you're a leader or a Jane Doe Christian like me. This anointing is for as many as follow God's open invitation to drink deeply of the waters of the Spirit (I Peter 2:9, I John 2:27). Yes, we must be abiding in Him. Yes, there is wisdom in godly counsel and scriptural confirmation. And yes—thank God, yes—this anointing of the Holy Spirit is directly available to every believer.

"So, what about Eneglaim?"

I confess, after I found all the exciting relevance of Engedi, I relaxed, like someone who had just finished a good meal. Pretty soon, though, the Spirit nudged me to investigate the significance of Eneglaim. I found that Eneglaim borders the Dead Sea. In contrast to the Spirit's thriving river, there is so much salt in this sea that absolutely nothing can live in it. There are no fish, no plants, nothing. In fact, any fish that might inadvertently swim into the Dead Sea from tributary fresh waters die immediately. Their bodies are covered with salt and are discarded on the shore. Though streams flow into the Dead Sea, there are no outlets. These are the dead-end waters of the world, utterly hopeless without God's power.

So, as we put this picture together, we see that from the temple of redemption, from the waters of baptism with the Spirit, we are taken through the preparatory desert of Arabah, to the refreshing fountain of Engedi, to the lifeless, quenched edge of the Dead Sea at Eneglaim, so in need of the Spirit's healing waters. All of this happens so that we can stand at the River and spread the net of the Gospel, which captures a bountiful harvest of souls. Notice that verse ten mentions that there are many fish, which, like the abundant Great Sea, are quite diverse. This speaks of God's desire to spread a broad net, to bring people of all kinds into His kingdom.

"This is getting over my head. I'd rather rest in the shallow water."

It's only natural to linger where we feel safe, but we should remember that resisting the Holy Spirit's prompting to move forward is a fleshy impulse that leads to stagnation. In verse eleven, we see a sobering warning that the shallow waters into which some wade are swampy marshlands where the fresh water of the Spirit doesn't run. Those who soak in the marshes rely on a historic experience in the Spirit. They refuse His call to move onward and will, as in Ezekiel's vision, be left for salt. Turn to Deuteronomy 29:23 to see what kind of salt this is. We're talking brimstone salt—a burning waste material, unfertile, unproductive, like Lot's wife at the overthrow of Sodom and Gomorrah—definitely not a good place to be.

This retreat of the flesh can be exceedingly subtle. It's not that we bolt for the marshes. Sometimes, waves of opposition wash us away from the center of the River's current. Sometimes we just drift along with others leaving the flow. Even if we're among those who were once rooted like trees in the Spirit, we let storms topple us. Bit by bit, we begin to rest on our past experiences in the Spirit without drinking afresh in the present.

We get lazy.

We assure ourselves that we're technically in the River, even when we've long left His dynamic current. We enjoy the company of the many marsh squatters, comfortable to watch what God is doing from a distance rather than being actively involved.

We let our association with the Holy Spirit become more social than personal, choosing to deny the Spirit's call rather separating ourselves from our marsh-dwelling peers. We shrink back from standing like the deeply rooted trees God wants us to be.

We're reluctant to righteously challenge church traditions that are in conflict with the flow of the Spirit, convincing ourselves it's better to keep things nice, to get along in the highly populated marshes.

We stagnate. We get root rot. We lounge in the shade of the trees that remain on the bank. We become unproductive, useless in the Spirit. We wonder why God abandoned us, when we are the ones who withdrew from Him.

Let's be real. No one wants to cop to being a marsh-dweller. I know I don't. But I also know I have been there. How can I tell? Fruit—or actually the lack thereof.

Read through verse twelve, which describes the productivity of God's river-fed orchard. These trees bear fruit every single month without fail. There is no falling or withering of their leaves, because they drink year-round from the fountain of regeneration. There is no winter. Not only is the fruit a constant source of nourishment, even the leaves are useful for the miracle of healing.

How is that kind of continuity possible? In the natural, it's not. In the natural we work our way up to vacations. We kick back. We schedule breaks. We age. We retire. But in the Spirit, the impossible happens. That life-giving spring bubbles up eternally for all who would answer Jesus' call to drink of the waters that will never run dry.

Notice how the description of these trees in verse twelve tracks with the psalmist's description:

"The righteous shall flourish like the palm-tree: he shall grow like a cedar in Lebanon. They are planted in the house of Jehovah; they shall flourish in the courts of our God. They shall still bring forth fruit in old age; they shall be full of sap and green."

Psalm 92:12–14 ASV

If we're vitally drinking from His River, there will be evidence. Our branches will reach out toward others. Fruit will be continual. Therapeutic leaves will pop out in a perpetual spring, for the purpose of healing the nations (Revelation 22:1–2). There will be no withering with age, no leanness, only the enduring vitality of the Spirit, His anointing raining down on us continuously, making us acutely aware of God's presence with us and His desire to move in power through us.

CHAPTER SIX

Going Deeper Without Going over the Deep End

Once, when I shared an amazing move of the Holy Spirit with a small group I was new to, a very bright believer shook her head with a smile and said, "I don't know, Susan. Sometimes, you're sort of half 'praise the Lord' and half cuckoo." She circled her finger around her temple for emphasis. Unaccustomed to modern-day displays of God's supernatural power, part of her wanted to shout hallelujah, and the other part reasoned that I must be kind of crazy, over the deep end. It wasn't many months before another example of the power of the Spirit prompted a second "cuckoo" from her. A couple of years later, however, when I shared the true story of how a woman I know had been raised from the dead, there were no more jokes about my sanity. There were only the tears of faith in her eyes.

Being called crazy goes with the territory of moving in the power of the Holy Spirit. It happened to Jesus (Mark 3:21); it's happened to me. I suppose it's to be expected that the world will think we've lost it. That's hard. But it can be even tougher to have our mental stability called into question by people who are an integral part of our lives, especially within the family of God.

I dearly love the woman who called me half "cuckoo" at first. I appreciated her honesty, and I respected that she had the integrity to voice what she was wrestling with to my face. It represented her sincere, cautious wading into unfamiliar waters; it spoke of her desire to explore the possibility that God still moves in power through everyday believers. And ultimately, we became good friends as we experienced the Holy Spirit's work together over time.

"But what about my reputation?"

Before we venture into God's River, let's put all our fears about the potential of losing face onto the table. The fact is: we like it when people think well of us, particularly within the body of Christ. We enjoy their fellowship, their approval, and their respect. We secretly savor the esteem hard work can garner. But even though we may humbly bow as those affirming crowns are placed on our heads, even though it was God who gave us everything we have and are in the first place, it's easy to slip into a subconscious guarding of what people think of us, especially as we become better known within their ranks. And if we're not incredibly watchful against it, we can allow the glittering reputation God has blessed us with to become an idol before Him.

Think of the children of Israel, miraculously rescued from slavery in Egypt. In Exodus, we learn that God gave the Israelites favor with those they had toiled for all those years, and that just before their release, God instructed all of the men and women to ask their masters for gold and silver jewelry. In fact, the Israelites had received so much favor from God that they were handed a virtual treasure trove. Thus, they left Egypt, having plundered their captors, and celebrated it as God's triumph. But before long, we find them dancing around a golden calf, likely fashioned from the very gold jewelry that God gave them both the favor and the idea to acquire.

Flash forward. Think of the rich young ruler, that man who sought Jesus out, wanting to inherit the kingdom, then turned back sadly, unwilling to walk away from his wealth and respected position to answer Jesus' call.

Flash forward again, this time to the present day. Honestly examine your life for the idol of a prized reputation, also known as *the pride of life*. It's a snare rooted in the fear of man. Will you choose to dance around the golden calf of public opinion? Will you celebrate the ideas, favor, and spoils you've received as if they weren't blessings from God? Or will you cast all your crowns before Jesus and follow wherever He leads?

Think about this: you'd never go swimming laden with gold and silver, weighed down by such things. You know they'd make you sink like a stone! So, let's examine our hearts for every weight or encumbrance that could be holding us back from flowing with the current of the Holy Spirit (Hebrews 12:1).

Are you afraid of what your family, friends or colleagues will think? Are there those, even within the body of Christ, who just wouldn't understand?

If you answered "yes" to either question, then you're in good company. Stop for a moment and call each person's name to mind. Be specific. Confess that these are the relationships that stand between you and fully following Jesus. Pray down your list of names, one at a time. Ask the Lord to touch their hearts with understanding and to give you the courage to put Him first.

In your mind's eye, take another look at the vision detailed in Ezekiel 47:1–12. Review that passage, taking time to observe each element:

> *Visualize the grounds surrounding the house—the temple of God. See the spring, bubbling up from the foundation of the sanctuary, running along the base of the altar of atonement. See the redeemed, congregated inside. Now, watch Jesus as He walks outside and around the temple, into the world. Hear Jesus calling, beckoning those inside the church to follow the course of the stream outward, as its flow expands into a mighty river. See Jesus leading those who approach the deepening waters of the Holy Spirit— gently drawing each individual in—to the ankles, the knees, the thighs, then deeper still, till the waters overwhelm human control. Notice the inhabited marshes along the edge. Turn to those well-rooted trees along the bank, along the river as it climbs through the Arabah's desert, leading to its glorious peak where the waters cascade off the cliffs of Engedi, its spray anointing the valley below, all the way to the barren Eneglaim, refreshing the dying sea of humanity. See the fishermen at the bank, pulling in an abundant catch. Study those never aging trees absorbing the mist from the waterfall, bearing fruit continually.*

Linger here. Honestly look at this picture. Ask the Lord and yourself:

"Where am I in this vision?"

Resist the urge to abandon this question until you honestly identify where you'd draw yourself into this picture at this moment. Try to pinpoint an exact location. If it helps, map out the vision in a sketch, then draw yourself in, knowing that He loves you, no matter where you are.

You may see yourself as a seeker, peering into the temple from a distance, curious to see what's there. If so, no matter who you are or where you've been, know that you are welcome. The Holy Spirit has personally drawn you to this place.

If you're already a believer, you might see yourself inside the temple like I was for a while. Maybe you've ventured into the River with Jesus, up to the ankles or knees. Perhaps you're a tree, drawing daily on the life-giving flow. You might realize you're in the marshes, or in the Arabah. You may be bearing fruit under the anointing of that waterfall.

Wherever it may be, realistically acknowledge your position in this vision to God. Now ask yourself:

"Where do I want to be?"

Look at the picture again. Tell your Father where you'd like to be in that vision.

Did you see yourself as a seeker? Maybe you're realizing you want to accept Jesus as your Savior and Lord. Know that God is calling you by name. If you're ready, just stop and answer His call. Tell the Father that you are opening your heart to Jesus. Ask Him to forgive your sins. Welcome the Holy Spirit to live inside you.

Maybe you're already a committed believer, but you spotted yourself lingering inside at the altar. Maybe you want to take those first steps outside the temple and into the River with Jesus. Maybe you've waded into the water—up to your ankles or knees already—and you want to go deeper still. Maybe you want to be a tree under the cliffs of Engedi, continuously under the Spirit's anointing. If it's forward motion, it's good, even if it's your first tentative baby step into these waters.

Remember: how deep we venture into God's River is entirely up to us, in our individual free will to choose. God continues to call, and He is there to embrace anyone who chooses to go deeper into Him. If you're a little scared, like I was, picture yourself taking Jesus' hand as He leads you into the River (Isaiah 41:10). He will let you take your own pace. He won't pull you deeper. He won't push you faster than you want to go. He will, however, ask you to trust Him. As He did with Peter, He will call you to step out of the comforts of the natural and into the waters of the Spirit.

"But how do I do that?"

As much as we tend to think we have to do or be something grand, remember this is all about grace. This is all about what God has freely done for us, not something we could ever buy, do, or earn. Turn to Luke 11:11–13. We see here that the Father will give of the Holy Spirit to those who ask.

So, let's ask. He adores you. He loves it when you look to Him. You are free to ask God to light your path every step of the way. If you get confused or don't understand something, stop and pray. Invite the Holy Spirit to help and teach you.

"But what if I'm afraid of the Water?"

You're not alone. I was afraid, too.

Though I know it's perfectly safe for you to venture into this River alone with God, I realize it can be helpful to have another believer at your side, in a kind of spiritual buddy system. Maybe you have someone who can partner with you in this. Maybe there's another believer who is ready to move forward alongside you. In Ecclesiastes 4:9, we're assured that two are better than one. You may want to make yourself accountable to another person, to pray for and encourage each other, to keep each other on course.

If there is no one in your life you can partner with in this way, still do not let fear deter you. Know that God is not the author of any fear that would prevent you from answering the Holy Spirit's call. Be frank in prayer. If you feel fear, confess it. Then ask God to help you move past it. Hear what the Spirit is saying to you now:

> *"And the Spirit and the bride say, 'Come.' And let the one who hears say, 'Come.' And let the one who is thirsty come; let the one who wishes take the water of life without cost."*
>
> *Revelation 22:17*

Isn't that an amazing invitation? If you hear Him, come. If you're thirsty, come. Add to that: anyone who simply wants to come is invited to drink of these waters over the entire course of earthly life for free! You don't earn it. You needn't wait to hear from anyone else. The Spirit and the bride are already calling you. The door is open for every believer to move forward in the Spirit, while still vitally connected to the sanctuary where we were first redeemed.

POP QUIZ:
When does the Holy Spirit come to reside in believers?

If you're not sure, look back at Ezekiel's vision for the answer. The waters of the Holy Spirit are present within the temple at the altar of regeneration.

Numerous Scriptures confirm that upon receiving Jesus as Savior and Lord, the Holy Spirit immediately indwells every believer. This priceless deposit of the Spirit is a grace Timothy is repeatedly exhorted to guard (I Timothy 6:20, II Timothy 1:14).

The fullness of the Godhead bodily indeed dwells in Christ. That means the complete package—the Father, Son, and Holy Spirit—travel and dwell as One in the believer. Still, in this vision, we see Jesus calling the Spirit-inhabited believer beyond the temple and into baptism with the Holy Spirit, where the waters of the Spirit go beyond filling us to immersing us in Him, and onto where that initial deposit can readily refill, multiply, and overflow.

Think of your body as a cup. Upon regeneration, your cup is filled to the brim with the waters of the Spirit. Then, Jesus takes your full cup and immerses it into His River. Now, the Spirit's waters are not only inside the cup, they also envelop it. Even after emerging from the

River, the limitless fountain of the Spirit continues, available to refresh and refill the cup perpetually.

"Does that mean I've got it all at regeneration or is there a second experience?"

Perhaps the most hotly debated issue about the Holy Spirit is the controversy over when baptism with the Spirit happens to believers today. Is there an all-in-one experience with the Spirit at redemption, or is baptism with the Holy Spirit a "second blessing?"

All-in-oners assert that every believer is baptized with the Holy Spirit at the moment of rebirth, backing their position with chapter and verse; however, believers in a second blessing cite other Scriptures to defend their persuasion. Who is right and who is wrong? Don't both sides have to ignore certain verses to refute the other's claims? Is it spiritual arrogance to suggest that we've got all there is to get when we're born again? Does preaching a second blessing encourage spiritual elitism or imply that it's possible to separate the Godhead and thereby get Jesus minus His Spirit? And just what is the promised baptism with the Holy Spirit anyway? Boy, can we get in a bunch about this!

Before giving me clearance to teach this study to a traditional women's group, the pastor cautiously inquired if I believed in a second experience, sensitive to the controversy within his denomination. First, I assured him that I believe Scripture supports that the Holy Spirit indwells at regeneration. The pastor nodded in relieved approval. I went on to say that yes, I also believe there can be a second experience, and a third and a fourth and a fifth and a sixth and a seventh... By then, the pastor was laughing in enthusiastic agreement at my point, that we can look forward to as many experiences in the Holy Spirit as our hearts are open to receive.

We tend to be task-oriented with these things. Instead of moving on a continuum in the Spirit, we target this goal or that so we can check it off of our holy "to do" lists. Drawn to repentance: *Check!* Redeemed: *Check!* Spirit-baptized: *Check!* You know it's true. There's a real danger in looking at these past experiences and kicking back, thinking we're done, instead of infinitely moving forward into all the many experiences God has for us ahead. Relationship with God has a past, present, and a future, where we can look forward to many works of the Spirit.

So, is the Bible in conflict with itself? No. Remember, we shouldn't cherry-pick verses to support our mind-set. Rather, we should only adopt views that are consistent with the Bible as a whole. That means, to embrace all of Scripture on this question is to accept the view that the mighty River of the Holy Spirit moves on a variety of people in a variety of ways and timings.

"Are some people regenerated and baptized with the Spirit at the same time?"

Yes. Turn to Acts 10:44–48. Here, we read about Peter, preaching Jesus to Gentiles who gathered at Cornelius' house. Notice, in verse forty-four that while Peter was *still* telling them about redemption through Jesus, the Holy Spirit fell on everyone who heard.

Imagine Peter's shock that these Gentiles believed and were baptized with the Spirit before he even finished his sermon! He hadn't even had a chance to make an altar call, and here they were manifesting gifts, evidence to Peter that both redemption and baptism with the Holy Spirit had already taken place. Rather than getting ruffled because God chose to move in an order Peter didn't expect, Peter rolled with it. He congenially affirmed the authenticity of the Spirit's move by directing the newly redeemed, freshly baptized with the Spirit Gentile believers to be welcomed into another type of baptism, that is, water baptism in the name of Jesus.

"Is everyone regenerated and baptized with the Spirit at the same time?"

I wasn't. Even though we're indwelt by the Spirit at regeneration, Scripture confirms my experience that not everyone is regenerated and baptized with the Spirit at the same time. Look up Acts 8:14–17. In this instance, which precedes the events of Acts 10, Peter and John minister to Samaritans who have already been redeemed and water baptized in the name of Jesus for some time. We see that the apostles prayed for these believers that they might *receive* the Holy Spirit who was yet to fall upon them. Clearly, as believers, they were already indwelt by the Holy Spirit, but Peter and John still laid hands on them and prayed that they'd *receive* the Spirit, that He would fall *upon* them.

This is a point of confusion for some. Many tout this passage as proof positive that baptism with the Holy Spirit is always a completely separate experience, and that believers aren't filled with the Spirit upon regeneration. They erroneously suggest that Jesus is not the "fullness of the Godhead" (that is Father, Son, and Holy Spirit), which Scripture elsewhere assures us that He is. Many others simply avoid the implications of this passage because it conflicts with their traditional "all-in-one" at redemption theology.

Is the Bible in conflict with itself? Absolutely not. Then, how do we wrap our heads around this apparent conundrum? The lightning rod word of this passage is the word *receive*. Rather than throw out Scripture or stiffen in our respective ranks, let's think about that word *receive*. Consider the parallels of the following scenario:

> *I am at home, working on a demanding project. I have invited a friend and her sisters to move in with me. Though they're triplets, each has a name and distinct personality. I have only met two of the triplets before, but have heard good things about the third. The triplets arrive simultaneously. My friend understands that I'm on a major deadline, and because I have given her a key, she and the sister I've met enter my study and say hello, while the unmet sister goes to the kitchen and begins to arrange fresh fruit she's brought. I briefly receive the two sisters I know before they leave me to my work. Later, when I choose to put aside my task, I go into my living room and formally **receive** my third new roommate, long after her actual arrival. Overflowing with excitement, the third sister I'm just meeting envelops me with an embrace. She offers me wonderful housewarming gifts, power tools that I desperately need for my work.*

You see, the third sister has been in my home for some time already and yet, the act of actually receiving her, then allowing her to envelop me and give me gifts comes later, depending upon my choice of when to formally receive her. That doesn't mean she wasn't in my home before I received her. That doesn't mean I hadn't previously received her two sisters. It also doesn't negate the possibility that another person might have stopped what she was doing and received all three new roommates simultaneously upon arrival. It just means that, in my case, the act of receiving the third sister was separate from and later than the moment she first entered my dwelling.

In a similar way, some receive Jesus and are baptized in the Holy Spirit at the same time, and other believers may have the Holy Spirit living in them for some time before having a separate, later experience of being baptized in the Holy Spirit and being equipped with gifts.

Still iffy on this point? Let's look at another biblical account of distinct multiple experiences.

Acts 18:24–19:6 plainly exemplifies separate experiences, all without negating the simultaneous outpouring in Acts 10. Here we meet Apollos, a man who is mighty in the Scriptures and already teaching diligently about the Lord in accordance with the baptism of John, who had been martyred years prior, after declaring Jesus to be the long-awaited Messiah. Notice that Apollos is not just preaching about a Messiah yet to come. Apollos is preaching about *the Lord,* which implies accepting John's identification of Jesus as Messiah.

Paul further clarifies the meaning of John's baptism just below in Acts 19:4. For the people of Apollos' day, receiving John's baptism meant repenting and believing in Jesus as Messiah, Savior, and Lord. What's more, verse Acts 18:25 says Apollos was *fervent in spirit.* The Greek word for fervent has a liquid connotation, like water bubbling to a boil. So, Apollos had received Jesus. He was also bubbling with the indwelling Spirit. But when Priscilla and Aquila heard him preach, they realized that Apollos was only familiar with John's baptism into Jesus and not with Jesus' promise of baptism with the Holy Spirit and fire.

Notice the example Priscilla and Aquila set for us in how they dealt with this situation. They didn't shout Apollos down or embarrass him in public. They took him aside and carefully explained to him what he didn't know about God's ways, no doubt clarifying the distinction between the baptism of John into Jesus and being baptized with the Holy Spirit and power. Notice that after Apollos became acquainted with baptism with the Holy Spirit, he was encouraged in his gift as an evangelist and his preaching was thereafter described as *powerful.*

In Acts 19:1–6, Apollos' story is immediately followed up by yet another example of disciples who had not yet *received* the Holy Spirit at the time when they believed. In fact, these believers hadn't even heard that there was a Holy Spirit to receive, even though time had clearly passed since their regeneration. They also hadn't undergone John's baptism, which Paul quickly rectified, baptizing them in water in the name of Jesus. Then, in verse six, we see that Paul laid hands on them, and the already indwelling Spirit came *upon* them in a new way, evidencing His baptism by gifts of tongues and prophecy.

"Is baptism with the Holy Spirit a separate experience for some?"

Yes. This doesn't conflict with the fact that some are baptized with the Spirit at regeneration. It simply means that the Bible demonstrates that the timing of these experiences can vary. Whether the believer receives baptism with the Holy Spirit immediately upon regeneration, or whether days, months, even years pass in between, Jesus invites us all, knowing how powerfully baptism with the Spirit equips believers for ministry and harvest.

If you're already in the River, great! Challenge yourself to go deeper, bear fruit, and use your gifts. If you're still inside the temple and you're just realizing the Holy Spirit hasn't fallen on you in this way yet, I encourage you to take Jesus' hand and let Him lead you into that River. It's not something you have to work your way up to or that you have to be spiritually mature to receive. Newborn believers received this baptism in Acts 10. More mature believers received it in Acts 8, 18, and 19. Whatever the timing of these experiences has been for you, wherever you are on His continuum of grace, answer Jesus' invitation to move onward, step-by-step in the Spirit.

"Once the Spirit indwells aren't we always filled with the Spirit?"

If our cups were always filled to the brim with the Spirit, then Paul wouldn't have needed to exhort believers to be filled with the Spirit (Ephesians 5:18). Yes, the Holy Spirit can flow like a fountain, keeping our cups full to capacity, but when we chose to make way for the flesh within our finite cups, we displace the Spirit.

Think of fleshy choices as if they are stones that you are dropping into what was a full cup of Spirit water. The more stones you put in, the more of the Spirit gets displaced. Maybe a pebble lodges in the tube that was feeding the Spirit's fountain. Now, the process of refilling gets compromised. Evaporation takes place. The once fresh water in your cup starts to stagnate. It collects dust. Tell the truth: would you want to drink from a cup that had been sitting open and dormant for a week? Plus, day-by-day unattended, the level slowly drops, till there is no water left at all.

Though the fresh water of the Holy Spirit is completely accessible to believers, we can quench the Spirit, stopping up the flow. We can take up so much room with those fleshy stones that we leave Him little room to fill. It is not that He has withdrawn from us. Rather, we displace Him. We all do it. No one is exempt from this struggle. In Romans 7:14–25, Paul writes about this ongoing war we wage with the flesh. Our enemy will do everything he can to subvert us. That's right. We're not wrestling with flesh and blood. This is spiritual warfare. No kidding.

The bad news is: when we give into the flesh, we quench and displace the Spirit. But the good news is: when we deny the flesh, the Spirit floods back to refill us, rendering the enemy defeated, while the believer moves beyond the battlefield, refreshed and empowered.

"How do I know if my cup is low in the Spirit?"

The better I've gotten to know the Holy Spirit's presence, the more acutely I sense when I've displaced Him. We can do some quick diagnostics. Just as the Spirit manifests Himself in us in detectable ways, so does the flesh. Spot-check yourself with Galatians 5:16–25. Are you struggling with envy, outbursts of anger, jealousy, hatred, strife, sexual impurity, substance abuse and the like? Those are evidences of the flesh. Are you overflowing with love, joy, peace, patience, gentleness, goodness, faith, meekness, and self-control? Those are the fruits of the Spirit.

If you find your cup is low or even almost empty, be encouraged. It is the still present deposit of the Spirit who is giving you the discernment to diagnose your spiritual condition. Not only that, He stands ready to help you clear out the fleshy stones that compromise the flow of fresh water.

What to do? The Holy Spirit is your Helper. Ask Him to help you identify every fleshy impediment that's in your cup. Repent and enlist His help in purging the debris. Some stones will be harder to remove than others, particularly if you've carried them for years and have grown attached or even addicted to them. Sometimes, as Jesus suggested, you may need to fast and pray in order to eject a particularly stubborn boulder. Sometimes, it's helpful to make yourself accountable to a trusted prayer partner.

Whatever you do, remember that God will not violate your free will. He has provided the Holy Spirit to help you as you choose to allow Him access; however, the Spirit will not barge in uninvited or forcefully claim space you refuse to relinquish. Still, to the extent you submit, the weight of those fleshy stones will be lifted and the current of His River will rush in to refill.

CHAPTER SEVEN

Passing the Power Torch to You

At the end of our Christmas Eve services, we always sang a carol by candlelight. Even the children got to hold a candle, its flame representing the Spirit, which we were to carry out into the world. As kids, my siblings and I used to have an informal competition to see who could keep the candle burning the longest. We'd all manage to keep them lit inside the sanctuary, but once outside, our cupped hands provided little protection against the brisk December night. Within moments, the ocean air would whip through and snuff our fires out.

Water, Wind and Fire—these are three powerful forces, all associated with the Holy Spirit. Ezekiel's vision concentrates on the Spirit as water—a spring, a fountain, a river. Genesis and Acts depict Him as the life-giving breath and mighty wind of God. Now, let's take a look at another aspect of the Spirit's work: as a purifying, consuming, eternally blazing torch, conferring the Spirit's anointing of kingship throughout history.

From the beginning, it was God's will to be our King, but God's people rebelled against His authority. By Samuel's day, they were demanding an earthly king. In I Samuel 8:5–10:11, you'll see how God told Samuel to warn the people of the hardship they'd bring upon themselves under a human king, but Israel stubbornly insisted. So, God let them have their way and instructed Samuel to appoint a king, then showed him precisely what man to appoint: Saul.

When Samuel anointed Saul as king, the torch of the Spirit's kingship anointing was passed to Saul and he began to prophesy. However, just as God anticipated with any earthly king, Saul stopped obeying God, resulting in the torch being passed to King David. Despite the corruption of successive human kings, the torch was picked up by prophets, who foretold God's promise of an eternally reigning King, in the line of David, leading up to the advent of Jesus.

In Matthew 3:11–17, we read the account of how John the Baptist preached that, while he baptized in water for repentance, the promised Messiah would baptize with the Holy Spirit and fire. When John baptized Jesus in water, he saw the heavens open up and the Spirit of God descend like a dove upon Jesus, accompanied by God's voice, identifying Jesus as His beloved Son. These signs tracked with the prophetic word John had received from God, telling him that the One upon whom he would see the Spirit descend would be the One who would baptize with the Holy Spirit. This prompted John to affirm Jesus as the One who would take away the sin of the world, the Son of God (John 1:33–34).

So, at Jesus' baptism, after centuries of flawed human kings, we see God returning to His rightful position of kingship over us, passing the torch of the Spirit's anointing to Jesus as the promised eternal King, a Sovereign who stands ready to baptize every believer with the Holy Spirit and fire, making even commonplace believers kings and priests to Him.

"Isn't fire kind of dangerous?"

There is something both attractive and fearsome about fire. As you are enveloped in the blaze of the Holy Spirit, people will be drawn to you. Believers and unbelievers alike will watch you, like Moses' burning bush, on fire, yet safe, not consumed. Fascination with the spectacle will give way to curiosity about how this could possibly occur. The heat of the fire will prompt a thirst, a longing for relationship with God.

Check out Daniel Chapter Three. Read how Shadrach, Meshach and Abed-nego were miraculously safe in Nebuchadnezzar's fiery furnace. See how Nebuchadnezzar was awestruck to witness a fourth man walking with them in the fire unharmed, appearing *like the Son of God*. Notice how dramatically this event changed Nebuchadnezzar's heart toward Shadrach, Meshach and Abed-nego, as well as their God.

Many believers fear the very fire of the Spirit into which Jesus calls us. They back away, afraid that the miraculous won't happen for them, that they'll just get burned. They cower behind bad experiences or the errors of others. They caution fellow believers not to get too close, to leave the tending of God's fire to the clergy. They distance themselves from teaching on this subject, neglecting to feed the very flame that could make them more like Jesus.

The question you'll be left with is: *Am I going to trust people or my eternal King Jesus who kindles this fire?* As we walk through the Gospels, we'll see that Jesus had a lot to say on this subject. He carefully explained how the Holy Spirit would keep the torch of the anointing ablaze, manifesting His presence to the children of all generations.

> *"He who believes in Me, as the Scripture said, from his innermost being shall flow rivers of living water. But this He spoke of the Spirit, whom those who believed in Him were to receive; for the Spirit was not yet given, because Jesus was not yet glorified."*
>
> *John 7:38–39*

Notice that Jesus described the Spirit as a river, tracking with Ezekiel's vision (Ezekiel 47:1–12). The Greek words for *were to receive* in this verse are *mello lambano*, which can also be translated to mean *are yet to take hold of.* So, these verses confirm that the torch of the Spirit had not yet been passed to the disciples at this point. Indeed, the power accessed through baptism with the Holy Spirit and fire would not be given to them until after Jesus was glorified, that is, after His crucifixion, death, resurrection, and ascension.

> *"Truly, truly, I say to you, he who believes in Me, the works that I do shall he do also; and greater works than these shall he do; because I go to the Father."*
>
> *John 14:12*

Jesus made an astounding claim there, didn't He? Consider all the supernatural works Jesus performed. Casting out demons, multiplying food, healing the sick, and raising the dead were all regular occurrences in Jesus' ministry. Was Jesus saying we could actually do these kinds of spectacular works as well? Absolutely. But Jesus didn't stop there. He said we'd do even *greater* works!

I don't know about you, but it's hard for me to wrap my head around doing greater works than Jesus did. How do you top calling Lazarus out of the grave? The Greek is helpful when it comes to clarifying the word for *greater* as *more* or *larger in quantity.* Jesus was essentially saying that believers would have the time and numbers to do even more than He was able to accomplish in three years of earthly ministry.

So, yes, we really can do greater works. It's possible because the same Spirit who burned in Jesus, supernaturally empowering His ministry, can burn in every believer, across countless generations, who answers Jesus' call to baptism with the Spirit and fire. That's where the impossible becomes possible! Ask yourself:

- *Am I seeing works like Jesus did in my life?*
- *Am I seeing even greater works?*

If your honest answer to both questions is no, then you're like most people. There is a lot of room to grow in the Holy Spirit. There are ways you really can be more like Jesus than you already are, not only in character, but also in Spirit-empowered service.

Jesus was very clear that He would maintain a presence with all believers in the Holy Spirit, and that this fire of the Spirit would burn eternally, even after He had left the earth in bodily form:

> *"And I will ask the Father, and He will give you another Helper, that He may be with you forever; that is the Spirit of truth, whom the world cannot receive, because it does not behold Him or know Him, but you know Him because He abides with you and will be in you. I will not leave you as orphans; I will come to you. After a little while, the world will behold Me no more; but you will behold Me; because I live, you shall live also."*
>
> *John 14:16–19*

Jesus' foregoing words concerning the continuing work of the Holy Spirit were spoken just prior to Jesus' passion. Jesus knew that He would be leaving his disciples (in physical form) and that the Spirit would be given as His continuing presence. After the resurrection, when Jesus appeared to the disciples, we read of another important step in the disciples' spiritual process. The Bible says: *"...He [Jesus] breathed on them, and said to them, 'Receive the Holy Spirit.' "* (John 20:22)

"Whoa. Back up. What exactly happened here?"

Remember: Jesus had died for the sins of the world. He had conquered death, and the disciples believed in Him as the Son of God. So, as their accepted Savior and Lord, Jesus breathed on them, imparting the Holy Spirit to regenerate and take up residence in them. I believe John 20:22 marks the moment when the disciples were born again, borne of the Spirit. When Jesus breathed on them, the Holy Spirit went from being WITH them to dwelling IN them; however, the Holy Spirit had not yet fallen UPON them with that fire-power to witness that was still to come. If we place them into Ezekiel's vision, they would be in the temple, indwelt by the Spirit, but not yet baptized with the Spirit and fire at this point.

Okay, watch Peter's first big move after being born again (John 21:3). Gotta love this guy! Think of it. The miracle-working, crucified Jesus, whom Peter denied, had appeared alive and had administered regeneration first hand. What did Peter decide to do next? *He decided to go fishing!* Huh? Was that the non sequitur of all time or what? Actually, he was just like we are. That's why we relate to him so easily. Jesus did a stupendous work in Peter's life, and what did Peter do? Peter went right back to what was natural for him, what he did before he ever met Jesus. He went fishing and convinced the rest of the newly redeemed disciples to go with him.

Maybe it was all a little too much for Peter. Maybe he was just hungry or needed to make some money. Whatever. Jesus still used Peter's retreat to the natural to demonstrate a point in the Spirit. Read on in John 21 to see what this professional fisherman caught that night in the natural. Zip! Nada! Not so much as a little guppy. Peter may have wondered what was up with this. After all, Jesus had promised Peter would do the same works Jesus did, once the rivers of living water were flowing through Peter in the Spirit. *Aha!* There's the answer. Again, though Peter was regenerated, he had not yet been empowered by baptism with the Spirit and fire, a work that was yet to come, as detailed in Acts Chapter Two.

Back to our story—we see that Jesus appeared to the disciples again, after their fruitless night of fishing. Under the anointing of the Holy Spirit's power, Jesus instructed them to cast the nets out again. This time, the harvest of fish was so enormous that their nets could not contain them, hearkening to Ezekiel 47:10.

Think back, about Jesus' first words to Peter (Matthew 4:19), when he initially called him from casting nets into the sea: *Follow me, and I will make you fishers of men.* Though Peter was indwelt by the Spirit at this point, he was still operating largely in the natural. Once again demonstrating the power of the anointing, Jesus urged Peter on, to be equipped to bring in an overwhelming harvest of souls. Therein lies the primary purpose for baptism with the Holy Spirit.

We read about the disciples' next major step in the Spirit in Acts One, where we learn that, just prior to His ascension, Jesus gave the following orders to the apostles in parting:

> *"And gathering them together, He commanded them not to leave Jerusalem, but to wait for what the Father had promised, 'Which,' He said, 'you heard of from me. For John baptized with water; but you shall be baptized with the Holy Spirit not many days from now...but you shall receive power, when the Holy Spirit has come upon you: and you shall be my witnesses both in Jerusalem, and in all Judea and Samaria, and even to the remotest part of the earth.' "*
>
> *Acts 1:4–5, 8*

That's right. Jesus instructed the born-again, Spirit-inhabited disciples to wait for another experience, referred to as *the promise of the Father*, which is baptism with the Holy Spirit.

"They already have the Spirit. What's the difference?"

When a person is regenerated, the Holy Spirit indwells as an initial deposit, filling the inside of that person's cup. It's an important internal work of the Spirit, limited by the capacity of the person. Jesus urged His disciples to wait for baptism with the Holy Spirit, knowing they needed to be equipped to go beyond an internal work to a supernaturally empowered work of outreach, to spread the Gospel throughout the world.

Whereas regeneration brings about an in-filling of the Spirit, baptism with the Holy Spirit brings about an overflow, a falling upon, an enveloping anointing for service, ministry, and harvest. Yes, we've seen examples of these two major works happening seemingly simultaneously; however, the disciples are an additional example of those who were indwelt by the Spirit, then had to wait for baptism with the Spirit and fire, as others did later in the book of Acts.

"Why would God make me wait? I hate waiting."

You're in good company. Who likes to wait, especially for something we need? In this instance, the apostles needed to wait because Jesus had not yet been glorified, which Jesus had said would happen before the rivers of the Spirit would flow out of them (John 7:39). Others in Acts just didn't know there was more to be received (Chapters 8, 18 and 19).

The latter was my experience. I was born again for some time before I had even heard there was such a thing as baptism with the Holy Spirit. As with Apollos, another believer quietly took me aside to affirm Jesus' invitation to be baptized with the Spirit and fire. More time passed as the Holy Spirit helped me to unplug faulty church traditions and plug into what the Bible really has to say. I went from fearing baptism with the Spirit to being taught by the Word about it. Finally I reached the point where I deeply wanted Jesus to empower me for harvest in this way. Then, because the Holy Spirit had already been poured out at Pentecost, baptism with the Spirit was available to me as soon as I took the step of faith to ask.

Just prior to His ascension, Jesus had instructed the apostles to wait in Jerusalem until they were clothed with power from on high (Luke 24:49). Why wait for the Holy Spirit's power? First, because Jesus told us to, but also, because it's a spiritual battleground out there. Would you rush into battle undressed? Of course not. We need to be clothed with power to get the job done. On a practical level, those regenerated disciples were still running primarily on natural strength, pulling in empty nets after fishing all night. Like born again babies, they were spiritually naked and vulnerable till they were clothed with the Holy Spirit's power.

Take a cautionary look at the events of Acts 19:13–16 if you want to see just how vulnerable a person can become when rushing ahead of God into a spiritual battle while unclothed with this fire-power. These exorcists were unrecognized on this battlefield, but notice that the demons knew Paul and Jesus. As for the exorcists who presumed to battle these demons without Jesus' name or the power of the Holy Spirit, the Bible says the evil spirits attacked and overpowered them so that they ran away wounded and naked, literally unclothed.

I like the Greek word *enduo*, which is used in Luke 24:49. It means *to invest in clothing*. I invested a great deal of time, thought, and desire into receiving the spiritual clothing I have been given. I invested that time and continue to invest day-by-day, decades later, because I take Jesus' final orders about the Holy Spirit to heart. Anyone who reads this book is investing in being clothed with power. Anyone who seriously searches the Scriptures and finds the strength to turn from man-made doctrines invests in this clothing. So, let's investigate, confirm answers, follow through, bravely take Jesus' hand, get into that river of Spirit baptism, take up His torch, and wear His clothing of power.

"So, I'm supposed to just wait and do nothing?"

Jesus told the apostles to wait for the Holy Spirit. He ascended to the Father. The ordered wait began. Everyone went into the upper room. They devoted themselves to prayer. But apparently, the waiting got to Peter. Still under the natural power that failed him at fishing, he seemed to have had enough waiting. Once again, he decided to do something.

If you read Acts 1:15–26, you'll see what Peter did. He decided to replace Judas so that there would be twelve apostles again. They drew lots and the lot fell to Matthias, who was then incorporated as the new twelfth apostle. Now, maybe Matthias proved to be an asset. I hope that he did. I like to think that God used this appointment for the good, but all I know is that there is not a single biblical mention of Matthias accomplishing anything from this moment forward. Luke was known for his attention to accuracy and details, and yet there's not one anecdote, not one reference, not even so much as Matthias' name being dropped in an epistle. Maybe he was a quiet servant, even a martyr, but we're left to wonder whether Peter came up as empty by enlisting Matthias as he did when he dropped his nets to go fishing.

Let's not be too hard on Peter, though. We all do it. We have things to do, people to appoint. Instead of simply staying and focusing solely on obeying Jesus' command to wait, we multitask. But when it comes to generating supernaturally empowered harvest, we can just be spinning our wheels.

Take a moment and ask yourself: *Am I trying to do things for God au natural without waiting to be clothed with the fire-power of the Holy Spirit?* If so, take heart. The torch of the anointing that was given to Saul, David, then passed down by the kings and prophets, that same blaze of fire that burned in Jesus' earthly ministry was about to be passed again.

"So, then what happened?"

All heaven broke loose. Read Acts Chapter Two. Celebrate as our victorious King Jesus passes the torch of anointing to His disciples, baptizing them with the Holy Spirit and fire. Everything changed dramatically for the disciples at this point. It began with the Spirit blowing upon them like a mighty rushing wind, releasing the floodgates of Spirit baptism. They saw His fire come, tongues of flame resting on each of them, evidencing the conveying of this supernatural power. The disciples began to speak in languages unknown to them, but understood by those outside, people of diverse languages who were reportedly amazed to hear and understand the disciples in their own respective native tongues. This demonstration of the disciples' empowerment drew a huge crowd.

The same Peter who had floundered so in the natural was now clothed with the promised power of the Holy Spirit. The same guy who cowered away from a servant girl, denying that he even knew Jesus, took the floor, boldly preaching Jesus to a multitude. We don't know how many thousands heard Peter's testimony, only that three thousand souls were caught up into the kingdom's net that day, fulfilling Jesus' promise to make Peter a fisher of men.

Peter openly acknowledged that this was the outpouring of the Holy Spirit foretold by the prophet, Joel (Joel 2:28–29). He confirmed that there would be more prophecy, visions, and dreams given in the Spirit, gifts that would be given to men and women, to young and old alike. In essence, Peter accepted the torch of the Spirit's anointing himself, and then offered it to anyone willing to receive. Peter preached that this baptism of power is for every believer. He said it was for them, for their children, and for all who are far off, as many as the Lord would call to Himself (Acts 2:39). In doing so, Peter echoed Jesus' promise of Acts 1:8, that this supernatural baptism of power would extend to the ends of the earth. The Greek word often translated as *ends* or *uttermost* is *eschatos*. This word speaks to both time and place, assuring us that this fire-power will be available to all believers throughout the whole earth and till the conclusion of earthly time, literally till the ends of the earth.

Don't miss the personal implications here. Peter passed the torch of the anointing across countless generations all the way to each of us! Baptism with the Holy Spirit and fire is given freely, without limitation of time to all generations throughout history. Jesus extends an open invitation to all who believe. Still.

This is not just for spiritual superstars. It's not just for the clergy. It's certainly not meant only for first century believers. Today's believers are also numbered among the passing generations who have answered the Lord's call to pick up His power torch. This promise of the Father is for us!

"How do I know I've really been baptized with the Holy Spirit?"

This is a real hot button. Because baptism with the Holy Spirit was often recorded as being accompanied with supernatural signs such as tongues and/or prophecy, there are many who consider those signs, tongues in particular, to be an essential evidence of Spirit baptism. The Bible, however, never cites tongues as a necessary proof. Though gifts of tongues and prophecy are often recorded following Spirit baptism and are valid evidences, these signs are not always mentioned.

Check Acts 8:14–17. Here, Peter and John prayed for believers who were baptized with the Holy Spirit, and yet there is no record of tongues from them, or from Apollos, whose baptism with the Spirit is evidenced by empowered preaching at the end of Acts 18. Maybe they did speak in tongues; maybe they didn't. But to answer this question faithfully, we must embrace all of Scripture, including I Corinthians 12:30, and allow that it's possible that some don't speak in tongues when they receive baptism with the Spirit. I was one such believer.

In Luke 11:13, we learn that the gift of the Holy Spirit will be given to those who ask. Ultimately, I did just that. I asked Jesus to baptize me with the Holy Spirit. Though I felt a rush of overwhelming assurance that I had received what I'd asked for, that fire lit in my heart, there were no outward signs.

I did not speak in tongues that night.

I did not prophesy to anyone.

I simply went home and jotted down a poem that came to me, as if inspired to commemorate the experience. Yet despite the lack of an unknown tongue, I knew that I knew that I had been baptized with the Spirit after simply asking.

I have never doubted that experience, though it was almost two years before any manifestation of tongues. The Lord knew that, at the point of Spirit baptism, I was still fearful of tongues, and He understandingly waited until I was ready.

There were, however, two immediate internal manifestations to my baptism with the Holy Spirit. That night I received two gifts that evidenced that the Spirit had indeed come upon me: faith and distinguishing of spirits. I discerned the presence of the Holy Spirit, falling on me in a new way. That discernment was met with an unshakeable faith that I had received what the Father had promised, despite the lack of outward evidences.

Soon, I discovered that my testimony had a more powerful effect. I became instrumental in leading others to Jesus. Whereas I had been largely unfruitful before, once baptized with the Spirit, I became a fisher of men.

"Can I be baptized with the Spirit and fire at any time?"

Like salvation, baptism with the Holy Spirit is a free gift that has already been offered to you. You don't have to work your way up to it. You can't pay for it (Acts 8:20). You don't even have to finish this chapter before you ask. All you need to do is sincerely accept Jesus' open invitation into the river of His Spirit for baptism, ask, and believe that you have received.

You can ask alone, or if it helps to agree with a few other everyday believers as I did, that's fine, too. You can ask with the laying on of hands of your elders. You can ask hands free. Just ask, believing. Follow Jesus into the river of Spirit baptism. Open your heart and let His mighty wind blow through you, feeding the unquenchable fire of God.

CHAPTER EIGHT

Would God Really Give Power Tools to Children?

Ever get a gift you didn't want? Despite the availability of computers, I continued to hang onto my familiar typewriter into the early 1990s. I convinced myself that I didn't need the hi-tech tools so many of my colleagues were using. The fact was: I was computer phobic. I was afraid of what I didn't understand, fearful that I'd never learn how to use even the simplest of programs. Finally, my boss plunked a computer on my desk. He asked me to start using this power tool, promising it would increase my productivity for him. Resisting progress was no longer an option. He left me alone with that thing. Gulp! I didn't even know how to turn it on.

That's pretty much how it goes for a lot of us when it comes to the supernatural manifestations of the Spirit. I know that's how it went for me. Even after reading all about the power gifts in the Bible, I didn't trust God to distribute them to me as He willed, despite their potential for increasing my effectiveness in serving Him. I relaxed into the traditional resistance taught by my leaders. After all, I was just a spiritual babe and babies need milk, right? Power gifts were for the mature. They seemed way too meaty for me. Surprise! Just like my boss with that computer, God presented me with the power tools I feared most, some while I was still in spiritual infancy.

Maybe you're braver than I was. Perhaps you're one of those openhearted souls who longs to receive all God has for you. Like a child at Christmas, you can't wait to unwrap your presents and find out what our Father has given especially to you. But no matter your background as a believer, when it comes to spiritual gifts, we are assured that no one Jesus baptizes with the Spirit is meant to go empty-handed. Each one will be given a manifestation of the Spirit that will profit us all.

That's right. Spiritual gifts, though they can be personally edifying, are primarily purposed as equipment—as tools for *service, ministry,* and *harvest.*

Using three different Greek words, I Corinthians 12:4–7 helps us understand three distinct varieties of gifts—tagged respectively with the names of the same *Spirit,* the same *Lord,* and the same *God*—the whole Trinity joining together to equip us with everything we need to serve. You can use the acronym S.A.W. to remember the three different categories of tools we are given:

- **S**upernatural Gifts *(charisma)*
- **A**id Gifts *(diakonia)*
- **W**orkings Gifts *(energema)*

First, this passage mentions SUPERNATURAL GIFTS *(charisma),* all in conjunction with the same *Spirit.* These spiritual equippings are like divinely charged power tools. They are miraculous endowments with no natural counterpart. The supernatural *charisma* or "grace gifts" are both wholly undeserved and distributed precisely as the Spirit wills. These sometimes-spectacular manifestations can dramatically increase the effectiveness of even the lowliest of believers, facilitating the spread of the Gospel through demonstrations of God's superhuman power.

Second, verse five cites various ministries, or what can be called AID GIFTS *(diakonia).* These services, associated with the same *Lord,* encompass a number of support gifts such as helps, encouragement, administration, teaching, giving, and hospitality. While all of the gifts are service-oriented, Aid Gifts are marked by a sacrificial willingness to spend one's time, efforts, and resources attending upon those in need. Believers with Aid Gifts are often the unsung heroes of their communities, selflessly shouldering responsibilities many avoid. They intercede long after others forget. The Lord Jesus said that the greatest among us would be our servant *(diakonos).* Those who utilize Aid Gifts follow the Lord's giving example by humbly laying down their lives in the interest of others.

Third, there are diverse effects or WORKINGS GIFTS (*energema*), which I'll also call Talents, those *God*-given skills believers can choose to operate for His glory rather than their own. Exceptional musical, technical, creative, mental, or physical abilities could fit into this category. Like the master artisans in Exodus 31:1–6, there are people God gifts in all kinds of crafts and specialties.

You may be a linguist, a designer, a mathematician, an athlete, a seamstress, a performer, an architect, or builder with *energema* gifting. You may have effective culinary, scientific, or public speaking skills. The list goes on and on—but whatever talents God may have given to you can be employed to advance the kingdom both within the church and in your everyday working world.

Finally in verses 7–10, Paul refocuses our attention back to a specific list of manifest gifts from the first category—the Supernatural Gifts of the Spirit—the power tools that are as vital to the harvest of souls as they are marginalized in traditional Christian teaching.

Why the big secret about the *charisma* gifts? No one shies away from *diakonia* and *energema*. Many traditional churches have whole ministries set up to mobilize these widely used hand tools. Members are openly encouraged to offer up their God-given affinities and talents—the things we seem naturally good at, the things we like to do. But what's all too often missing is balancing support for and operation of the Supernatural Gifts of the Spirit, those gifts we hesitate to talk about, at least in a contemporary context.

Certainly, it's incumbent upon us to use our Aid and Workings Gifts, but let's be honest. There are a lot of churches today running predominantly on natural talent and effort, despite the fact that a wide array of supernatural power tools is available to every congregation, endowments that can divinely complement Aid and Workings Gifts.

How much more effective could teachers be if they were additionally equipped with the power tool of the word of wisdom? Think how physicians could benefit their patients through supernatural gifts of healing. What Bible translator couldn't use interpretation of tongues? How many administrators could use words of knowledge or distinguishing of spirits? And what hosts couldn't increase their witness to the lost by the effecting of miracles?

There's no question that Aid and Workings are invaluable gifts, but God also has Supernatural Gifts to bestow upon each body, tools that Paul carefully instructs the church to use. And check it out: when he exhorted us to earnestly covet the best gifts, the specific Greek word Paul used for *gifts* was *charisma* (I Corinthians 12:31).

The fact is, though there are many other important gifts listed in the Bible, it's the supernatural manifestations of the Spirit Paul listed in I Corinthians 12:7-10 that are tragically absent in so many traditional churches. It's the *charisma* gifts that spark so much debate. So, while every believer should be strongly encouraged to identify and utilize their Aid Gifts and Talents, for the remainder of this book, we'll examine those gifts so many don't talk about, those supernatural power tools I never heard about in church, but found all over my owner's manual: the Bible.

Perhaps, after years of hand tools, power tools don't look safe to you. Maybe you're concerned that the Holy Spirit will distribute a gift that will burn you or put you in over your head. You might be intimidated by His power, like I was. If that's you, be assured by Luke 11:9–13. There's not so much as a single snake or scorpion among the manifestations of the Holy Spirit.

Really.

Even we know not to give venomous creatures to our kids. God's gifts aren't poisonous; they're for the good of young and old alike. They're given to equip even common believers for uncommon ministry and harvest. Practiced in daily life, they make us more like our wonder-working Savior.

Tell me: if you had to literally move part of a mountain, say to build a highway, would you even think to use a shovel? Of course not. You would seek out the best power tools available. You'd use dynamite on the hardest places. Jesus used power tools all the time. He said those who believe would use them, too, to an even greater extent than He did. If we truly want to be like Jesus, that means the power tools are standard operating equipment, even for new believers. The power of the Holy Spirit can be like that dynamite for us, breaking through the hardest of hearts.

"Does God let new converts have power tools?"

It's counter to our cautious nature, but yes. He does, sometimes. In the book of Acts, we see power tools given to even infant believers. Again, these are grace gifts. We don't earn them with works or years of devotion. The Holy Spirit simply distributes these gifts exactly as He wills (I Corinthians 12:11). Receiving a gift does not necessarily make us more mature spiritually. But we are urged to mature in the Holy Spirit, and in the ways we use the gifts He gives us. Notice Paul's exhortation to Timothy and its connection to evangelism:

> *"Do not neglect the spiritual gift that is within you, which was bestowed upon you by prophetic utterance with the laying on of hands of the presbytery. Take pains with these things; be absorbed in them, so that your progress may be evident to all. Pay close attention to yourself and to your teaching; persevere in these things; for as you do this you will insure salvation both for yourself and for those who hear you."*
>
> *I Timothy 4:14–16*

When my boss gave me that computer, I'm sure he would have been disappointed in me if I had never learned how to use it and just left the instruction manual he gave me unread. I could have stubbornly clung to my typewriter, when the computer was right there, the better tool for the job. What a waste it would have been if I had accepted the computer, played around with it for an hour or so, and then didn't put it to any continuing use. What if I'd never even turned it on? Can you imagine how my boss would have felt? How much more should we want to show our gratitude to our Father God by receiving and learning about all the gifts we've been given, and by diligently continuing in them?

Rightly used, these power tools are real attention grabbers. They help us to demonstrate the power of God, so those who gather around listen to what we say about Him. They also help us demonstrate the love of God. Think of how tenderly Jesus loved through supernatural signs and wonders. Once people were miraculously healed or fed, you can bet they wanted to hear what Jesus had to say. Harvest naturally follows when we sow seeds through power ministry. These power works can be particularly striking through children.

I have a friend, Sandy, whose daughter, Holly, grew up unable to carry a tune. Sandy assures me that this child wasn't even a good enough singer to bury in a chorus. Clearly, singing was not her talent. She just wasn't born with the chords or the ear. Then, on two separate occasions, at two different churches, two different men, visibly stirred by the Holy Spirit, prophesied over Holly in the presence of her parents that God was giving her a major music ministry of tremendous influence, that she would be leading and encouraging people in worship. This seemed impossible. Holly was no more a leader than she was a singer; however, the repeated prophecy from two men they didn't even know was too striking to disregard, even though there was no immediate manifestation.

Two years later, the Holy Spirit fell on Holly powerfully. Suddenly, this formerly untalented girl could sing, not only in tune, but also captivatingly well. At the same time, the Spirit began to inspire beautiful songs of praise in her. Original melodies, harmonies and lyrics began to pour out of Holly in far less time that it would take to compose them naturally. By age sixteen, Holly was leading worship as well as sought after by new churches to come and train their worship teams. Before long, during prayer ministry at church, Sandy observed as the Holy Spirit added a prophetic dimension to her daughter's gifting, spontaneously giving Holly specific songs for each person to whom the pastor ministered, even when what little had been shared by these people was completely outside of Holly's hearing.

Now a grown woman, Holly continues to lead others into the presence of the Lord, not only in America, but also in other countries across the globe. Holly knows there is nothing natural about her gift. Her voice and songs are pure wonders of God, empowered by the Holy Spirit, the same Spirit who is available to move miraculously through you.

"Isn't it bad to look for signs?"

If you're looking for signs as an end-run around faith, then yes. In fact, the Bible says that it's a wicked and perverse generation that looks for signs, and that no signs (beyond Jonah) will be given to those people (Matthew 16:4). There's a difference, however, between faithless insistence upon signs as proof and the rightly confirming signs that naturally follow believers, attesting to the power of God. Consider Jesus' parting words in the Gospel of Mark:

> *"And these signs will accompany those who have believed: in My name will cast out demons, they will speak with new tongues; they will pick up serpents, and if they drink any deadly poison, it shall not hurt them; they will lay hands on the sick, and they will recover."*
>
> *Mark 16:17–18*

Many remind that Mark 16:9-20 doesn't appear in the earliest manuscripts found, but the essential point of verses 17-18 (that signs would occur through believers in Jesus' name) is well supported by many other widely accepted biblical passages (Acts 10:46; 28:3-6, Matthew 10:18, etc.). This passage doesn't mean that we should needlessly drink poison or pick up snakes to prove God's power. Rather that, as we're serving God, if something like this unavoidably happens, God has the power to protect us and will receive glory out of doing so.

Remember, God doesn't do purposeless tricks. God's signs are for the holy purpose of spreading the Gospel. Jesus said: *Unless you people see signs and wonders, you simply will not believe (John 4:48).* Jesus punctuated his point by healing a nobleman's dying son, resulting in the man and his whole household believing.

Christians don't require signs or supernatural gifts as proof, but the more given over we are to the Holy Spirit, the more the fire-power of God will flow through us, making us more like Jesus who regularly moved in the miraculous. When we believe in Jesus, when He baptizes us with the Spirit and fire, signs will naturally follow, just as they did with Jesus. We could keep picking up our familiar hand tools, the way we're accustomed. But the harvest is ripe, the job is too big, so the Holy Spirit distributes power tools to help win the lost, even to the children among us.

"But my church isn't into the spectacular gifts."

Maybe not. Mine wasn't either, but God is. How do we know about this, even if our leaders discourage or downplay contemporary supernatural manifestations? We look to the Bible, which shows us these three major purposes for signs and wonders:

1. To EMPOWER the preaching of the Gospel
    (Isaiah 61:1–3; Luke 4:18–19; Romans 15:18–19)

2. To DEMONSTRATE the authentic power of God
    (Mark 16:20; John 4:48–50; Acts 4:16; I Cor. 2:4–5)

3. To ATTRACT unbelievers to God
    (John 6:2, 12:9–11)

Do you want to be equipped for service? Do you want to truly be like Jesus, in all His wonder-working power? Do you want to maximize your outreach to the lost? If so, then don't seek the signs and wonders as proof or in and of themselves, simply answer Jesus' invitation into His powerful River and you'll find power-gifts flowing, right along with the full complement of fruits.

"My church doesn't allow certain gifts of the Spirit."

If this frustrates you, think how the Spirit of God feels when His gifts are marked *Return to Sender!* Paul addressed all believers about the supernatural gifts in no uncertain terms:

> *"If any man thinketh himself to be a prophet, or spiritual, let him take knowledge of the things which I write unto you, that they are the commandments of the Lord. But if any man is ignorant, let him be ignorant. Wherefore, my brethren, desire earnestly to prophesy, and forbid not to speak with tongues. But let all things be done decently and in order."*
>
> *I Corinthians 14:37–40 ASV*

As the Holy Spirit inspired Paul to write this letter, the propensity of believers to quench certain gifts was anticipated, particularly prophecy and tongues. So, he distilled the message of I Corinthians 12–14, into the following bullet points:

- *Accept these as God's commands*
- *Earnestly desire prophecy*
- *Do not forbid tongues*
- *Allow the ignorant to be ignorant*
- *Let all things be done in order*

All too often, the first three directives are thrown out in the interest of the fifth: maintaining order. The irony is that when tongues and/or prophecy are forbidden in the church, there's no disorder related to these gifts left to handle. For all practical purposes, most of the list has been negated, and only the fourth point has been served, as ignorance is allowed to continue.

After centuries of leaders failing to acknowledge or teach these commandments, many congregants don't even realize they exist. Many church leaders rarely have to deal with maintaining order because the corporate practice of these gifts has died off by attrition. Few have to correct anyone's use of tongues or prophecy because no one dares to operate these gifts or even knows the Bible still encourages them.

Take another look at the Scriptures on that last point. It doesn't say *maintain order*. It says *let all things be done decently and in order*. It is both a commandment to *let* these gifts come forth and an instruction as to the way these things should be *done*: in order.

Though some defend maintaining ignorance within the church based on verse thirty-eight, let's look back at this verse in context with verse thirty-seven. In this couplet, Paul mentions two basic categories of people: 1) brethren and 2) the ignorant. Here's how they break down:

1. **Brethren:** the spiritual (prophets and all believers)
2. **The Ignorant:** the unspiritual (all unbelievers)

Now, let's remind ourselves of the broader context within Paul's letter. Notice how Paul opened this three-chapter section on the manifestations of the Holy Spirit: *"Now, concerning spiritual gifts, brethren, I would not have you ignorant."* (I Corinthians 12:1 ASV)

Clearly, Paul addressed this letter to brethren and he did *not* want them to be ignorant. The Greek word for *ignorant* is: *agnoeo*. Sound familiar? It's the same root as our word *agnostic*. It encompasses those who ignore God and are disinclined to know Him or abide by His commandments.

So, I don't believe that Paul is saying that the spiritual should shy away from teaching the Lord's commandments to those within the church who don't know or understand them yet. It's not even an excuse for everyday believers to remain uninformed. Rather, I believe he's saying that he doesn't want any of the brethren to be ignorant, and that all who are spiritual should put these commandments on spiritual gifts into regular teaching and practice.

Paul drew the dividing line between those who know God (the sheep) and those who don't (the goats). He didn't want the church to be divided about the orderly exercise of supernatural gifts. He wanted the church to be united in correct observance of them as God's commands. Paul wasn't writing to agnostics. He was writing to a church that needed instruction agnostics don't care to heed. He wanted them to stop diverting focus to those who don't believe and to take these commandments to heart personally.

Perhaps there were those within this church who needed to be stirred up to earnestly desire prophecy. Perhaps there were those who were inclined to forbid even interpreted tongues. Paul set the record straight, citing in the authority of the Lord that these gifts should be allowed to continue within the church in God's prescribed order.

Frankly, in many Christian leadership circles, revelatory gifts are viewed as an unmanageable can of worms. It took centuries to get those messy things into that can, sealed up and stashed, and they sure don't want to let them out again.

Believe me. I know how messy it can seem, especially at first, to follow the Lord's commandments in the operation of these particular gifts in church. But even if you do think of these gifts as worms, think of what worms do, how worms can till the soil of hardened hearts, breaking up the fallow ground of man-made tradition so the whole family of faith can mature through the practices God has commanded (Hosea 10:12).

Better yet, instead of worms, think of these gifts as instruments in God's orchestra to be played unplugged from the distortions of human tradition. When many instruments are played out of order, it can sound like a confused mess. But when a skilled conductor directs those same instruments to cooperate in order, beautiful music can come forth.

"I don't want to overemphasize the gifts."

Honestly, in my traditional upbringing there was absolutely no danger of overemphasizing the importance of supernatural gifts today. Instead, the supernatural gifts were unilaterally under-emphasized, completely absent within church functions. Teaching on the subject was taboo. Sure, we talked about the wonders Jesus worked. But I don't recall even the slightest hint from that pulpit that we could manifest the supernatural power of God in the here and now.

Years ago, as a wave of the Holy Spirit moved through our area churches, I became aware that some congregations were actively discouraged from scriptural practice of the manifestations of the Spirit during services. Some pastors went so far as to forbid the operation of supernatural gifts, finding them too controversial. Frustrated, many newly gifted believers left their traditional churches in search of fellowships that were more open to the power of the Spirit, like I did. Others wilted on their thirsty vines, unable to combat the long-held traditions of men.

Admittedly, many have erred by focusing too heavily on the gifts in and of themselves, but the solution is not to marginalize or forbid the gifts altogether. The solution is to keep the gifts in perspective, to remember that the purpose of the gifts is not to draw attention to the wonders, but to draw attention to our wonder-working God. It's not about the gifts. It's always about the Giver. And in accordance with Scripture, a healthy body should manifest power gifts on a regular basis, like Jesus did.

Jesus is our example for balance related to the use of the gifts. If you're really concerned about this, go through the Gospels. Get a fresh sense of how often Jesus operated in the supernatural power of the Spirit. Study the graceful correlation between Jesus' miraculous works and the crowds who gathered to hear Him. Jesus kept the gifts in perfect balance. Jesus is the one who told us that we'd need this supernatural power to witness (Acts 1:8).

Does it get messy? Sure. Will there be error? Yup. Will church leaders need to offer correction? Uh-huh. But tell me—do we boycott cars because some people cause accidents with them? No. So, let's not quench the Spirit and neglect our gifts just because people make mistakes. Rather, let's study to show ourselves approved. Let's learn to operate our power tools properly and in order. Let's invite the Holy Spirit to distribute supernatural manifestations as He wills, trusting that His will is always perfectly in balance.

"Is it Christmas yet? I want to open my gifts!"

Every day can be like Christmas in the body of Christ. Isn't it amazing to think that the Creator of the universe watches us, truly pleased when we want to receive and use what He has given? In the following chapters, we'll open up each of the power tools God has for us. We'll spend extra time looking at those that are more widely feared or misunderstood.

Once again, I'm going to ask you to stop and say a prayer before you start the next chapter. Thank God for providing you with power gifts for service, ministry, and harvest, even if you don't know what those gifts are just yet. Ask Him to give you the gifts He knows you need. Invite the Holy Spirit to be your teacher as we proceed in Jesus' name.

Go ahead, now. Don't rush. Just be with Him for a moment. Talk to Him about this in your own words. Delight yourself in the Lord, knowing that He will give you the desires of your heart (Psalm 37:4).

CHAPTER NINE

The Word of Wisdom

What it is:

Receiving and communicating God's understanding of a matter; Holy Spirit-guided application of knowledge; insight to be used in teaching, counseling, and/or problem solving

What it's not:

Intellectually deduced human counsel; the voice of human reason

> *Though I was raised in the wisdom of the Bible, the Lord has since shown me that the seed of my rebellion against my parents' counsel took root when I was thirteen. The summer before entering high school, I was thrilled to be invited to a slumber party with the popular girls in my class. That night, an informal poll was taken, and descriptive labels were assigned to each girl. Others were dubbed things like Prettiest, Funniest, or Most Likely to Get Dates. I was mortified to be voted Most Sensible. It seemed more like an indictment than a prize. As a teenager, the last thing I wanted was to be known for was good judgment. It made me feel old school, not cool like the others. I made many foolish choices in the years that followed, all geared at ridding myself of that dubious distinction of wisdom.*

My parents endured much as I showed my peers just how insensible I could be, but in time, I returned to tend the good seed my mom and dad had faithfully planted in me. The wisdom I had once spurned became a deep desire of my heart as I matured in the Lord. I realized that wisdom really was a prize, a gift to be cherished. I learned that words of wisdom, given in the Holy Spirit, far surpassed any human sensibilities, blessing us with the understanding of God.

This divinely imparted wisdom, listed among the manifestations of the Spirit (I Corinthians 12:8), is purposed to equip believers to serve the body, even in situations that may confound natural solutions. No matter how complex a conflict or conundrum, the word of wisdom is given to help us understand and embrace God's superior point of view. This gift helps us to go beyond simply knowing God's Word to applying it in the day to day of practical Christian living.

One thing is for sure: we know God loves it when we seek Him for wisdom. Turn to I Kings 3:3–14. (II Chronicles 1:1–12 tells this same story.) We read that David's son, a young King Solomon, went before the Lord in worship. That night, God visited Solomon in a dream. It's telling to track their dialogue. After God prompted Solomon to ask Him for something, Solomon's initial response was gratitude for all that he had already been given in his father's kingdom. Next, he humbly admitted how his youth and inexperience made him feel unequipped on his own to lead the people. Then, of everything a young man could have requested of the Almighty, Solomon asked only to be given wisdom to rule his subjects rightly. God's great pleasure at Solomon's request was demonstrated in that He not only gave Solomon wisdom, but also riches, honor, and long life, if Solomon would walk in His ways.

Immediately following Solomon's dream, we see an intensely practical application in I Kings 3:16–28. Newly gifted, young Solomon was faced with settling a now famous conflict between two women, both claiming to be the mother of the same infant son. These mothers were harlots, outcasts. Yet Solomon humbled himself to consider their complaint and, in so doing, demonstrated his newly given wisdom in such a profound way that word of his judgment spread throughout the kingdom.

You can read more about Solomon's wisdom in I Kings 4:29–34. Solomon's inspired book of Proverbs abounds with references to wisdom. Solomon knew where he got this wisdom (Proverbs 2:6). He appreciated what a blessing wisdom was (Proverbs 3:13). He exhorted sons to adhere to the advice his father, David, gave him to acquire wisdom (Proverbs 4:1–7).

"What does this look like today?"

After two days of working on this chapter, I went to a prayer meeting and received prophetic ministry. These people didn't know anything about me, or what I was working on, but God did. Much of what was prophesied over me was specific to God giving me wisdom and revelation; I was told that I would receive the counsel of the Lord. There was even a direct reference to Solomon from someone who didn't hear the initial prophecy. Interestingly, there was also an indication that I was on the verge of something big, that something wonderful would happen to me within a very short time frame.

As you might imagine, the prospect of a blessing right around the corner engaged my hopes. I quickly asked myself what I would hope to see happen soon. Various business opportunities flashed across my mind, but none felt like the right place to set my hopes, especially in light of all the blessings that I already enjoy. Then, I thought: *What if God spoke to me with the wisdom of His counsel during this time? What if He gave me revelation or a special impartation of His presence?* As unworthy as I feel to be graced in these ways, I decided that any interaction with the God I love would be the most wonderful thing I'd ever hope could happen in fulfillment of that prophecy.

The next morning, it hit me. The Lord showed me that, on a small scale, I had been granted an opportunity very much like Solomon's! As my hopes had been triggered by that promise of something wonderful just ahead, it had paralleled God asking Solomon what he wanted in that dream. Without realizing it, I had been given the unconscious chance to evaluate what I'd like God to give me. I could have chosen to hope for a financial windfall or new work, but instead I chose to invest my hopes into receiving wisdom and revelation from God. This wisdom, which I had rejected in the foolishness of my youth, I now value far above any of this world's temporal blessings.

Solomon realized that godly wisdom is of great worth, much more than any notoriety or wealth it can bring about. Though Solomon became fabulously rich and famous, he continued to value wisdom above all the gold or silver that he could ever possess (Proverbs 16:16). Solomon was not alone in recognizing the surpassing worth of God's counsel. Even secular kings, like Nebuchadnezzar, recognized the superior value of God-given wisdom over the insight of human sages (Daniel 1:19–20).

A word to the wise: no matter how rich or powerful we may appear to be in the natural, always remember that, from a spiritual perspective, we are just unworthy paupers, blessed to be God's humble servants. It's just that, when we operate under His anointing, our tattered rags are covered while we are clothed with priceless power from on high. Notice Joseph's humility when he told Pharaoh that it was not in him to interpret God's counsel, and how Joseph went on to assure Pharaoh that the answer would come from God (Genesis 41:16).

Old Testament examples of wisdom dovetail right into the new covenant. In Isaiah's messianic prophecy, we read how the Spirit of God would come to rest upon Jesus, giving Him wisdom and understanding (Isaiah 11:2). Indeed, Jesus fulfilled Isaiah's prophecy, manifesting an astonishing spirit of wisdom in His hometown synagogue (Matthew 13:54–58), so much so that they took offense at Him. We're looking at a first class power struggle here between the traditionalists and the promised Messiah.

While Jesus' wisdom powerfully demonstrated that He was more than just a man, the traditionalists, in an effort to disparage Him, made sure to point out that His family was entirely human. Verse twenty-eight reports the resulting tragedy. Because the traditionalists didn't believe, Jesus didn't do many miracles there. Think how many could have been healed, fed, or delivered if they had only received Jesus' wisdom as from God.

Lest we get the wrong impression that wisdom places us into passive positions, notice how this gift put Jesus into the thick of conflict resolution. In John 8:3–11, we read of one such challenge when the scribes and Pharisees brought a woman caught in adultery to Jesus, pointing out that the Law of Moses required her stoning, trying to get Jesus to speak against the authority of Scripture. Instead, Jesus' God-given words of wisdom disarmed the opposition completely.

Check out Matthew 22:15–22. Here we see how the Pharisees plotted to trap Jesus into saying something against the authority of Caesar. Jesus not only discerned their test, but also answered in such a way that left them marveling. When challenging Jesus on issues of church or state, the Pharisees pitted Jesus against the two strongest power-systems known to man, power-systems desperately in need of God's wisdom to this day.

Opposition doesn't just go with wisdom's territory; opposition *is* the territory. Swirling at the center of every conflict are the questions wisdom answers:

- *What is the right thing to do?*
- *What should we say when opposed?*
- *How can we best navigate this world's problems?*

A friend approached me for help concerning his daughter. This senior had been abruptly expelled from a respected private academy for accepting answers from another student on an open book test, bringing about her transfer to an undesirable public high school. My friend asked if I would help him write a letter, appealing for mercy from the headmistress who had made a strict zero-tolerance example of his daughter. He hoped the letter would persuade the headmistress to consider a lesser form of discipline so that his daughter could graduate from this more prestigious school with her twin sister.

Never having reared a child myself, I don't begin to understand the challenges of godly parenting. At a loss as to how best to respond, I asked the Lord for words of wisdom. The next morning, counsel came to me quite spontaneously, deposited within a matter of moments. There was no doubt about its source. It was not a reasoned process. I simply accepted the message of wisdom I was given and delivered it to my friend, crediting the counsel to God.

The Holy Spirit had counseled that all of life is like an open book test. No matter how well-intentioned or sincerely composed, a letter coming from anyone but the daughter would only repeat the original offense by giving her life-test solutions she needed to search out and implement herself. Rather than helping write this letter, I was to help encourage this parent to embrace the headmistress as God's instrument of correction to his daughter, a blessing at this pivotal juncture in her life. His daughter would survive that undesirable school. She would grow through suffering the consequences of wrongdoing. The importance of integrity would be written on her heart, as she would soon graduate and leave the nurture of her parents' admonitions, to embark on an independent future. Though the direction of this counsel called for a significant change in this father's approach to helping his daughter, he received and followed it gratefully, as words of wisdom from the Lord.

I have no formal training in counseling. But through the word of wisdom, the mind of God becomes like an open book through which any believer can search for answers in the Spirit. We can choose to consult others. We can follow the desires of our hearts and take what seems the easy or safe way out. Or, like my friend, we can press in to understand the big picture, as our all-wise Father God sees it.

The word of wisdom is given so that, in the Spirit, even the unlettered among us can access God's mind, the mind of Christ, as we navigate the everyday challenges of this world. That's right, the power of the entire Godhead is there to help even the least of us deal with all sorts of human conflict—from parenting issues, to business disputes, to bitter life and death struggles.

Read how Jesus counseled His disciples about the coming persecution in Luke 21:10–15, promising that He would give them the wisdom and the words to refute their opponents. These men weren't doctors of psychology. No one had a degree in counseling. Jesus was offering real God-given wisdom to navigate real persecution that He knew would occur after His ascension. This promised wisdom would be distributed to them in the Holy Spirit, beginning at Pentecost and continuing for all believers of all future generations.

"Sounds great. Where do I sign up for this gift?"

The Holy Spirit distributes these gifts as He wills, but you are encouraged to earnestly seek God for wisdom. No doubt, words of wisdom are sorely needed within the body. But let's not get cavalier about the realities of this gift. Though it may attract those who want to tell others what to do, with a sort of cowboy, step in, take charge and fix it mentality, this gift isn't about elevating humans. It's about serving to bring the mind of Christ to bear in difficult, even dangerous situations.

Take Stephen for example. In Acts Chapter Six, we read that the apostles needed help serving the growing church by waiting tables. Now, one would think this would be a good chance to involve the newbies among them; however, notice the job qualifications the apostles cite:

> *"But select from among you, brethren, seven men of good reputation, full of the Holy Spirit and of wisdom, whom we may put in charge of this task."*
>
> *Acts 6:3*

Sound overqualified to you? I mean, why would wisdom be a prerequisite for serving food? The thing is, as simple as food service might sound, the apostles were making a leadership appointment. Leaders are groomed through service, following the example of Christ. And look who got the first slot on the church wait-staff: Stephen, a man noted for being full of the Holy Spirit and of faith.

We read in verse eight that Stephen was also performing powerful signs and wonders in the Spirit. As these miracles validated Stephen's testimony, they also landed him smack in the middle of a huge controversy with the Libertines that required Spirit-given words of wisdom.

This is where it gets really ugly. The Libertine synagogue's argumentative traditionalists couldn't cope with Stephen's wisdom, so they spread lies about Stephen, stirring people up to testify falsely against him, accusing Stephen of speaking against God and Moses. Notice how the hot spots mentioned in verse fourteen reveal how threatened these traditionalists felt. They didn't want the testimony of Jesus preached. They didn't want what they'd built to be destroyed, and they certainly didn't want their customs changed. Imagine the havoc of this heated debate. Yet, at the center of it all was Stephen, aglow with grace, so much so that everyone who sat in the council saw his face as if it had been the face of an angel (Acts 6:15).

Acts Seven records the words of wisdom given to Stephen by the Holy Spirit. The Libertines listened until Stephen entreated them to understand that humans don't rightly build God's house. Stephen frankly identified these traditionalists' problem: They were stiff-necked.

Their hearts and ears were uncircumcised. They chronically resisted the Holy Spirit, just the way their fathers did, by trying to build God's house by human standards.

Stephen's words of wisdom were the sword of the Spirit to them, and God's expressed mind cut them to the quick. They began to gnash their teeth at Stephen. But in the moments before they would drive him out of the city and stone him to death, Stephen—still full of the Holy Spirit—was given a glorious vision of Jesus, standing at the right hand of God.

With his dying breath, Stephen set the example for all who would seek this gift. Stephen entrusted Jesus to receive Him, and in a voice loud enough for his rock-hurling executioners to hear, he asked the Lord not to hold to his murder against them. Beautiful Stephen, full of wisdom, died like his Lord, radiantly forgiving till the end.

"Conflict? Opposition? Martyrdom? Is there an 'up side' to this gift?"

We should all ask ourselves: is it more important for us to please even powerful people or to please our supremely powerful God? People-pleasers quench the Spirit of wisdom. Like Stephen, God-pleasers fix their eyes on Jesus, even through rejection by the world, even through horrific treatment at the hands of traditionalists.

Know that you must trust God with the results of serving in this gift, results that are not always pleasant on a human level. Whereas Solomon's wisdom hailed him to his subjects, Stephen's led to a painful, undeserved stoning. Both men pleased God. Neither was able to please all the people. Even Solomon was left with a disgruntled, bereaved mother who was undoubtedly upset with him for the wisdom he expressed.

Though I am often approached for counsel, there are times when even my Christian friends avoid seeking Spirit-given wisdom from me. These days, there are those who openly admit that I'm not the one they call on when they want to be weak. They say they call me when they're ready to face up and be strong, when they want to get undergirded by the wisdom God gives. It's not that I'm any great shakes at problem solving in the natural. They know I'm not lettered as a counselor. They know I have my own struggles, that I'm just an imperfect everyday person. But they also know I will seek the Lord for His words of wisdom, and that I'll honestly deliver whatever understanding God gives me, even if it's not what they hope to hear.

Despite the social challenges it presents, for me, a big "up side" to this gift is that we have the chance to know God's mind. Every glimpse of His mind helps us to know Him better (Proverbs 9:10).

I want to know God better, don't you? I want to help others to understand His divine viewpoint. But if, in our humanity, we're shopping for gifts based on what we want out of them—like oh, wow, wouldn't this help me win friends and influence people—we've lost perspective. These are gifts we give back to God by humbly serving Him.

"What do I do if I want wisdom from God?"

Ask in Faith

When you ask, ask in faith (James 1:5–8). Know that God wants to reveal His mind to His people. Know that He wants to be known in this way.

I've lost count of how many times I've asked for words of wisdom. I'm a serial asker. I ask every time I sit to write this book, knowing that I'm just one lowly person stepping into a hornet's nest of controversy that has raged for thousands of years. I desperately need God's mind. I long for His understanding. I need His Spirit to give me words of wisdom to communicate His holy counsel to those within the church who are entrenched in the traditions of man. So, if you find any error in these pages—even so much as a typo—know it is from me. But on the other hand, if you find any wisdom here, please recognize it as beyond my limited human capabilities, and rather as a demonstration that the Holy Spirit still distributes this much needed gift to everyday believers in the here and now.

Study the Scriptures

I exhort you to study the Bible daily (II Timothy 2:15). Don't just reread your favorite passages. Scour the whole Bible, over and over, even those passages that seem difficult. As you do, ask the Holy Spirit to teach you and give you understanding.

Since wisdom involves applied knowledge, increasing your knowledge of the Scriptures provides a firm foundation for this gift. The more you absorb, the more the big picture of what the Bible is really about comes into focus. Biblical stories are arrows in your quiver to help you target modern-day conflicts with God's already imparted wisdom. Even the foibles of our heroes of faith help us to avoid the pitfalls of sinning ourselves. The Bible is rich with both positive and negative role models, all of which are instructive to us today.

Watch for Counseling Ops

Don't be surprised if problem-solving ops start showing up on your doorstep, or maybe even within the walls of your own home. Recognize that the Holy Spirit may be apprenticing you in wisdom.

You may be given words of wisdom spontaneously; however, if you're not sure you have God's mind about a matter, just listen. Resist the urge to argue or spitball solutions in the natural. It's okay to say, "*I don't know yet.*" Simply assure the conflicted person that you've heard them, you're taking their problem seriously, and you'd like to pray about it for a short while to give opportunity for the Holy Spirit to guide your answer.

Seek the Lord for Wisdom

- Faithfully follow up.
- Pray about it.
- Search the Bible for pertinent knowledge on the subject.
- Ask for wisdom and understanding.
- Allow time to listen for what the Holy Spirit could speak to you about that particular situation, understanding that the Spirit will never speak in conflict with Scripture.

Remember: there is no problem too complicated for God. The depths of His wisdom are rich beyond the capacity of human beings to even fathom (Romans 11:33). Trust that there is wisdom available for those who seek it from Him.

Stand and Deliver

Once you are confident that you have received the Lord's wisdom, pray that the Holy Spirit will prepare the person's heart to receive His counsel. Contact the person and give him or her the words of wisdom you have received. Welcome that person to seek confirmation, especially if it involves a major decision.

Rest in the Lord, regardless of the earthly results. Let go of the need to have the person say you're right, or even for that person to heed God's counsel. Your responsibility is simply to deliver God's message of wisdom.

Minister the Spirit in the Spirit

As we serve with words of wisdom, we should always do so with the full complement of the fruits of the Holy Spirit. Think of those fruits as an inseparable unit, always operating together (Galatians 5:22–23). Our conversations with those who disagree should mirror God's wisdom:

> *"But the wisdom from above is first pure, then peaceable, gentle, reasonable, full of mercy and good fruits, unwavering, without hypocrisy. And the seed whose fruit is righteousness is sown in peace by those who make peace."*
>
> *James 3:17–18*

Highlight each of those key characteristics of Spirit-given wisdom. If you are walking in Spirit-given wisdom, you will be pure, you'll be gentle, approachable. You'll be merciful, abounding in the fruits. You won't be partial, strident, arrogant, self-righteous, or hypocritical as you deal with controversy. You will sow the seeds of righteousness in peace.

One thing is for sure: God never calls upon us to administer the word of wisdom in the flesh. If you start to feel argumentative, critical, angry, frustrated, cynical, or superior, you're slipping into the flesh, which deafens you to the still small voice of the Holy Spirit. When the voices of the flesh rise in debate, maintain quietness in the Spirit. Listen. Think of yourself as a tree whose roots must drink deeply of

His fruit-generating river (Ezekiel 47:12). Don't let yourself get tossed about by winds of controversy. Stand, peacefully grounded in His Word of truth.

Caution Counsel Shoppers

Be aware. There are those who seek out multiple counselors, searching for someone who will tell them what they want to hear, someone who will give them permission to disobey God's already spoken Word (II Timothy 4:3–4). If you encounter such a person, clearly speak God's truth in love. No matter how much your flesh wants to sympathize with someone else's, never take anyone's side against God. If they claim God is unfair or unloving, gently correct their misunderstanding. Weep with those who weep. Show the compassion of Jesus. But weep with your hand solidly clasping your Savior's as you deliver His unrivaled words of wisdom.

I Corinthians 2:6–16 gives us a strong perspective on speaking words of wisdom to those who are mature, even to our leaders in the faith. You may be just an everyday congregant like I am. But you, too, can listen for the voice of the Holy Spirit, who searches everything, even the depths of God. I echo Paul's words as a prayer for you:

> *"For this reason I too, having heard of the faith in the Lord Jesus which exists among you, and your love for all the saints, do not cease giving thanks for you, while making mention of you in my prayers; that the God of our Lord Jesus Christ, the Father of glory, may give to you a spirit of wisdom and of revelation in the knowledge of Him."*
>
> *Ephesians 1:15–17*

CHAPTER TEN

The Word of Knowledge

What it is:
Information that is directly and solely imparted from God

What it's not:
ESP, telepathy, psychic readings, mental illness, or acquired via natural sources

> *As a young adult, I had an older Christian friend who was as wary as she was skeptical about the modern-day operation of power gifts. One day, when this friend was requesting prayer for an unnamed guy from her hometown, the Holy Spirit distinctly spoke his first name to me. When I told her his name, my friend was astonished. She quickly confirmed the information as true, realizing that I couldn't possibly have guessed his name on my own. I must admit, I was kind of stunned, too. It was my first experience with the word of knowledge.*

It's a good thing that it's the Holy Spirit's job to distribute these gifts as He wills, because each one is so fascinating and desirable, I would hardly be able to choose what's best for me and the local body of which I'm just one small part.

Exhortation to acquire knowledge is common in the Bible; however, this gift is not about the natural learning process we'd all be wise to pursue. God created each of us with varying abilities for natural education. Some find learning and retaining knowledge quite challenging, some are more adept, and still others are born with photographic memories.

Though a person might have a high natural capacity for amassing knowledge, the word of knowledge listed in I Corinthians 12:8 is a different thing. It's a manifest power gift of the Holy Spirit, distinct from all forms of natural learning in that the word of knowledge involves speaking forth information that has been supernaturally retained or imparted from God to the believer, in the Spirit.

"What's the difference between prophecy, the word of wisdom, and the word of knowledge?"

All three of these power gifts involve communication from God. While aspects of the word of knowledge and the word of wisdom could be considered under the broader umbrella of the prophetic, not all prophecies would necessarily be considered words of wisdom or words of knowledge. However, these three gifts often work hand in hand, complementing one another in the Spirit as knowledge's information + wisdom's understanding = God's prophetic counsel.

The word of knowledge can be interpreted as mingling with foretelling aspects of the prophetic when God-given knowledge is related to something that is yet to come, as when Jesus foreknew the colt would be there in Luke 19:30–31. However, since disclosure of things yet to come is most regularly associated with prophecy, let's focus on distinguishing the word of knowledge as unlearned, Spirit-disclosed information about things in the past or present.

"Does a person with this gift know it all?"

As it is with prophecy, words of knowledge are given in part (I Corinthians 13:8–9). God is the only one who knows it all, and the Holy Spirit distributes this gift of unlearned knowledge exactly as and when He wills, sometimes when we're neither expecting nor requesting that knowledge.

Virginia and I have been friends since we were Brownies together in grade school. We've shared many landmark events over the years. We both rebelled as teenagers, and then got saved around the same time. We've worked together at important junctures. I celebrated with her when she married her wonderful husband.

For a while we lived on opposite coasts, so I went to visit Virginia while in her town on business. As I parked, I saw Virginia emerge from their building. I wasn't expecting to hear from God. All I was thinking about was how happy I was to see my friend, when the Holy Spirit softly spoke a word of knowledge to me, something I could not have known in the natural. He informed me that Virginia was pregnant. There was no physical evidence of pregnancy that I could see. Virginia and I hadn't even talked about their family plans.

Before I'd barely even said hello, I delivered the Holy Spirit's message. This news took Virginia completely by surprise. Even she didn't know that she was expecting at that moment. God knew, though, and this word of knowledge served as a joyful annunciation. It also encouraged her to take a confirming test. Indeed, Virginia found that she was already in the early weeks of pregnancy with her first and only child.

"Isn't that like being psychic?"

No, it's not like being psychic because this knowledge came from God. What clearly separates the word of knowledge from psychic phenomenon is the source of the information. ESP, telepathy, psychic readers (interpreting tarot cards, palms, tea leaves, crystal balls, and the like), astrologists, and mediums all get their information from the enemy, who occasionally throws just enough truth into his lies to dupe people into buying his poisonous wares (Deuteronomy 18:10–13). The reason believers shouldn't have anything to do with these practices is that they amount to putting the false god of this world before the true God of the universe.

Friends, remember: the enemy is a wolf in sheep's clothing, disguising his ugliness as an angel of light, hoping to deceive even the elect (II Corinthians 11:14–15). No matter how innocent or positive the information the enemy offers may seem at first, the Bible is clear that Satan's end-game is to lure sheep away from God's flock and into destruction.

The enemy also has a Plan B. If he can't entice you into buying his wares, he'll trash-talk God's gifts, trying to convince you to fear valid scriptural forms of communication with God. But as clearly as we should realize that the source of any psychic phenomenon is the enemy, how much more clearly should we embrace the fact that the single source of information for the word of knowledge gift is our omnipotent God?

So, let's make a point to give credit and praise only where it is due. There's a lot of misunderstanding on this subject, leading the uninformed to stick enemy labels on God's gifts, even under seemingly benign labels like "women's instinct." If God gives you a word of knowledge and someone comments that you must be psychic, lovingly correct his or her misunderstanding and give the credit to God. Resist taking pride in how God has used you. Refuse to stand on anybody's pedestal. Revel only at God's glory.

If someone supposes that you read their mind, let them know that it was God who knew their thoughts and gave you the information in the Spirit. If they size you up as generically *spiritual*, a moniker the world has co-opted to encompass all kinds of enemy counterfeits, make sure to let them know that the Holy Spirit is your source. If they ask what zodiac sign you are, tell them that you were born under the sign of the cross. Identify yourself with God, just as Job did when he declared:

> *"I will fetch my knowledge from afar, and I will ascribe righteousness to my Maker. For truly my words are not false; One who is perfect in knowledge is with you."*
>
> *Job 36:3–4*

Be assured that if the Holy Spirit distributes the word of knowledge to you, the information you receive will be accurate, not because you're personally insightful or worthy of any higher esteem than anyone else within the body of Christ is. It'll be true simply because it comes from your Maker, the one who is perfect in knowledge, your omniscient God.

"So, God gives us knowledge we can't learn naturally?"

Yes! Amazing, isn't it? But that's our powerful God. When I was growing up, my mother hired an indigent housekeeper who had been raised as a migrant worker. Though I don't think Tina was ever tested, I would guess that her IQ was very low. She couldn't read, write, or even take a phone message. She "signed" her paychecks with an X.

Precious Tina had very little natural ability to retain even the simplest bits of oft-repeated information. I remember when Tina returned from a family reunion to gleefully announce that she wasn't 57 as she'd thought; she was 64! What's more, she'd found out that her given name wasn't Tina at all; it was Jackie!

Work-wise, though Tina did laundry every Monday morning for the better part of two decades, every Monday she still had to ask what to do. That's why my mom and I were so amazed to hear Tina sing numerous hymns from memory all day as she worked. She may not have known or remembered anything else, even her real name and age, but somehow, in the Spirit, this completely illiterate woman could quote the Bible. She knew the Gospel well and communicated that knowledge regularly. Mom and I shared a confidence that despite the fact that Tina couldn't read, recall, or learn almost anything of significance in the natural, God had given her a specially empowered capacity to speak from His Word and to sing hymns of praise.

"What does the Bible say about words of knowledge?"

Those of us who can read can see first-hand what the Bible has to say about God-given knowledge. Believe it. Day and night, God pours out words of knowledge (Psalm 19:2). This knowledge comes directly out of His mouth, knowledge that is pleasant to our souls (Proverbs 2:6, 10), knowledge that is there for the hearing if we will only listen. Proverbs 19:27 cautions us against plugging our ears to the Almighty, warning that if we stop listening to His words of knowledge, we'll stray into error.

God is our ever-present help, and one way He helps us is by imparting information, knowledge that we should highly value. We are at war, Army of God. Spirit-given words of knowledge are a strategic form of intelligence, even for common foot soldiers. If earthly knowledge is power, think how much more we should value the superpower the word of knowledge brings, straight from the mouth of our God.

Proverbs 20:15 advises that the lips of knowledge are more precious than gold or rubies. Solomon exhorts us to apply our ears to words of knowledge (Proverbs 23:12). Paul bubbled over with thanks to God for the way the Corinthian church was enriched in Christ Jesus, in all words and knowledge, that they weren't short of a single gift, but rather were in a state of eager expectancy, waiting for revelation from the Lord (I Corinthians 1:5–7).

"How is the word of knowledge manifested?"

It is articulated. This gift isn't just called *knowledge*; it's called *the word of knowledge* (I Corinthians 12:8). That means that there is communication involved. The Greek for *word* in this case is *logos*. This carries the meaning that this knowledge from God is spoken forth, preached, or conveyed in some manner. It could be signed to or by the hearing-impaired. It can even be sung, by a humble housekeeper like Tina.

"Doesn't this gift require a level of maturity?"

The Spirit gives the word of knowledge to believers as He wills, when He knows they are ready to start growing in this gift. When I heard the Spirit speak that guy's name to me, I wasn't even old enough to vote. Honestly, at that point, I didn't fully understand what a word of knowledge was. I wasn't anybody special. I just knew the Holy Spirit had given me a way to validate His work to someone who was clinging to the traditional view that these things don't happen any more. So, I yielded to the flow of that Voice I recognized and spoke the word of knowledge the Holy Spirit had given to me, demonstrating the modern-day operation of this power tool to my skeptical friend. It was much later that I had the "aha" moment, as the Spirit taught me, line upon line, the Scriptures concerning this gift (Isaiah 28:9–10).

Fear and control issues prompt many traditional leaders to reject modern-day words of knowledge, and they do so at their peril. Hosea prophesied that God's people were destroyed for lack of knowledge, and that, because they'd rejected knowledge, God would also reject them as priests (Hosea 4:6). We should never discard such a valuable manifest gift of the Spirit, nor limit God to just giving it to elders; rather, we should embrace the knowledge God gives, regardless of the youth or lack of stature of the messenger (Daniel 1:17). We should appreciate how it can stabilize us in truth, even when the entire world is shaking around us (Isaiah 33:6).

Admittedly, this gift can be unsettling to skeptics, especially if the secrets of their hearts are revealed. The Lord can use the word of knowledge to break up fallow ground, to stir hardened minds to consider the truth. This can happen to sheep like me and also to shepherds. I have seen pastors stop, mid-sentence, because the Holy Spirit has given a word of knowledge for someone present who needed to know He saw them in their private desperation (Jeremiah 3:15).

Jeremiah 11:18 explains how the Lord makes the deeds of others known to us in this way. That's how it worked when Jesus ministered the word of knowledge to the woman at the well (John 4:7–29). Jesus told her what He could only have known in the Spirit, that she'd had five husbands and was presently with a sixth man outside the bonds of marriage. Certainly, it unsettled this woman, but in a good way. She had been stuck in a destructive cycle and needed unsettling. Because she knew immediately that Jesus' words of knowledge concerning her were true, it helped her to believe the most important information Jesus shared with her, that He was the promised Messiah.

In fulfillment of Isaiah's messianic prophecy, Jesus moved powerfully in the Spirit of knowledge (Isaiah 11:2, Colossians 2:1–3). Jesus communicated Spirit-given knowledge that His friend Lazarus had died, two days before that news was delivered by natural means (John 11:11–15). That same Spirit rested on Peter as he spoke forth knowledge that Ananias and Sapphira were lying about withholding a portion of their proceeds (Acts 5:1–11).

My friend, Allie, often operates in the word of knowledge. Sometimes, the knowledge imparted has been momentous, but God also uses this gift to help us with the simple details of our lives. Once, during a prayer meeting, the Holy Spirit gave Allie a clear piece of information, that someone in the group was eating too many bananas. Allie was almost hesitant to speak out this word of knowledge because it seemed so unlikely, almost ridiculous. She risked looking like a kook if she were wrong. Still, convinced of what she heard in the Spirit, Allie asked the group if anyone had been eating too many bananas lately. A man sheepishly admitted that he'd been on a fad diet, eating nine bananas a day! Allie was able to deliver the message to that brother, that the Lord wanted him to know that he was jeopardizing his health and that he should return to a more balanced diet.

As you can imagine, some information that the Holy Spirit imparts can be sensitive in nature. We might enjoy a good laugh about something like the bananas, but I'm sure you can understand why believers should use discretion as they operate in this gift (Proverbs 5:2). There are some times when a word of knowledge should be reserved until it can be delivered gently in private and other times when it should be delivered in front of witnesses. For that reason, if the Holy Spirit gives you a word of knowledge, pray for wisdom about how and when to deliver the information.

"What purposes does the word of knowledge serve today?"

Serve is the operative word (II Corinthians 6:4-10). The word of knowledge helps us to admonish each other (Romans 15:14). It informs intercession, cutting through the secrets of the heart to the truth of our neediness before God. As with Jesus and the woman at the well, it validated His testimony to a woman in bondage to sin. When Jesus spoke the words of knowledge about Lazarus, he told the disciples so that they would believe. Spirit-imparted information helps us to partner with God to combat lies and speculation with the confirmed knowledge of the truth (II Corinthians 10:5). It gives us a glimpse into the mind of our omniscient God.

Jesus died to restore us to active relationship with God. Through gifts like the word of knowledge, anyone who believes can experience the power of God Jesus promised, even the very least of us. That's what the priesthood of all believers is about. In addition to providing needed information, the word of knowledge demonstrates that direct communication with God is still possible for everyday people in the here and now. These vital messages are given by the Holy Spirit so that we can encourage others to seek God themselves, so we can point them toward Jesus, in whom all treasures of knowledge are hidden (Colossians 2:3).

CHAPTER ELEVEN

The Gift of Faith

What it is:
Supernatural impartation of assurance concerning what God is going to do before He does it, defying all natural reason and circumstances

What it's not:
Naturally mustered positive thinking or striving to maintain conviction

> *As a college freshman, I learned that my left leg was shorter than my right. It's not that I needed healing of what was there. I needed the creation of new lengthened bone and tissue to make up for what was lacking. That's when the Holy Spirit gifted me with faith to believe that He would miraculously rectify this situation. He gave me such certainty that I called four unbelievers' attention to my lopsided legs. I asked them to measure and be absolutely sure that my left leg was shorter than my right. Granted, it was only as scientific as we could get in a dorm, but after repeated measurements, they were convinced. I said I wanted them to be positive so they would believe me after God grew my left leg out to match the right one. They thought I was nuts!*

Was this the gift of faith at work or simply my youthful presumption? The answer wasn't long in coming.

Soon, I got together with three other students for prayer. In earnest, I began to ask the Lord to grow my left leg. A friend lovingly stopped me and said that we didn't need to beg the Lord. All we needed to do was praise Him for what we all had faith that He would do. I began to simply thank and praise Him in faith. Within moments, my left leg grew out before our eyes. Skeptics may scoff, but I know what I saw and felt. It was persistently tingly at first, a few inches below my left knee. For the next day or so, I could literally feel the new tissue God had created, all while I went back to show the evidence of His miracle-working power to the dumbfounded secular students who had been so sure when they first measured me.

In the light of I Corinthians 12:7's assurance that there is a manifestation of the Spirit available to equip each believer, the skittish among us might quickly review the list of nine supernatural manifestations and choose their gift as faith. They know they believe already and that they couldn't do that if they didn't have faith. Faith seems a lot less controversial than tongues or interpretation, not so scary as distinguishing of spirits, less demanding than the word of wisdom, less dangerous than the word of knowledge or prophecy, much less taxing than healing or miracles. Faith is something they can wrap their heads around, so, *pshew*! They feel like they're off the hook from following Paul's exhortation to earnestly seek other power gifts.

Not only does this line of thinking presume to usurp the Holy Spirit's position to distribute these manifestations to every believer as *He* wills (I Corinthians 12:11), it could also make for a body with disproportionate numbers of this one body part, when we need a balance of all nine of these manifestations of the Holy Spirit to function at full potential (I Corinthians 12:17). But if you've been relaxing into the idea of calling dibs on the gift you view as the safe one, the usual one, the one that won't raise any traditional eyebrows, you might want to dig a little deeper into how this amazing gift operates.

Did you ever notice that faith is the only gift that's also a fruit of the Holy Spirit (Galatians 5:22)? Interesting, huh? Actually, the fruit and the gift have much in common. They're alike in that both are the substance of things hoped for, the evidence of things not seen (Hebrews 11:1). Both produce an assurance about what God is going to do. Because both are given, in the technical sense, both might be thought of as gifts. However, there seems to be a difference between the abiding fruit of faith and the manifest supernatural gift of faith listed in I Corinthians 12:9. Paul's prayer for the Thessalonian church gives us a clue to the distinction:

"To this end we also pray for you always that our God may count you worthy of your calling, and fulfill every desire of goodness and the work of faith with power."

II Thessalonians 1:11

See that? Paul prayed that they would experience a *work of faith with power*. James linked power-works with faith, too, when he encouraged prayer for the sick, assuring that the prayer of *faith will restore the one who is sick* (James 5:14–15). Peter explained that it was through faith in the name of Jesus that the lame beggar was healed (Acts 3:16), another power-work facilitated by the gift of faith. Stephen, a man known to be full of faith, was used to manifest signs and wonders. That's why I believe that, in addition to the fruit of faith, Stephen also manifested the gift of faith (Act 6:5, 8). Maybe Jesus was talking about the gift of faith when he indicated that if we had just the tiniest seed of faith, we could move mountains (Matthew 17:20). Powerful artillery, this gift.

Whereas the fruit of faith is a saving, abiding faith, a measure of which is given to every believer (I Corinthians 13:13, Romans 10:13–17, Romans 12:3), the supernatural gift of faith, distributed to some as the Spirit wills, manifests alongside works of power. In that way, the gift of faith facilitates the operation of all the other manifestations of the Holy Spirit listed in I Corinthians 12:7–10.

The manifest supernatural gifts are like a set of power tools and faith is like the power cord through which the current of the Holy Spirit flows. Or, if you extend Paul's metaphor of the church as a human body, you might think of faith as the circulatory system, expediting the flow of power to the other body parts (I Corinthians 12:14–26).

The gift of faith, distributed to me for my leg, facilitated the effecting of the first miracle I'd ever seen, and has likely saved me from back trouble later in life. Most importantly, it demonstrated God's wonder-working power to the lost. When I was gifted with faith to pray for the instantaneous healing of my friend's ankle (Chapter 1), it served two purposes. First, my friend was relieved of recovering from a painful injury and the hassle of hobbling around on crutches. But second, it served as an eye-popping sign to her unbelieving hall-mates. They knew a miracle had taken place, something beyond the capacity of any human being, and my friend freely testified that it was Jesus who had done it.

I know from both of these experiences that there was nothing I did to muster up, pray up, or in any way work up this faith. I didn't coax God into giving it to me. He just did. In both instances, it was purely the Holy Spirit, willing to distribute the gift at that moment. The gift of faith was like a power cord that suddenly appeared in my hands. All I did was plug it in to facilitate the healing God wanted to do.

There are many examples of how Jesus manifested the gift of faith, coupled with the faith of others, in conjunction with various power gifts. You can read about the great faith that resulted in the healing of the centurion's servant (Matthew 8:5–10), or how the blind men were healed in accordance with their faith (Matthew 9:28–29), or how the Canaanite woman's daughter was delivered, facilitated by faith (Matthew 15:22–28).

Though I love all the stories of Jesus' compassionate works of power partnered with faith, one of my favorites centers around a woman who had been hemorrhaging for twelve years (Mark 5:25–34). Seriously. Take the time right now to read this vivid account. Notice the transfer of power that resulted when she, in faith, touched the hem of Jesus' garment and instantly received her healing. Her faith wasn't in the wisdom of men, certainly not the many physicians who had failed her; rather, her faith was fixed on the power of God, demonstrated in the Spirit through Jesus (I Corinthians 2:4–5).

Faith teamed up with prophecy when Paul was being shipped to Italy. Storms battered the vessel, until hope of survival was gradually abandoned (Acts 27:1–25). See the prophetic manifestation in Acts 27:23–24? Keep in mind, this ship was in terrible shape. They had jettisoned the cargo and tackle. They had already gone a long time without food. They fully expected to perish. Enter an angel of God, mingling the assurance that none would be lost with Paul's Spirit-empowered conviction of their yet to be seen salvation. Paul spoke out the faith that accompanied this prophetic visitation:

"Therefore, keep up your courage, men, for I believe God, that it will turn out exactly as I have been told."

Acts 27:25

Paul's words ring with the essence of the gift of faith. Paul didn't just hope. He was convinced that God would intervene powerfully, that He would do the impossible, just as He had promised. There was no doubt (James 1:5–8). Though they ran aground, though soldiers plotted to kill the prisoners rather than see them swim to safety, ultimately every last one of them made it to shore, just as Paul prophesied in faith.

There is something palpable about this kind of faith. Though invisible in the natural, it can be readily observed in the Spirit, in ourselves and in other people. Paul saw this kind of faith in a man who had been born lame. It led to a miraculous healing (Acts 14:8–10).

"What about the kind of faith it took to raise Lazarus?"

Years ago, I received a call to come to the hospital after a friend's mother had suffered a devastating heart attack. When I arrived, I was told what had just transpired.

Family members had already rushed to the hospital, desperate to say their goodbyes, but they had no access while the medical team was working. Despite their best efforts, my friend's mother's heart and breathing had stopped. All attempts to resuscitate her had been unsuccessful. The doctor had called out her time of death, which was noted in her medical record, and then had gone out to tell the family.

Meanwhile, my friend was in the waiting room, interceding along with others there. When the doctor approached to tell the family of their mother's passing, my friend started to pray in faith that her mother would come back to life. Overcome with grief, the only thing my friend could do was to repeat Jesus' name over and over, and pray in the Spirit for God to intervene. The doctor persisted, explaining that they had done all that they could, but there was too much damage. Her mother was gone.

That's when a woman who worked at the hospital approached, attempting to pull the doctor aside. Because it seemed a terribly timed interruption, the doctor asked the woman to wait while he finished informing the family. Again, the woman broke in and once more the doctor silenced her. Finally, the woman blurted out, *"But doctor...she's back."*

Indeed, though recorded as dead, a few minutes later, when no one had even been working on her, my friend's mother was spontaneously resurrected, as my friend called upon the name of Jesus in faith.

Those who needed to make amends did so; those who longed for closure got it, and my friend had the chance to say meaningful good-byes before her beloved mother finally went to be with the Lord nine days later.

"How can I get that kind of faith?"

Here's the thing about faith: people who need it are often in very difficult situations, having exhausted all natural solutions. Not everyone who prays is gifted with faith to work miracles or heal the sick. I've prayed for the sick many times, believing God can heal, but not receiving that certainty that He would in that particular case. One thing is for sure, though: no matter how ordinary a position we hold in the body of Christ, we are all welcome to cry out to the Lord for help, even while struggling to believe.

Maybe your heart resonates with the cry of the father who brought his seizure and unclean spirit-plagued son to Jesus (Mark 9:17–29). As he asked Jesus for help, the father's words *if you can* communicated desperation more than faith, prompting Jesus' response that *all things are possible to those who believe.* The father recognized that Jesus operated with a faith more powerful faith than his own, and responded that he did have [some] faith. What he needed Jesus to help him with was his *unbelief.*

Aren't we all a bit like that? We have that measure of faith, that fruit of faith God gives. In principle, we believe in what Jesus can do. But in the weakness of our plight, when the rubber hits the road of our need, we have to ask God to help that human part of us that simply isn't strong enough to believe Him for the big stuff, especially if our problem hits close to home.

After healing/delivering the boy, even Jesus indicated that this situation required more than the usual kind of faith. Though Jesus had previously given His disciples authority over unclean spirits (Mark 6:7), they'd been unable to help this boy. Jesus' response to the disciples was telling when he advised them that this kind of spirit could only come out through prayer and fasting. In other words, there can be a connection between the wonder-working gift of faith Jesus manifested and time spent denying our flesh and inviting the anointing of the Holy Spirit.

Though the Spirit distributes gifts as He wills, we are all exhorted to earnestly seek the greater gifts (I Corinthians 12:31). While prophecy alone is identified in I Corinthians 14:1 as being among those greater gifts, the clear implication of these verses is that there are other manifestations of the Spirit that should be earnestly pursued, gifts that serve to edify others. Because the gift of faith works together with all the other power gifts, it may well be one of those greater gifts we should earnestly seek.

Friends, remember the Bible says *seek*, not *stress over*. It's not a matter of earning this gift of faith through the works of prayer and fasting, certainly not by vain repetition. It's a matter of loving God with a heart so pure that we long to serve and spend time with Him, even at the expense of our human needs, and staying open to the Holy Spirit showing us what God is going to do.

Even on earth it's clear that self-sacrificial communication builds relationships. That is no less true with our relationship with God. Talk to Him. Listen for Him. Pray with your mind. If you've been graced with tongues, pray in the Spirit, knowing that it's a way to build up your faith (I Corinthians 14:15, Jude 1:20). Ask, ask again, and keep on asking. Then, as you go through the normal course of living, maintain an internal sense of readiness in the Spirit.

If God gifts you with wonder-working faith, trust that you'll know it. This isn't "name it and claim it." We don't get to call dibs on the gift of faith or manipulate God into distributing it to suit our presumptions of what accompanying power-works we think He should do. We just open our hearts, ready and willing if He should choose to distribute the gift of faith to us.

When the gift of faith is truly bestowed, there'll be no doubt, no pushing, striving, or hesitation, just the know-that-you-know-that-you-know joy of serving our magnificent God, and the wonder of seeing the impossible happen, just as He foretold.

CHAPTER TWELVE

Gifts of Healing

What it is:
Supernatural working of physical, mental, emotional, or spiritual cures

What it's not:
Psychic healing, quackery, generated by humans, at our whim or constant disposal

> *Weeks in advance of my annual physical, I noticed that I had an irregular mole. This mole had been there for years, but had begun to grow and change quickly. Concerned, I decided to get it checked at my upcoming appointment, but it occurred to me to pray about it first. I put my fingers on the mole and prayed for healing in the name of Jesus. Over the next twenty-four hours, I noticed that the mole had started to peel away at the edges, a process that I watched, amazed, as it continued until the entire mole completely fell off, leaving only a pink mark underneath as a reminder of where it had once been. By the time I went to my doctor, even that tender skin had faded into my normal flesh color.*

If gifts of healing aren't the most sought after of the gifts, it certainly isn't for lack of need. There have always been far more sick and diseased than those truly moving in gifts of healing. As soon as Jesus started healing people, crowds started to gather. Talk about a power-harvesting tool! Even if they didn't know Jesus was the Messiah, word quickly spread that the deaf were suddenly hearing, the blind were seeing, and the lame were walking. It was no different once the apostles began to move in the power of the Holy Spirit (Acts 5:14–16).

Gifts of healing, administered in the name of Jesus, can persuade even the hardest of hearts of their need for a power beyond their own. Because this gift strikes so deeply at the core of human need, it is a phenomenal people magnet, a mighty tool to be sought especially by those who are also sent out as apostles or evangelists.

"So, this gift is just for leaders?"

Clearly, this gift empowers the ministry of those in leadership, authenticating their testimony for Jesus; however, when healing is mentioned as a sign that accompanies believers (Mark 16:17–18), there is nothing to say it's only for leaders. I know I haven't been in any form of leadership when God has chose to use me in this way. I find no "leaders only" limitation elsewhere in Scripture, either. Again, this is among the manifestations that are distributed as the Spirit wills. I've seen Him distribute it to leaders and everyday believers alike.

"Don't you think some faith healers today are kooky?"

For starters, when Scripture calls us a peculiar people, in context, peculiar doesn't translate to kooky or woo-woo, as some like to say (Deuteronomy 14:2, I Peter 2:9). It means that we're a people of God's special possession, a holy treasure, purchased and set apart for Him. In some ways, being possessed by God makes us look different to the world, just because godliness is an unnatural state. That understood, we should guard against fleshy behaviors that undermine our effectiveness by being just plain odd or off-putting.

No doubt, some have been fairly "out there" in this department. There have been downright charlatans. There have also been believers who started well and then lapsed into error, vainly repeating actions that may have worked in the past rather than listening for God's present instructions.

Even sincere believers can get off track into inappropriate showmanship, particularly with the availability of TV time and the allure of celebrity. I have no problem with the appropriate use of modern media; it's the business I was called into, and many have used it very well. But lo and behold, TV time turns out to be expensive, prompting competition to draw an audience. For some this has degenerated into marketing gimmicks, look-at-me wardrobe, eye-popping theatrics, and hyped personalities pleading for financial support. In some cases, it looks more like commerce than a move of the Holy Spirit.

Dear Lord, have mercy on us.

But rather than pass judgment on those who may have fallen short of our high calling, let's look to Jesus as our behavioral example—Jesus, our servant Savior who, even though He was God, carried Himself with the kind of humility and discretion we should all emulate.

As we seek to move in the healing power of the Holy Spirit, let's keep flashy mannerisms, catchphrases, and speech patterns in check. There will always be mockers, but let's not invite their taunts by giving them legitimate ammunition to fire at us. Jesus' words and works were revolutionary, but there was nothing weird or kooky about the way He moved in God's power. There is no record of Jesus showboating in any way as He healed. To the contrary, He consistently adorned Himself with the fruits of the Holy Spirit, setting the example for all those who would follow to bring healing in His name.

How much personal style is too much? Well, if people are starting to mimic or caricature your mannerisms, on-stage antics, or speech patterns, it's possible that your personal style is upstaging the Holy Spirit within you. If you're more often described by your pronounced makeup, hair, or clothes than by your likeness to Jesus, it's probably time to simplify your look and thus rightly return the focus to the God you serve.

When it comes to using gifts of healing, men and women alike would do well to consider Peter's exhortation to wives, when he advised them to prioritize beauty of the heart over showy external adornments (I Peter 3:3–4). Peter isn't saying we can't wear gold jewelry, appropriately nice clothes, or enough makeup to look normal under bright television lights. He's saying that our internal adornment is infinitely more important.

When we're representing Jesus, let's represent Jesus, in all the beauty of His genuine humility. Let's dress with moderation, and first and foremost, put on that gentle and quiet spirit that's so precious in the sight of God.

Sure, God can use you no matter what you're wearing. But Friends, let's not allow the world to squeeze us into its manufactured mold. There was no physical attractiveness about Jesus that drew the multitudes to Him for healing (Isaiah 53:2, 5). Jesus didn't dress to impress or strive to draw a crowd. No. People came in droves because Jesus was genuine. He simply lived in the manifest power of God. Since Jesus is our example, it is more than fitting that we should walk in the way He walked. That means that, instead of calling attention to ourselves in any way, we should always direct attention and glory to our empowering, healing God.

The same Holy Spirit who anoints us with gifts of healing is also full of wisdom and self-control. He is authentic in every way. There is nothing put-on or fake about Him. He only wants to call attention to Jesus. The more we set our flesh aside and give way to the Holy Spirit, the more His healing grace has room to flow through us to those who need His touch.

"Praying for the sick freaks me out. What if they don't recover?"

There is a difference between praying for healing and operating in distributed gifts of healing. All believers should demonstrate the compassion of Christ with a willingness to pray for those who are sick, injured, or diseased. At the same time as we pray in faith, we should be careful not to move ahead of or presume upon the Holy Spirit's anointing for healing to take place. We shouldn't coax people out of wheelchairs or declare that they're healed based upon our own drummed up enthusiasm. While hopes may soar momentarily, the resulting crash of realization that a healing has not occurred can be devastating.

Years ago, my precious friend, Hope, was dying of cancer. Never have I been at a bedside more surrounded by prayer. Praise music played continually. Hope comforted herself in her agony by singing along with those worship songs, even when she was half conscious.

While I prayed for Hope fervently, the Lord had gently shown me that her healing would not be in this life, but rather, in eternity. I remember being greatly concerned for Hope's husband when other well-meaning believers exhorted him that if he only had enough faith, God would heal Hope and raise her up, even from her deathbed. Please know that I believe God could have done just that.

While Hope trusted that He might choose to allow her death, she also believed in His capacity to heal her with all her heart. But sadly, there were those who stepped outside of the Spirit's leading, presuming that it was God's plan to heal Hope physically. This put a pressure on Hope's husband that the Lord never meant for him to bear. It added the worry that he was somehow personally responsible to the already overwhelming sorrow of watching his beloved wife's suffering.

As we consider this gift, we should keep in mind that even though there is a time for physical healing, there is also an appointed time to die (Ecclesiastes 3:2). For Hope, that time was only days in coming. Though she was just in her early forties, the Holy Spirit assured me that her life was not cut short. Hope adored God. She followed Jesus with every fiber of her being. She didn't die because of a lack of faith. She passed into eternal life because it was her time.

So, why do I spend time in a chapter on gifts of healing to tell you about someone who wasn't healed? Friends, at the same time as I exhort you to seek this powerful gift, please accept my counsel to be sensitive to the prompting of the Holy Spirit who gives it. When we venture outside the Spirit's anointing for healing, we can do more harm than good. When we're declaring this or that as "done" in Jesus' name and it doesn't turn out the way we presume, not only does it damage our own credibility as believers, it may lead others to doubt the power of Jesus' name.

Major caution flags go up for me with the whole "name it/claim it" healing-on-demand approach, which smacks of people trying to lead God, rather than God leading people. Never forget: when God chooses to heal, it is a grace gift. That means it is a totally undeserved blessing, not something God somehow owes us, or something we can somehow shame, obligate, or manipulate Him into doing.

We can all take the example of Luke 7:1–7 to heart. Notice how the centurion's messengers positioned the centurion as being *worthy* for Jesus to grant his request. But as Jesus approached, the centurion himself sent friends to tell Jesus that, to the contrary, he didn't even feel worthy for Jesus to come into his home. In faith, he went on to express that he recognized Jesus' authority. He believed all Jesus had to do was say the word and he'd know his servant would be healed.

There is a fine line between presumption and faith, isn't there? Though the centurion's messengers presumed upon Jesus to heal because the centurion was worthy in their estimation, the centurion humbled himself and entreated Jesus to heal in faith. It was a faith that prompted Jesus to commend the centurion to all those who were following Him.

So, absolutely, pray in humility for the sick. Know that God can heal even the most devastating diseases, but wait for the Holy Spirit's clear prompting before you declare any yet to be manifested healing to be a done deal. Especially if God has used you in healing before, resist the urge to cite that as a personal track record. God alone is the healer, so He gets all the glory.

After prayer for healing of medical conditions where the healing is not readily apparent, the recipient of prayer should *seek medical confirmation of healing before treatment is discontinued.* Jesus didn't hesitate to tell people to show themselves to others after they'd been healed and neither should we (Luke 5:14). Not only does this serve to document what has taken place, it can also open doors to witness. Many a doctor has been moved to consider God's healing power by the testimony of a miraculously healed patient. That's how it was for my friend, Christian.

Even with modern medical advances, a diagnosis of Hodgkin's disease is not taken lightly. Though successful treatments exist now, in 1946, Hodgkin's was incurable, a death sentence. Imagine yourself as a young mother just after World War II. Imagine that your five year-old son has been diagnosed with this then fatal disease. Consider going through the strain of six months of antiquated, ineffectual treatment, only to be told that your suffering child had just six to eighteen months to live. Picture your friends, urging you to celebrate Christmas early, fearful that your child wouldn't survive the season. This is where Andrea found herself, an everyday mom, praying desperately for the life of her son, Christian, knowing that the doctors had done all they could and that the only one who could help Christian was her Lord.

Early one morning, at one of her lowest points, Andrea hesitated in the kitchen doorway. Emotionally and physically drained, she leaned against the doorjamb for support. Suddenly, slumped in weakness,

Andrea felt a powerful presence reach around her from behind. This distinct, undergirding presence literally lifted her up from under her arms, helping her to stand up and move on in faith.

That divinely therapeutic visitation marked the end of Christian's physical decline. Within four months, there was no longer any indication that Christian had ever even had Hodgkin's disease. So complete was Christian's healing that, in 1963, when Christian attempted to enlist in the Navy, they refused to believe that he could have had Hodgkin's, as Christian had declared on his medical history. The Navy remained unconvinced until their own pathology lab confirmed Christian's history through tissue samples taken in 1946. Knowing how incurable Hodgkin's was at that time, they viewed Christian as a documented medical miracle. At this writing, Christian continues to thrive, a testimony of the power of God to heal, even through the prayers of unassuming lay believers like his mother.

"What if someone thinks I healed him or her?"

Lovingly and clearly correct that person's misunderstanding. Explain that you're just a human being who is following Jesus. Direct all thanks, praise, adulation, and glory to God. Make it clear that any healing that takes place has been performed by God and that you are only a human instrument in His hand. Finally, encourage that person to follow Jesus and seek how he or she, too, might serve Him.

"If I'm not healed after prayer, is it my fault?"

Years ago, I remember hearing some false teaching on this subject. The preacher was adamant that if a person wasn't healed, then it was that person's fault because they must have sin in their lives, either unconfessed active sin or the passive sin of unbelief. I was disturbed to see how many nodding heads and *amens* signified agreement with this error.

Yes, there are times when our sin can be an impediment to healing. But there are also times when a person's chronic sickness is not because of sin. Consider John 9:1–3, in which Jesus advised that the man wasn't blind because of his own sin or his parents' sin.

Instead, it was all about God being glorified through his ultimate healing. Additionally, Paul understood that some ailments remain to keep us from exalting ourselves and to demonstrate how God's power is made perfect in our weakness (II Corinthians 12:7–10).

"Should a person who has manifested this gift be able access it all the time?"

Though God always has the power to heal, this gift, like other manifestations, is distributed as the Holy Spirit wills, and not as we will (I Corinthians 12:11). This gift is not at the believer's constant disposal, but rather at God's. If gifts of healing were on demand, then why did Paul suffer a continuing thorn in the flesh or Timothy with stomach ailments (I Timothy 5:23)?

If you think of healing as if it were a power tool, that tool doesn't seem to be resident in the believer's tool box, there to be picked up and manifested any time, at the believer's option, the way a prayer language can be. Rather, it seems that believers may be visited with this gift each time the Holy Spirit wills to distribute it. Some seem to be visited with gifts of healing more often than others, and some only on occasion.

We can ask for this power. We can do our part to keep the flesh from impeding the flow. But each time these wonders occur, no matter how seldom or often, ultimately, it is because the Holy Spirit has willed to distribute healing. Perhaps this repetitive distribution is why Scripture says *gifts of healing* (plural) instead of the singular *gift* of healing (I Corinthians 12:9, 28).

Notice that, whereas those who are gifted to teach are referred to as *teachers* in verse twenty-eight, those who manifest gifts of healing are not called *healers*. Although believers are distributed the power to heal in Jesus' name, scripturally, God alone is considered our healer (Exodus 15:26), making the moniker *faith healer* a bit of a misnomer when applied to a human being.

Though God has graced me to manifest gifts of healing on occasion, it has not been a regular or even frequent occurrence. It has also been this way for me with other manifestations of the Holy Spirit. Even though gifts of healing have been given to flow through me, I don't think of gifts of healing as a possession. I just think of myself as

His possession, and I simply make myself available to use whatever power tool He chooses to put into my hands.

While there are those who have operated in this gift numerous times, even those who have developed healing ministries, healing does not always take place for a variety of reasons. It might be that the timing is not yet right. It might be that God has good reason not to remove a person's thorn in the flesh. It might be that unbelief has compromised the flow of healing (Matthew 13:58). It might be that the believer who started out well, has drifted into the marshes of error (Ezekiel 47:11), away from the healing current of God's River (Ezekiel 47:12). It might just as easily be that God wants us to trust Him, even if He allows the natural physical course of sickness to continue.

"How will I know if God is anointing me for healing?"

As we can tell from Jesus' experience with the woman who had a chronic issue of blood, there was something sensory about the healing power that went out of Jesus when she, in faith, touched His garments (Mark 5:30).

While the Holy Spirit anoints believers for healing in different ways on different occasions, there is a frequent accompanying gift of faith for healing. I've also seen gifts of healing team up with the word of knowledge or prophecy as God informs someone of an unknown physical need and/or a desire to heal.

Though a believer may discern that there is an anointing for healing without physical cues, I've heard numerous reports from friends that the Holy Spirit has directed them to lay hands on a person for healing by giving them a physical sensation of tingling or warmth. Sometimes it's in one hand or in the area needing attention, alerting the believer to the Spirit's imminent desire to manifest healing power.

I remember one night when a friend of mine was instantaneously healed under such an anointing of the Holy Spirit. She was blind in one eye, and when this anointing fell, she requested ministry. There was nothing showy about it, no big prayer—she was just touched by a Spirit-anointed hand in Jesus' matchless name, and instantly her blind eye was opened.

"Is the laying on of hands required?"

No. Remember that Jesus never even met the centurion's slave. That healing took place across a distance. He didn't lay hands on the woman with the issue of blood, either. It was she who, in faith, touched only the hem of His garment. While the laying on of hands isn't common to all healings, it is, however, common to many in Scripture.

In Luke 4:40, Jesus laid hands on every one of the sick and healed them. Now one would think, if there were ever a time for not laying on hands, it would have been when Jesus encountered a leper in Luke 5:12–14. This man was unclean, an outcast. No one wanted to be anywhere near him, much less touch him, for fear of catching his disfiguring disease. Perhaps that is exactly why Jesus chose to touch this man in faith. Turn to Acts 28:8–9 and you'll see that Paul also laid hands on Publius' father for healing of fever and dysentery.

Though the context of Paul's caution to Timothy not to lay hands on anyone too hastily likely concerns promotion to sacred office, it is also understood by some as having application to laying hands on the sick (I Timothy 5:22). No matter how you interpret this verse, I would encourage you to listen carefully for the prompting of the Holy Spirit when praying for those who are contagious.

You can be confident that if the Spirit indeed wills to distribute healing power through the laying on of hands, He will protect the instrument through which His healing power flows. Jesus was in no danger of infection when He touched the sick under the unction of the Holy Spirit. But when we step out from under the Spirit's protective guidance, we can expose ourselves to sickness, even sin. That said, there are times when things like calling on church elders for the laying on of hands and anointing with oil for healing are very scriptural things to do (James 5:14).

Not long after my friend, Jenna, began to grow in her experience of God's power, she consulted with her doctor about long-term escalating symptoms she was experiencing from what her doctor said with virtually 100% certainty was endometriosis. She was told that the only way to get relief from this pain would be to have the abnormal tissue surgically removed.

Jenna set a date for surgery, and then asked if leaders from our church would lay hands on her and pray in advance of the procedure. She could have shied away from revealing this private female problem to men, but Jenna humbled herself undeterred. Like the woman with the issue of blood, she just wanted to press through in every way she could to touch the hem of Jesus' garment in faith.

Though Jenna's request wasn't common at that time, two men from our pastoral staff joined Jenna's husband and me to lay hands on Jenna, anoint her with oil, and pray for her healing. It was just a quiet circle, gathered behind the scenes. Since her symptoms continued, we didn't know exactly how God had ministered to Jenna that day, but the presence of the Holy Spirit had been palpable.

Soon, the surgery date came. Jenna's doctor had her prepped and went in to perform the laparoscopic procedure. To the surgeon's great puzzlement and Jenna's delight, he found nothing of what he fully expected to see. He just shook his head repeatedly, saying there wasn't a single spot of endometriosis there to remove! And though the surgeon closed without doing anything that would have treated the symptoms Jenna had been having, afterwards Jenna had recognizable relief. God had indeed heard Jenna's cry as she stepped out in faith and submitted herself to prayer for healing, then waited to see it manifest in a way her doctor could witness.

"How will I know what to do as I pray for the sick?"

The key is to remain in vital communion with the Holy Spirit and to follow His instructions, which may differ with each situation and person. Sometime Jesus healed with a touch or just a word. Perhaps it would seem strange if you saw someone spit on the ground, make clay, put that clay on a blind person's eye, and ask them to go wash, but Jesus did it (John 9:6–7).

While Jesus healed in a variety of ways, the constant for Him was flowing with God in the Holy Spirit. The more Jesus healed, the more clamored for His attention. If you think you don't have time for personal prayer, think about Jesus, traveling with a band of twelve constantly, multitudes hanging on His every word and deed, religious leaders questioning Him right and left. But still, Jesus made time to pray alone. He often purposely withdrew from the crowds, into the place no one really wanted to go: the wilderness (Luke 5:16). Jesus knew the value of time alone with His Father and He made their time together a priority.

Those who would seek to operate in gifts of healing would do well to follow Jesus' example. The better we get to know God's voice privately, the more easily we'll be able to hear Him over the din of this world, and the more we'll be sensitive to that still, small voice of the Holy Spirit, prompting us to manifest that same healing power that flowed with such grace through Jesus.

CHAPTER THIRTEEN

Effecting of Miracles

What it is:
God performing what is naturally impossible through a human being

What it's not:
Magic, psychic phenomenon, possible through human effort

> *The forecast called for a downpour that morning along with thundershowers all day. Indeed, there was a pervasive, dark cloud cover, though we needed a full day of sunshine for the twelve hours of work set before us, making a film about a young man's journey to faith. We had a full cast and crew on the clock and a scant budget that didn't allow for rescheduling or overtime. We needed an immediate full-scale change of a massive weather system. Without a word to anyone, I stepped aside from the crowd. Knowing Jesus had calmed storms, I quietly asked for just that kind of help. I looked up and immediately, a single patch of blue sky broke through those dark clouds. Within minutes, we were working under completely sunny skies. It held up all day, confounding the meteorologists, in bright testimony to the wonder-working power of God.*

The word *miracle* gets thrown around pretty liberally these days. We might proclaim it a miracle that we got a parking spot, that a job came through, or that a baby was born. While all of these things can be wonderful, and while there is something to be said for the miracle that is life, created by God, when we talk about this gift, we'll be considering those things that don't immediately occur in the natural, those physical wonders requiring God's supernatural intervention, that He uses us to effect.

Nonbelievers can claim babies are naturally born every day; however, if a person who is known to be dead is raised right out of his coffin, then we're talking *miracle* (Luke 7:12–17). Believers serving with this gift are empowered to effect what's physically impossible, as a sign to unbelievers (Exodus 4:1–8). It's not that we do the miracle. God does. We're just the vessel God uses to accomplish His wonders.

It is physically impossible to walk on water, yet Jesus not only did it Himself, He also bid Peter to work the same miracle, which did occur until Peter took his eyes off Jesus (Matthew 14:22–33). There's a very important lesson in this for all who would work miracles in Jesus' name: The connection to Jesus is an absolutely essential component. The minute we take our eyes off of Jesus, the power flow is broken and we sink like stones into the limitations of the natural world.

We have no power whatsoever in and of ourselves. Zero. One hundred percent of the power to work miracles comes from God. Friends, do not allow verse twenty-three to escape your notice. Though it might seem disjointed from the rest of the passage, it is actually key. Jesus' alone time with God directly preceded the manifest miracle. Vital connection to God through prayer should never be bypassed or underestimated in its importance.

One Easter, a close friend of mine prepared enough food for twelve to fifteen family members. There was a ham large enough for fifteen or twenty. She had vegetable dishes, a package of thirty-six tiny rolls, and dessert. What she didn't know was that an open invitation to come to her home had been issued to those at church who had no place to go for Easter dinner.

When almost forty people showed up, my friend knew she couldn't possibly feed everyone. There were more people than the dinner roll count on the bag, even if each person only took one! There was no time to go to the store. That's when she decided to pray over the food before serving it, believing that God would feed all her guests.

They began to slice the ham. They kept slicing and slicing, yet the ham didn't seem to deplete in any proportion what was being cut. People filed past the service table, loading their plates, completely unaware that not enough food had been prepared. My friend watched with a little concern as each person took at least two of those tiny rolls. Some of the men took as many as four rolls each, yet my friend said nothing, trusting that the Lord would supply. The food never ran out. People ate as much as they wanted, never knowing that there hadn't been even nearly enough. In fact, there were leftovers of everything, including the dinner rolls that had proved so popular. Sound at all familiar to you?

Read over the miracle of food multiplication in Matthew 14:15–21. While many of us would rather leave the working of miracles to Jesus (or to our leaders), notice how Jesus invites the disciples' participation in the impossible, telling the disciples that the crowd of five thousand men (plus women and children) did not have to leave to be fed. Jesus said: *You feed them.* Jesus prayed over the five loaves and two fishes before they were served, just as my friend did. Then, rather than Jesus serving the food Himself, He told the disciples to distribute the food to the multitude. It wasn't that the Lord was above the task of serving food. No. Jesus wanted to involve the disciples, to partner with them in effecting this miracle, the same way He wants to partner with us in the Holy Spirit today.

Interestingly, though there are times that God seems to initiate the miraculous, there are also times when humans initiate, asking God to move miraculously like my friend did with Easter dinner. Peter asked Jesus to allow him to walk out toward Him on the water. Mary initiated at the wedding at Cana (John 2:1–10); however, she did not take over or presume to make demands of God. She simply alerted Jesus that their host had run out of wine, then allowed room for His response, instructing the servants to do whatever Jesus told them to do. In like manner, those of us who entreat the Lord for the impossible today should attentively listen for any instructions that may come in the Spirit, trusting God's sovereignty, even if He doesn't choose to intervene in the way we hope.

"Is the effecting of miracles one of the greater gifts we're supposed to seek?"

While the Bible doesn't specifically identify this as a greater gift, it just might be. If we think of the manifestations of the Spirit as power tools for witnessing, this one is like a supercharged evangelistic harvester. This is no cream puff, barn-kept equipment. The entire Bible teems with stories of the miraculous. Jesus' ministry was regularly characterized by operating in this gift, a gift He passed on to the Church via baptism with the Holy Spirit, for the purpose of validating her witness.

When God cleared that storm at my request, it validated my testimony to those standing by, some of whom were wrestling with what to believe. They knew my human limitations. They knew I was powerless to change something as wildly beyond my control as the weather. So, it served as striking evidence that God is real, that He hears prayer, that He can and does move in power.

Miracles are attention-grabbers. People who won't respond to talk will quickly bow to manifest power. Miracles are tools God uses to increase the population of His church. Just look at the way the early church grew at such an astonishing rate, sometimes thousands in a day. That's why we still need this gift today and every day, to help reach the lost.

"If miracles still happen, how come I haven't seen any?"

If you're looking for a miracle as proof that God still does them, you may want to examine this underlying question: *Do I believe God before I see or because I see?*

From my rank and file position in the body of Christ, I have been graced to see and hear of many modern-day wonders, all attesting to the continuing gift of the effecting of miracles. I never looked for miracles as proof, I simply believed God, and then I started seeing them, consistent with the testimonies of Scripture. Miracles happened to Peter and Paul (Acts 9:36–42, Acts 20:9–12) and, yes, they still happen, even to the least of God's servants today. They happen in fulfillment of Jesus' prophetic word, that the wonder-working power that flowed through Him in the Holy Spirit would course through believers, equipping them to be witnesses of His glory to the ends of the earth (Acts 1:5, 8).

An interesting thing I've noticed about miracles is that they seem to happen repeatedly to those who believe in God's power to do them.

God doesn't intervene miraculously all the time, but the people I know who have seen one miracle can usually cite multiple instances of God's manifest power in their lives. Whereas miracles are a sign to unbelievers, to believers the effecting of miracles is a gift, a by-product of the Spirit-empowered life.

It's especially sad, within the church, to see just how locked up in unbelief we can become. Even though we say we believe and we know the Bible tells us that these signs are there to empower our testimonies in the Lord, even though we pray fervently—when it comes right down to it, we reflexively revert to natural expectations.

Consider Acts 12:1-17. The early church had just experienced a grievous loss when Herod had James put to death. There was no small threat when Herod also arrested Peter and threw him into prison, posting four squads of soldiers to guard him. Though the Bible says fervent prayers went up for Peter from the church, those prayers were not noted for being expectant.

Still, God saw the need and intervened. An angel appeared, roused Peter from between two sleeping soldiers, then told Peter to get dressed and follow. Even Peter didn't know if what was happening was real or a vision, but he faithfully followed the angel's instructions. Imagine Peter's amazement when the iron city gate opened by itself! It was only after the angel disappeared and Peter found himself freed that he knew for sure what had actually happened.

Now, remember the church that was so fervently praying? Peter went to their house and knocked on the door. When the servant girl, Rhoda, joyfully reported that Peter was at the gate, did they believe her? Hardly. Though they had not ceased to pray for Peter, they told Rhoda she was out of her mind! It wasn't until they saw Peter with their own eyes that they believed God for the very miracle they'd been praying would happen.

Friends, we're not so very different from that church, praying much more fervently than we're believing. It's understandable how it happened. After all, they'd probably prayed for James, too, and God hadn't stopped James' execution. That's how unbelief creeps in to imprison us, even if we've once witnessed the miraculous. More recent blows of persecution, ridicule, and disappointments compromise our expectancy. We pray fervently, but we're essentially praying in unbelief.

So, why did this miracle happen, even though it seems there was unbelief? First and foremost, because our sovereign God knew it was not Peter's time. God used this miracle as a sign to Herod and the soldiers, as well as to encourage the church that was freshly bereaved of James. Did God work alone this time or did He involve any humans in working this miracle? Look back through this story for clues to how two believers partnered with what God was doing.

Peter was imprisoned under armed guards. If anyone would have seemed naturally keyed up, fearful, or anxious to the point of insomnia, it seems it would have been Peter, whose head was to be next on the chopping block. Do you really think you'd get a wink of sleep under those conditions, bound with chains between guards, knowing this night could be your last? But what was Peter doing when the angel showed up? He was *sleeping*. Even the bright light that filled the cell didn't wake Peter. The angel had to strike Peter to rouse him.

I don't know about you, but just the fact that Peter was sleeping so soundly looks like faith to me. I imagine that he prayed before he went to sleep and entrusted his life to the God who never slumbers. Then, waking, Peter participated in the effecting of his miraculous release by following the angel's instructions, even when he wasn't sure if what was happening to him was real or a dream.

Then, there was Rhoda, an everyday servant girl, who believed without seeing, after only hearing Peter's voice at the door. The evidence of Rhoda's faith shows in that she didn't even open the gate to be sure that it was actually Peter. Rather, she ran to the others, bursting with certain joy that the miracle they'd prayed for had happened. Even when the others called her crazy, even when they tried to convince her it was only Peter's angel and not Peter himself, Rhoda's faith was unshakeable. She insisted that the miraculous had occurred, even though she had yet to see it.

Though Rhoda wasn't at the prison to see Peter's release, it appears that any prayers Rhoda may have prayed for Peter were prayers of faith. While Scripture doesn't specifically name Rhoda as praying, we know that she was in that fervently praying household. We know that she received the miracle in faith. It's also very possible that this simple servant girl was a prayer participant in the effecting of this lifesaving miracle.

I don't know about you, but it moves me that God used a girl of such humble station to speak to the church about what He had done. Rhoda probably wasn't educated. She wasn't high profile. She wasn't a man who could naturally command respect or attention in that day. I imagine that she had probably been waiting on them, preparing food, cleaning up, hearing their fears, their grief, their concern for Peter, and adding her prayers to theirs.

I want to be like Rhoda, don't you? I want to be simple and uncomplicated enough by this world to believe and participate in what God is doing. But being like Rhoda also means being of humble station, a true servant to God's people. As much as working miracles makes us like the Lord Jesus, let's never lose sight of that picture of Jesus, picking up the basin and towel, humbly washing the disciples' feet.

The gift of effecting miracles isn't meant to put us into a spotlight. To the contrary, we are to be like that unseen worker in the rafters who joyfully trains the spotlight on Jesus, and revels that God alone gets the glory.

CHAPTER FOURTEEN

Distinguishing of Spirits

What it is:

The Holy Spirit-given ability to recognize and identify what type of spirit is at work

What it's not:

Natural instincts, a sixth sense, an excuse to entertain evil spirits

> *After a particularly challenging day, I asked God to minister to me while I slept. Before dawn, while dreaming, I felt a large right hand come to rest on my right upper arm. Scriptures committed to memory during waking hours reminded me to test the spirit. Within the dream, I quickly prayed that if this spirit didn't confess Jesus as Lord it would leave me immediately. In response, instead of leaving, the hand moved from my arm and came to rest on my upper chest, just below my throat. The hand was strong, warm, reassuring, and fatherly, exuding the effervescent love I have come to recognize from God. His hand on me had weight. It was so palpable that I can still almost feel it today. In fact, from time to time, I still put my hand over where His was, reminding myself of the reality of His abiding presence.*

Is this gift a little daunting to you? Okay, maybe it's downright scary. Maybe it completely freaks you out. Trust me, you're not alone.

Because distinguishing of spirits is normally associated with confronting demons, there don't seem to be too many believers lined up, earnestly seeking this much needed power gift. Though we tend to defer this kind of warfare to leadership, the enemy of our souls often attacks lone sheep when earthly shepherds aren't around. That's why every believer should be watchful, prepared with the assurance of God's superior power to protect even a little teen lamb like I was when I first encountered the enemy.

There is, however, much more to this gift than many realize. Distinguishing of spirits isn't only about recognizing when an enemy spirit is at work. It's also about recognizing godly spirits, including the Holy Spirit.

There are four types of spirits this gift helps the body of Christ to discern: 1) the Holy Spirit; 2) angels; 3) evil spirits; and 4) good or evil in human spirits. Let's look at these one at a time:

The Holy Spirit

What a relief, huh? This gift helps us to discern the presence of the Holy Spirit, so we can welcome His work in our midst.

Read John 1:32–33. Think about it. John had been baptizing for repentance, proclaiming the coming of the Messiah. Jesus approached John for baptism, and John said he didn't recognize Him (as the Messiah) at first. It was only after John discerned the Holy Spirit descending and resting on Jesus that John recognized Jesus as the Messiah, the promised One John himself had prophetically proclaimed would baptize with the Holy Spirit.

Consider how the Pharisees were compromised by not moving in this gift. They insisted that Jesus was empowered to cast out demons by the prince of demons, totally missing the same Holy Spirit John had ultimately discerned upon Jesus. The Pharisees were not alone in their blindness to the Holy Spirit. The religious people also accused Jesus of having a demon when they couldn't accept His teaching (John 7:20, John 8:48–49). Notice that, in both of these instances, it was God's people who failed to distinguish the presence of the Holy Spirit, and they dishonored the Lord Jesus in the process.

Body of Christ, we should all want to correctly distinguish the presence and work of the Holy Spirit. We should want to be like Peter, in Acts 10:44–48, when he recognized that the Holy Spirit had come upon the Gentiles. If we rightly discern the movement of the Holy Spirit, we can let go of the limitations of traditionalism and embrace what God is doing in the present, even if it differs from what we expect. This gift allows us to affirm the work of the Holy Spirit and to ascribe honor to God for His intervention in our lives, honor He richly deserves.

Angels

Since not all angels are sent from God, it's important to discern which are which. While God does appoint holy angels to render service to us, there are also fallen angels (disguised demons) in the service of our enemy, who share his evil mission to steal, kill, and destroy.

God's holy angels are ministering spirits, sent for our good (Hebrews 1:14). They protect us (Psalm 91:11–12), take care of us (Luke 22:41–43), and bring messages from God (Matthew 2:13, Acts 27:23).

But we can't just go by appearances, assuming any angelic being that appears to be lovely is from God. II Corinthians 11:14–15 warns that Satan will disguise himself as an angel of light. Like the mangy wolf in sheep's clothing that he is, the devil purposes to deceive even the elect, posing as something beautiful, helpful, and harmless when he is anything but that. Our eyes can literally deceive us. Our ears can hear what sounds like the right words. That's why we need the Holy Spirit to help us supernaturally distinguish just what type of angel is at work.

Scripture welcomes us to put all spirits to a test. Just before listing the manifestations of the Spirit, Paul gave us a simple two-way trial:

> *"...no one speaking by the Spirit of God says, 'Jesus is accursed';
> and no one can say, 'Jesus is Lord,' except by the Holy Spirit."*
> *I Corinthians 12:3*

Waking or sleeping, if you find yourself in the company of an angel and you're not sure, you will not offend a holy angel by asking that angel to tell you that Jesus is Lord, something a holy angel will be quick to affirm. On the other hand, a fallen angel won't be able to get those words out and can quickly be unveiled and rebuked in the name of Jesus (James 4:7).

Once, an angel of light appeared to me in a dream. Talk about putting on an attractive, harmless appearance! She looked like a bubbly little blonde, being overtly complimentary as she sashayed into a friend of mine's new apartment. Even while dreaming, the Holy Spirit immediately put me on guard about her, giving me the discernment I needed to identify her source, despite her deceptively wholesome appearance. While she gushed to my friend about how great the place was, as soon as he left, cynicism flashed in her eyes.

In the dream, I approached her face to face and sternly rebuked her in the name of Jesus. In an instant, she was unmasked. That pretty blonde exterior quickly melted away into a hideous snarling monster. Then, just as quickly as she had been outed as fallen, she disappeared, in mandatory submission to the superior power of the Lord, operating even as I slept. This dream was not only an exercise in discernment; it was also a reminder to pray for my friend as well as an alert for him to be watchful in his new environs.

"Sorry, but this sounds kind of nutty."

Yeah, I hear you. When I start talking about spiritual emissaries manifesting to human beings, I know I might lose more than a few readers. But here's why I believe in God-sent angels and fallen angels: The Bible says they exist. Jesus believed in them and encountered them regularly. They're there, waking or sleeping, whether we believe in them or not. We shouldn't worship holy angels and we shouldn't fear fallen ones. What we should do is pray for the gift of distinguishing of spirits so that we can tell the difference.

Demons

These are overt evil spirits, vile enemy henchmen that don't bother to disguise themselves. The only good thing about them is that they are rendered completely powerless against the authority of the name of Jesus, even from the mouth of an everyday believer.

While a lone demon can grip a human being, multiple demons have also been known to find strongholds within a single person. In Mark 5:2–16 we read how Jesus delivered the Gerasene demoniac of so many demons that their collective name was Legion.

Ever wonder why Jesus agreed to send the demons into that herd of swine? Perhaps it was a way to demonstrate the reality of demons to those who might have explained the man's possession and deliverance away as an elaborate act. Whereas people can simulate things, pigs don't have that capacity. Two thousand swine hurling themselves off a cliff and drowning themselves rather than live with those tormentors inside them make a persuasive point. Though the deliverance of the man was Jesus' primary concern, the story spread quickly through the swine-herders because of the pigs. In protecting themselves from the liability of having lost their herd, they defended themselves with the truth, that Jesus had brought deliverance to a man everyone had written off as hopeless by sending real demons into their swine.

But before the swine and before the deliverance, first, Jesus had to diagnose what was wrong with this man. Was he mentally ill or disabled in some way? Did this man need healing or deliverance? That's why Jesus needed to use this gift of the Spirit, enabling Him to distinguish that the man wasn't suffering from sickness, but rather from demonic possession.

Paul needed this gift, too. In Acts 16:16–18 we find Paul annoyed by a fortune-telling slave-girl who was actually announcing that Paul was a servant of God, proclaiming the way of salvation. Some might take issue with Paul, observing that this girl didn't seem to be against them. Why stop her from calling out the truth? Paul, however, recognized the spirit of divination within this girl, a spirit that might have identified with Paul while present, then used that association later to lead new converts astray. It's important to note that familiar spirits will often precede their lies with truth, associating themselves with goodness just long enough to lure the naive into their end-game of deceit. Paul saw this demonic spirit for what it was and cast it out, much to the disappointment of those who had profited from the slave-girl's divinations.

Like Paul, we should never allow demons to speak or act out unchecked, even if they seem benign on the surface. Rather, they should be immediately subdued, rebuked, cast out, and prohibited from returning. There is no reason whatsoever to fear, argue, or get physical with them. Know that the authority all believers have in the name of Jesus is absolute and should be exercised with expedient confidence.

Exorcism is not, however, to be co-opted by those who are not in personal submission to Jesus. Because Jesus is the one who exercises authority over demons, only those who are submitted to Jesus as Lord are guaranteed His protection from the forces of darkness. Remember what happened when those exorcists attempted to use Jesus' name without a direct relationship (Acts 19:13–17)?

When it's the human spirit vs. an evil spirit, the evil spirit's power is not only superior, it's dangerous, a lesson learned the hard way by those exorcists. But the same demon that poses such a threat to the unprotected human spirit can be rendered completely powerless, even by a baby believer standing under the authority of Jesus. Jesus vs. demons? It'll be Jesus by a knockout every single time.

This is not to say that believers should be cavalier about confronting demons, nor seek them out. It is serious spiritual warfare. While believers are protected in the name of Jesus, Jesus noted that there are some particularly stubborn demons that can only be exorcised through the disciplines of prayer and fasting (Matthew 17:21, Mark 9:29). Since we still struggle with the flesh, which can compromise our submitted relationship to Jesus, denying the flesh through fasting and living in close communication with the Father strengthens us in the Holy Spirit. It can make even the lowliest believer more like Jesus in His authority over demonic spirits, even legions of them.

"Shouldn't we leave casting out demons to priests?"

Absolutely. But guess what, everyday believer? We are the priests! Jesus came to make all believers kings and priests to God (Revelation 1:6). He has built us up into a spiritual house in which we are each to serve as members of a royal priesthood (I Peter 2:5, 9). We are all challenged to pick up the bright torch of God and to use it to call people out of darkness and into the liberating light.

So, yes, Everyday Believer/Priest. If you are surrendered in service to God, be ready to do some spontaneous spiritual housecleaning when needed.

During the final weeks of my dear friend Hope's life, I spent many days at her bedside. Hope was the personification of a gentle and quiet spirit. In all the years I'd known her, I'd never heard her get agitated or raise her voice. That's why I was so surprised to hear her frantically screaming from inside the house when I pulled into her driveway.

I ran inside. A woman was fruitlessly trying to calm Hope, who was flailing in her bed, screaming for the woman to do something about the sinister man in a dark coat that she'd just seen enter her home. The woman kept trying to tell Hope that no one was there, that it was just the pain medication tricking her mind. Hope continued to yell that this evil being was still standing by the door, right beside me as I entered.

I hadn't expected to do battle that day. But I had come as a sister-priest to serve at Hope's bedside. It didn't matter that I couldn't see an evil spirit there at Hope's door. Whether that spirit had manifested to Hope in the actual house or if he had used her medicated state to invade her mind, he was there, very real, very threatening, to torment my dying friend.

Without hesitation, the Holy Spirit showed me what to do. I went straight to Hope's bedside and affirmed that I believed her, that she was distinguishing the presence of an enemy intruder. I took her hand and asked her to agree with me in prayer. Hope readily cooperated. Together, we took authority over this vile spirit, to cast him out and bind him from re-entry. Whether from her mind or her doorway, Hope saw the demonic spirit leave, immediately upon hearing Jesus' name. Hope returned to a state of peace, having participated in this victory in two ways: she had discerned an evil spirit, and she had agreed with me to vanquish him by the far superior power of God.

Now, I suppose many would argue that this was no evil spirit, that this was simply a hallucination. It's ironic really. To the point of cliché, we admit that the mind is the enemy's go-to recreation spot, yet we're hesitant to believe it when he's entered through that portal, knowing full well that the mind is where we're particularly vulnerable to attack, especially when medicated.

So, even if it is a hallucination, are we going to give our insidious enemy permission to threaten us within our weakened minds? Are we going to allow him to attack us in our dreams? *Never!* Our bodies (including our minds) are the temples of the Holy Spirit. Why sit back and let the enemy waltz into through his favorite door? Instead, we should pray that the Holy Spirit would help us to identify and promptly evict any enemy intruders by means of this much-needed gift.

The Human Spirit

Finally, distinguishing of spirits helps us rightly identify the character of the human spirit in those we encounter. Given fallen humanity's propensity for posing, the Holy Spirit's assurance of good character or warning of bad character can aid us as we navigate business, personal, and ministry life. In a way, this gift can function like a spiritual lie detector. If you don't think so, consider how Peter distinguished the deceiving human spirits of Ananias and Sapphira (Acts 5:1–11).

Jesus distinguished Nathanael's spirit as guileless before He ever met him (John 1:45–49). Jesus merely saw Nathanael sitting under a fig tree and immediately knew him. In the Holy Spirit, Jesus recognized Nathanael's spirit as good (John 2:25). It took a little longer for Nathanael. Notice that when Philip initially told Nathanael he had found the prophesied Messiah, Nathanael was iffy about it, since Jesus came from Nazareth. Still, moments into Nathanael's first face-to-face encounter with Jesus, Nathanael declared something only the Holy Spirit could have helped him to discern, which was that Jesus was the Son of God.

Jesus also distinguished Judas Iscariot's fallen human spirit long before Judas betrayed Him; it was an association Jesus maintained in the interest of fulfilling prophecy. Though Jesus was discreet about what He knew of Judas, He was outspoken about the fallen character He discerned in the scribes and Pharisees, recorded in Matthew 23. This should serve as fair warning to anyone who would pose as a religious leader and, in fact, lead people into the doctrines of men and away from the truth of God.

"I thought we weren't supposed to judge people."

Distinguishing of spirits isn't about people judging people. What judgment we are used to deliver comes directly from God. This gift shouldn't be used as a cover for us to render our human judgment or opinions about people. It should only be used under the direct unction of the Holy Spirit, as He reveals God's judgment.

Take a look at Acts 13:6–12. Read that whole passage before you continue. Now, ask yourself: *Was Paul guilty of the sin of judging Elymas?*

Answer: not even a little bit. Not only does verse nine tell us that Paul was full of the Holy Spirit when he discerned Elymas' spirit as evil, that same power coursing through Paul brought about a stupendous sign. Paul went beyond delivering God's judgment to being used to sentence Elymas to a time of blindness, a display of God's power that resulted in the proconsul coming to faith in Jesus.

Even Elymas' punishment itself, gave opportunity for Elymas to consider his need to be led. Elymas, like Paul, had been leading people astray. The same way temporary blindness taught Paul submission to God, it offered Elymas the chance to follow the way of salvation through Jesus. So, as tempting as it might be to find satisfaction that Elymas got what was coming to him, we shouldn't gloat over those God judges or disciplines. Instead, we should pray for that person, humbly realizing that we were once just as blind before God showed us the light.

That's the bottom line with distinguishing of spirits. Whether your stature in the body is great, or modest like mine, it's about the formerly blind leading the still blind to see God in Christ. Admittedly, power over spiritual forces can be a heady thing. However, lest we lose perspective, instead of getting fleshy satisfaction in the idea that the spirits are subject to us, let's rejoice for the overarching reason that our names, like that proconsul's, are written in heaven (Luke 10:20).

It is always and forever the Giver we love and celebrate, not the power-gifts He gives us. The truth is, the only time the demons are subject to us is when they look at us and see Jesus. It's not about us at all. We are simply God's bond-slaves, using this gift to exalt Him.

CHAPTER FIFTEEN

Various Kinds of Tongues

What it is:
Speaking unlearned language in words given by the Holy Spirit

What it's not:
Gibberish, taught by humans, learned, or composed in the mind

> *Freaked beyond description to realize that God might have this widely distributed power tool for me, I closed the door, turned out the lights, and sat cross-legged on my bed. Trembling, I told God how scared I was of this particular gift, and then added that I'd still do it if I had to. I opened my mouth and waited for a minute. In my naiveté, I'd feared that it would be like some sci-fi alien invader, that the Holy Spirit would take over my mouth and start manipulating my lips and tongue, and that a stream of words would suddenly come pouring out, beyond my control. Pshew! Nothing happened. I crawled under the covers, mightily relieved to be off the hook.*

We've finally reached the gift that initially terrified me so. Maybe it scares you, too. Maybe you've been warned about it, like I was, or you've heard it and it wigged you out like it did me. Maybe you've been ambushed by an overzealous proponent of tongues. Maybe it's just so strange to you that you'd rather not accept this gift. Or, you might be among those who have really prayed, wanting this gift, and yet have been disappointed not to receive it.

No matter who you are or what your story is, when it comes to this often-controversial gift, all believers are well advised to prayerfully examine it in the light of Scripture. It may be a lesser gift, especially in corporate usage, but we know that all of God's gifts are given for our good, even if only to indirectly benefit the body by edifying the individual (Luke 11:13, I Corinthians 12:7, James 1:17). With that in mind, let's open God's Word and ask the Spirit Himself to teach us.

> *"Now we have received, not the spirit of the world, but the Spirit who is from God, that we might know the things freely given to us by God, which things we also speak, not in words taught by human wisdom, but in those taught by the Spirit, combining spiritual thoughts with spiritual words."*
>
> *I Corinthians 2:12–13*

Part of the confusion about this gift stems from the fact that there are different kinds of tongues (I Corinthians 12:10). While their usages and purposes may differ, what all varieties of this multi-faceted gift have in common is that they each involve uttering language/s that we have neither learned nor been taught through any natural means. Instead, tongues is language that is purely given by the Holy Spirit. The Spirit puts spiritual thoughts into spiritually given words, even for everyday newborn believers (Acts 10:46).

The Bible refers to three different outworkings of tongues, each with a specific purpose: 1) Unlearned Earthly Language; 2) Spiritual Language of Prayer; and 3) Tongues with Interpretation for the church.

Unlearned Earthly Language

We find this kind of tongues manifested on the day of Pentecost, when the promised Holy Spirit fell upon the waiting disciples (Acts 2:1–11). This must have been quite a holy hubbub! If there had been any doubt in the disciples' minds about how they'd know that the Spirit had fallen upon them, this mass distribution of unlearned languages proved a sure sign that their wait was over. Cloven tongues of fire, resting on each one, served as visual confirmation.

The disciples had, indeed, been baptized with the Holy Spirit and fire, and equipped with an attention-arresting means to witness in an array of unlearned earthly languages. Naturally, this caused a stir. Peter, the same guy who had fearfully denied Jesus to a servant-girl, began to preach Jesus boldly. Three thousand souls were saved that day (Acts 2:41). That's quite a harvest, directly assisted by one facet of this gift.

Tongues, in unlearned earthly languages, can still be a very compelling sign to unbelievers today. Consider this account of an everyday woman who experienced this variety of tongues quite unexpectedly. During worship at church, this woman was always careful to pray in tongues softly, at a level that was inaudible to those around her, in accordance with I Corinthians 14:28; however, this particular day, she felt led to pray in tongues loudly enough that those immediately around her could hear. Afterward, a man behind this woman asked if she knew Greek. When he learned that she didn't know any Greek, or even know that Greek was the language she was speaking, the man was astonished. He knew Greek well, and had understood every word. He had come in as a skeptic, and this was an undeniable sign, designed by God just for him.

Still another woman, my friend, Danielle, had noticed that the language she was given sounded kind of Semitic. Though Danielle is of Jewish descent, she knows nothing of those associated languages. Out of curiosity, she wrote down a sampling from the tongue she was given and showed it to someone very familiar with Semitic languages, asking the man if it were Hebrew. To her surprise, he replied, "No. That's not Hebrew. That's Aramaic." Imagine Danielle's delight to learn that she had been speaking in an unlearned language also spoken by her Messiah, Jesus.

Spiritual Language of Prayer

This is the variety of tongues that seems to be most widely distributed amongst the body, and it may also have been met with the most controversy. It involves speaking to God in an unknown private language of prayer, given in the Spirit. I Corinthians 14:2 says that no one understands this language, as believers speak in mysteries to God, in words given by the Holy Spirit.

"What does it mean to pray in the Spirit?"

In I Corinthians 14:14–15, Paul talks about two kinds of praying: *praying with the Spirit* and *praying with the mind*. Following Paul's context, to pray in the Spirit is to pray in tongues, using the unlearned language of the Spirit, whereas to pray with the understanding is to pray in words we generate and compose in our minds using our own learned and understood languages.

Spiritual language comes from the Holy Spirit. It isn't generated in our minds the way our natural speech is. Those of you who have this gift may have observed the same evidence I've seen that these tongues aren't generated in the mind. I know I can't pray two different English prayers simultaneously, one out loud and the other in my thoughts. Even the attempt to do so makes my head spin! Yet, I've found that I *am* able to pray aloud in the Spirit simultaneously with an English prayer generated in my mind. It's not that I've done that much. I usually pray with just one or the other. It's just something I noticed that helped me better understand that my prayer language isn't generated by my mind.

"If this is a lesser gift, why would I even want it?"

Friends, it's not so much about what *we* want as what *God* may want for us. Always keep in mind that the Holy Spirit distributes these gifts to each person as *He* wills, knowing what is best for us, knowing both our personal needs and the ways we can best serve the body (I Corinthians 12:11).

Since a prayer language is for personal edification, we may slough off its value, overlooking the by-product of being edified. However, I know that when I am uplifted in the Spirit, I am better equipped to serve the body in any number of ways. A beaten down believer may have a hard time seeing past herself. But an edified believer is more ready and able to edify others in the flock. Beyond that, I always want to be sensitive to the prompting of the Holy Spirit to pray in this way. There have been many times I've seen my private prayer language usher me into the flow of other manifestations that have benefited the body.

Do you know what I appreciate about spiritual language? For starters, it's a language that is pure (fulfilling Zephaniah 3:9). After a life marred with serial error related to words spoken in English, I'm grateful to have a Spirit-given language that has never once denied, profaned, or dishonored God, one that has never included so much as a word in selfishness or sin. That means I never have to repent for a single word spoken privately in tongues.

What's more, the Holy Spirit knows what we need better than we do. He can intercede for us in ways for which we don't even know we need prayer. He can praise God through us in a language of uncompromised exaltation, even when we're so beaten down by circumstance that we can hardly put a sentence together in English. I know I get that way, especially when it comes to prayer over a chronic need or a distressing turn of events. Sometimes, there simply are no English words. Sometimes there are no words at all. Paul explains this dynamic:

> *"And in the same way the Spirit also helps our weakness; for we do not know how to pray as we should, but the Spirit Himself intercedes for us with groanings too deep for words; and He who searches the hearts knows what the mind of the Spirit is, because He intercedes for the saints according to the will of God."*
> *Romans 8:26–27*

Whether through spiritual words or groanings too deep for words, it's all the expression of the Spirit, interceding for us, perfectly in line with God's will, helping us even when we are too weak to pray for ourselves. We may not know what these prayers mean, but God listens as the Spirit combines those spiritual thoughts with spiritual words for us (I Corinthians 2:13). As we pray in the Spirit, we follow the exhortation of Jude 20, to build ourselves up in the faith, praying in the Spirit, strengthening ourselves for service to God.

Though there may be other historic applications to the following verse, you can almost hear the regret in Isaiah's prophetic word when applied to tongues, as believers decline interest in this renewing gift:

> *"Indeed, He will speak to this people through stammering lips and a foreign tongue, He who said to them, 'Here is rest, give rest to the weary,' and, 'Here is repose,' but they would not listen."*
> *Isaiah 28:11–12*

Which one of us doesn't need rest when weary? Which one of us would turn down a refreshing straight from God? Which one of us would opt out of regular edification if the Spirit willed to give us this gift? You already know that I did.

Though I was fully redeemed and baptized with the Holy Spirit, latent fears made me shy away from this particular manifestation. Even after I realized that tongues was one of those good and perfect gifts God gives, and not the tool of the devil I'd been warned it was, I was scared. I resisted big time. Yeah, I told God I'd do it, *if I had to*, but I didn't follow Scripture in openly desiring whatever gifts the Spirit would will to give me. In doing so, I passively limited the Spirit. He was too much of a gentleman to force me to accept this gift when I clearly didn't want it. He knew I needed time. He waited patiently until I came to not only be willing to receive this gift, but also to actively desire it. He had this gift waiting for me about eighteen months before I opened it. Now, decades later, it's a gift I use with gratitude regularly, all from my everyday, non-leadership place in the family of God.

Intercession for others is a way we can use even this lesser gift in service of the body (I Corinthians 12:7). Half the time, we don't really know our own needs, and we know even less about the hidden needs of others. Intercessors can use this gift as they privately pray for others in the Spirit, following Jesus, who always lives to make intercession for us (Romans 8:34, Hebrews 7:25). Ephesians 6:18 follows the armor of God passage with an exhortation to pray in the Spirit in all prayers and petitions as we intercede for all the saints.

I remember one night when a friend of mine felt prompted to pray for an out-of-town sister in Christ. My friend had no idea why she felt so troubled, thinking of this sister, so she asked the Holy Spirit to intercede through her in tongues. The next day, my friend called our sister to ask how she was doing. Our sister said that she'd been desperately depressed the night before, and that she had despaired of life and had been on the brink of abandoning her faith. Then, completely unexpectedly, two believers came to this sister's door to minister to her. She viewed their visit as having been sent by God. It renewed her spirit and gave her the courage to press on with life. My friend asked what time this sister had felt so down and when the intercessors came. She learned that our sister hit bottom just as my friend was prompted to pray, and that the intercessors came very quickly afterward, dispatched through prayer in the Spirit.

"When is it appropriate to use a prayer language?"

There are no limitations in Scripture for private use of a prayer language. On the contrary, we're encouraged to pray *at all times* in the Spirit (Ephesians 6:18). There are simple protocols within church settings. I Corinthians 14 puts this into perspective. Verse five plainly subordinates the use of spiritual language to prophecy that edifies the church, unless the tongue is coupled with interpretation so the body can understand its meaning.

While Paul was grateful to speak in tongues privately even more than those to whom he wrote, he exhorted us to speak words that can be understood when we're in the corporate hearing of the church (v.18–19). While I believe the language of I Corinthians 14:28 allows for a believer to pray in tongues quietly (to himself/herself and to God) in church, clearly, prayer language shouldn't be spoken at any level that is audible to the whole church body or distracting to those nearby, that is, unless there is a specific prompting of the Holy Spirit to do so and an interpretation follows. In this verse, the Greek phrase that is often translated as *keep silent* can also be interpreted to mean *keep close* or *hold peace*. While some churches call for complete silence, others allow some latitude to pray in the Spirit in church as long as one's voice is held to a very close, private level, which maintains peaceful order and calls no attention to itself.

It seems that singing with the Spirit is meant to follow a similar protocol (I Corinthians 14:15). In close or private settings, sing with the Spirit to your heart's delight. In open church settings, sing with the mind unless your song is either interpreted or unless it softly blends into a corporate chorus, indistinguishable from others, lifted in a holy orchestra of praise.

Tongues with Interpretation

Like a prayer language, this is spiritual language, unlearned in the natural. The difference is that, whereas a prayer language is primarily meant to be used privately for the believer's personal edification, this form of tongues can be spoken out and interpreted in church for the edification of the whole body. It's a message in tongues, spoken in the language of the Holy Spirit, who then provides the message's meaning so that the church can understand what the Spirit is saying.

Employed in this way, this aspect of tongues is akin to prophecy, when the spoken mind of God is understood and declared. In fact, though prophecy is considered a greater gift than a prayer language, tongues with interpretation seems to be elevated to a similar stature with prophecy (I Corinthians 14:5). The protocol Paul recommends in I Corinthians 14:27 closely mirrors order for expression of prophecy in verse twenty-nine. Paul encourages two or three messages in tongues at the most, speaking one at a time, with interpretation following.

"What if I'm prompted to speak aloud in tongues, but I didn't get an interpretation?"

Sometimes, the Holy Spirit will give you the assurance you need that someone else will interpret the message. However, if you're not sure and you've never received interpretation yourself, then I'd suggest that you simply tell someone in leadership that you believe you have a message in tongues and you would like to know if there is anyone present who has been gifted to interpret.

God set up and respects the order with which the gifts should operate within the church and, if the prompting is indeed from the Holy Spirit, He will wait until you ask this question and the message can be delivered in proper order. Notice in I Corinthians 14:27 that those with messages in tongues are to wait their turn, directly implying that, though two or three might receive overlapping promptings from the Holy Spirit to deliver a message, they are able to stand in queue until the prior message has been delivered or until the presence of an interpreter is confirmed.

"Is the gift of tongues available to every believer?"

WARNING: Highly controversial issue ahead!

Seriously, no matter what you've heard or how you've answered this question in the past, pray for grace to understand those who may interpret the Bible differently. Theologians far more studied than I have disagreed on the answer to this question for many centuries. Still, I'll prayerfully address it, trusting that you will consider the pertinent passages of Scripture and ask the Holy Spirit to instruct you personally.

Even though the prayer language variety of this gift seems to be widely distributed, many devoted believers have earnestly prayed and yet not received it, even after manifesting other power gifts. Before Paul underscores the greater position of prophecy, he says he wishes that everyone spoke in tongues (I Corinthians 14:5); however, in his rhetorical question of I Corinthians 12:30 (*all do not speak with tongues, do they?*), the Greek implies a negative answer, that not all do.

So, if not all do, is that because the gift isn't available to them or because they *could* potentially pray in tongues but just haven't or don't? Many reason that since tongues is the one gift meant for personal edification, it must be available to everyone. After all, isn't God an equal opportunity edifier? Those of this persuasion explain that while not all *do* speak in tongues, all *could* potentially. Others stand on the apparent answer to Paul's question (that not all do), concluding that God never intended for all believers to speak in tongues any more than all believers would be expected to operate in any other particular manifestation of the Spirit.

Though I believe that a prayer language is available to many more believers than those who seek and receive one, I'm cautious about stating an absolute, especially in the light of Paul's implication in verse thirty. Tragically, I'm sure many gifts are never sought or received, even though the Holy Spirit would will their distribution. But even though I, like Paul, wish that everyone could enjoy the personal benefits of tongues that I enjoy, I don't find clear scriptural support for citing tongues as standard equipment, or as a required proof of Spirit baptism.

Ow! We've just hit the sharp point of this thorny issue, haven't we? Hackles are quickly raised when tongues are cited as an essential evidence of baptism with the Holy Spirit, especially when the Bible doesn't specifically identify this gift as holding that proving position. Whereas tongues have served to evidence when many have been baptized with the Spirit, Scripture doesn't say that a believer who doesn't speak in tongues hasn't been baptized with the Spirit.

While unlearned earthly tongues seem to have been distributed across the board at Pentecost, Acts 8:17 bears no mention of specific manifestations. That doesn't mean there weren't any. We just don't know how the Holy Spirit manifested Himself as these believers were baptized with the Spirit.

Acts 19:6 refers to tongues and prophecy being manifest at Spirit baptism. Maybe they all manifested both, but this also leaves room to consider that some may have manifested only tongues, and some only the greater gift of prophecy. Again, keep in mind that the Holy Spirit chooses to manifest Himself through Spirit-baptized believers, distributing a variety of gifts in the ways that *He* wills.

Read I Corinthians 12:11–27, which further illuminates this point, comparing those who have been baptized into these graces to a human body. Paul advises that one body part shouldn't feel any less a part of the body than another, neither should one member make another member feel unnecessary, inferior, or excluded.

For all practical purposes, when tongues is cited as an essential evidence of Spirit baptism, it's equivalent to stating that a person who hasn't spoken in tongues can't possibly be baptized with the Spirit. It effectively excludes those who haven't received that particular gift, even though they may have received other manifestations. This call to understanding and unity within the body directly precedes Paul's implication that every member doesn't manifest every gift, including tongues, even though they are all baptized into the same Spirit.

I was a late bloomer as far as tongues are concerned. Even though I didn't speak in tongues when Jesus baptized me with the Holy Spirit, I did manifest the gift of faith, as well as the distinguishing of spirits. A year or so later, I manifested the word of knowledge, still before I received my prayer language. This confidence tracks with Scripture, which allows ample room for a variety of other means of confirmation.

So, bottom line: at the same time that I don't find tongues to be an essential evidence of baptism with the Spirit, either in Scripture or in my personal experience, and I don't find that it makes one any better than another within the family of God, I do find tongues to be widely distributed, biblically encouraged, personally edifying, as well as a very valuable tool for intercession.

Yes, many do receive a prayer language as their first manifestation of the Holy Spirit. Yes, I believe tongues may still be available to many who have asked repeatedly, but have not yet received it. Yes, it is among the gifts that we're exhorted to seek, understanding that we should also seek gifts that edify the church body all the more earnestly (I Corinthians 14:1). Yes, there is scriptural room for the possibility that tongues simply isn't your gift. That wouldn't mean you're left giftless. It would mean that you should earnestly seek whatever other gifts the Holy Spirit would choose to manifest in you.

"Any tips for those who still earnestly desire tongues?"

1. **This is only one of many gifts** that God may have for you. We don't have to strive or beg for it. It won't be forced on you if you don't want it or fear it (I Corinthians 12:11).

2. **The believer will be in control** of the physical aspects of speaking in tongues and should not expect the Spirit to manipulate his/her lips, jaw, or tongue. *We speak* as the Spirit *gives us* the words (Acts 2:4). Once a prayer language is received, believers will be able to both pray in the Spirit and stop praying in the Spirit at will, so they can be responsible for observing order within church settings.

3. **We shouldn't try to teach tongues** to ourselves by repeating nonsense syllables generated in the mind, since the flow of the Spirit's words is not a pump to be primed by mind-generated, natural speech (I Corinthians 2:12–13). If someone encourages you to start making up some syllables or suggests some to get things started, graciously decline to do so and, instead, speak only Spirit-given words or praises in your natural language.

4. **The Holy Spirit gives us words** to speak that have not first formed in our minds (I Corinthians 14:14). Like Peter stepping out of the boat to walk to Jesus on the water, there is a letting go of the natural experience of forming words in the mind, and a stepping out of that natural mode of speech into the flow of words given by the Spirit.

5. **First steps may be small.** Sometimes only a few words or phrases are given that may expand with ongoing use; other times tongues flow liberally from the start. Whether many words are received or few, all words spoken in the Spirit are for our good and should be received and used with joy (John 6:63).

6. **Tongues may be received privately or with others.** Although some receive this gift privately, it's also scriptural to receive this gift through the laying on of hands and joint intercession (I Timothy 4:14). Since, in multiple post-Pentecost instances, gifts of tongues were not noted as having been interpreted when first received, it seems reasonable to accept that interpretation is not required when in the process of initially receiving this gift within a small company of believers, and that the receiving believer may feel free to audibly speak out in tongues at the time when the gift is given.

"Won't people think I'm weird if they know I speak in tongues?"

Quite possibly. There have been tongues mockers around since the day of Pentecost (Acts 2:13). But do you know what kind of person doesn't worry about what anyone else thinks? That would be a person who is in love. You see, when our love for God eclipses our desire to please people, mockers lose their impact. I'm sure there are plenty of people who'd think I was crazy to speak in tongues, but I'd rather be crazy about God than deterred by what people think, wouldn't you? In I Corinthians 4:9–10, Paul says that we have been made a spectacle to the world, that we are fools for Christ's sake. That means that we put down our pride, forget about jockeying for position in this world or even in the church, and we use the gifts that God gives us with unselfconscious gratitude.

"If I have tongues, is that my only gift?"

Though we know in our heads that we should always continue to grow in grace, there's a tendency to stop seeking greater gifts after receiving tongues, feeling that we've somehow arrived in the Spirit or at least met some minimum quota. Maybe we're intimidated by the greater gifts. Maybe we assume they're for someone else who seems more spiritual, or maybe just for our leaders. Maybe we've asked for other gifts a time or two, then abandoned seeking when nothing seemed to happen, abdicating our biblical responsibility.

It may be that tongues is your only gift, but then again, it's quite possible that the Holy Spirit has additional gifts for you. Since tongues is a widely distributed, personally edifying gift, and Paul stresses that we should earnestly desire greater gifts that edify the body, it stands to reason why many within the body may receive multiple manifestations of the Spirit. Paul manifested tongues along with a number of other gifts. Everyday believers may also be multi-gifted.

Remember: these are gifts we use in service to God, so there's no "just take one" limitation! In fact, everyone who speaks in tongues is specifically exhorted to seek at least two other manifestations. Know what they are? Check out I Corinthians 14:1 and v. 13 for the answers.

"Why all the fuss about tongues?"

Why do so many get so focused on this one gift? Why did Paul have to spend most of I Corinthians 14 explaining the merits of prophecy over uninterpreted tongues?

Here's the rub: there are a lot of people who've received this gift, so that increases the potential for human misunderstanding. Some may wrongly see receiving this gift as a mark of spiritual achievement, as if tongues were a diploma handed down to those who have reached some level of accomplishment. But, Friends, we've got to remember that these are all grace gifts, totally unearned, not a marker of personal advancement or even of spiritual maturity.

Case in point: the Gentiles of Acts 10 could not have been any more freshly reborn when they received tongues. We're all exhorted to grow in maturity, no doubt; however, receiving tongues doesn't mean we're any stronger or more mature than the next person. In fact, sometimes more honor is given to less honored members of the body (I Corinthians 12:22–23).

The ongoing dysfunction over tongues swings both ways. Some are made to feel "less than" by pushy proponents of tongues, and some without this gift react defensively to "those with" simply because they have it. Some feverishly pray for others to receive tongues in such a way that the person is made to feel unspiritual or rejected if they don't manifest tongues. Some forbid tongues, pronouncing it to be "of the devil" today. Some with the gift won't accept believers into their exclusive idea of the Baptism with the Spirit "club" without it. Ouch! Others still violate church order, praying aloud in the Spirit at church without interpretation. CLANG!

Excuse me, but…GONG! Hey, what's that? CLANG! GONG! (That would be the "I Corinthians 13:1 alarm" going off.)

> *"If I speak with the tongues of men and of angels, but do not have love, I have become a noisy gong or a clanging cymbal."*
> *I Corinthians 13:1*

Rule of thumb: if it's not said or done in love, it's not in the Spirit. God's love, coursing through your every thought, word, and deed, is more powerful than all the supernatural gifts put together. Let's remember Job One: *we are called to love God and each other.* We are evangelists for Christ, not for a particular manifestation of the Spirit. Yes, let's be diligent to seek the Lord about how we, ourselves, could be equipped with gifts to serve Him. But let's lovingly leave the ball in the Holy Spirit's court to distribute whatever gifts He chooses, when and to whom He wills.

CHAPTER SIXTEEN

Interpretation of Tongues

What it is:
Receiving and declaring the meaning of unlearned language given by the Holy Spirit

What it's not:
Translating, decoding, or understanding a known language by any natural means

> *Once, I was in a small prayer group with my friend, Robbie. Robbie isn't in leadership. She's just an everyday believer like me. As we entered into praise and intercession, Robbie overheard the whispered prayer language of the woman sitting near her. At first, Robbie heard only the language of the Holy Spirit, but suddenly, she began to hear the message as if it were being spoken in English. Afterward, Robbie told me there was no mistaking this experience, and that the interpretation came like bullets of thunder into her heart.*

If you've never heard tongues spoken before, it may be hard to wrap your head around this gift. In simplest terms, it's like automatically understanding a language you've never been taught. You hear that language of the Spirit and—boom—miraculously, you understand its meaning. There is no straining to learn or decipher. It's a spiritual equipping, not a mental process.

Interpretation of tongues is a gift that is given away, serving to edify the church by hearing what the Spirit of God is saying through unknown tongues. We don't guess at an interpretation or make one up, supposing what God might be saying given the current situation or mood. This gift is about receiving and repeating. Believers *receive* the interpretation in the Spirit, and then *repeat* what is heard to the church, two or three at the most within one service, in turn, with one interpreting each message (I Corinthians 14:27).

Although I've heard some say that interpretation does not mean a word-for-word translation, the Greek (*herme neia*) allows room for this gift to be expressed through either translation or interpretation. The word *interpretation* could encompass anything from a literal translation to an explanation of a message in tongues' overall meaning.

"What if I feel led to speak out in tongues but I don't know if there's an interpreter or anyone familiar with these gifts?"

There really can be a learning curve as we grow in these graces, but step by step, the Holy Spirit will instruct us if we remain open to His leading. Given the fear of what others may think, coupled with Paul's caution not to speak audibly in tongues while in church without interpretation, it can be challenging to step out in faith, even within private settings. But ever the gentleman, our divine Teacher eases us out of our comfort zones, giving us opportunity to learn about His ways over time, and often with multi-level application.

My friend, Ginger was the first in her family of four to experience the gift of tongues. A mother of two, though she received and began to practice tongues as a prayer language privately, she confided that she had received this gifting with her husband, Jeremy, a believer who hadn't experienced that gift himself.

I recall one day when Ginger and I had ministered in prayer to someone in a small group. Ginger told me that she had felt the impulse of the Holy Spirit to speak audibly in tongues, but she had been fearful about how the other women in this circle of prayer might react since many of them were unfamiliar with this gift that was so new to Ginger herself. I explained to Ginger that she may have felt that prompting because the Lord had intended to give someone the interpretation, as a message and an introductory demonstration, all at the same time. I encouraged her to step out in faith if she felt such a prompting again.

Some time later, Ginger felt led to privately pray over her young sons in tongues. Just a toddler, her youngest quickly grew fond of being prayed for in this way and, spontaneously, he began to request it by asking her to pray the "amados" prayer. *Amados* wasn't a learned word for him. His English vocabulary was very limited at that age, and he'd had virtually no exposure to any other languages. Intrigued, Ginger spelled the word out phonetically, and then searched on the Internet. She was astounded to find that *amados* means *beloved ones* in Spanish.

Encouraged, Ginger continued to answer the Holy Spirit's call to pray for her sons this way, till one night, her husband (who had never heard her pray in tongues) came into the boys' room unexpectedly. Respectfully, Ginger paused and asked Jeremy if he'd like her to stop, but Jeremy encouraged her to continue. He stood at the door, quietly listening, as Ginger resumed prayer in tongues over their sons. Though he'd never spoken a word in tongues himself, Jeremy was amazed that he began to understand everything Ginger was praying, just as if she'd been praying in English. Later, he shared the interpretation: that her prayers were overflowing with praises to our God.

"Are interpretations of tongues always verbal?"

While interpretations of tongues are usually thought of as coming in a verbal way, keep in mind that it's also possible that God may interpret what He's saying to us by visual means, gifting us to interpret the unknown language of symbolic visions or dreams (as we read in the Old Testament that Joseph and Daniel were gifted to do). A picture could communicate what God wants us to know even more clearly than words. So, let's remember to give the Holy Spirit the freedom to gift us to interpret as He wills, even if it's not exactly in the way we expect.

Once, a sister of mine was interceding in tongues for a man on her church's pastoral staff when she noticed that her prayer language had shifted into an unusually authoritative tone. As she continued to speak in this commanding tongue, suddenly, she was shown a detailed vision of multiple demonic forces coming against the man who was the object of her intercession. The phrase *minions of tormenting spirits* came to her mind. In an instant, the Holy Spirit explained why He had been praying through her so forcefully. The tongue took on a scolding tone. Then, when prompted to do so, this sister dismissed the enemy's minions and they promptly fled, defeated.

"Who should be praying for this gift?"

Turn to I Corinthians 14:13. Do you see it? Everyone who speaks in tongues should also pray to interpret. Since tongues have been so widely distributed, there should be a lot of people praying to serve through this gift.

Those of you who speak in tongues, think about this for a moment honestly. When was the last time you sought the Lord to interpret tongues? Have you ever? If not, I would exhort you to follow Scripture in praying for this complementary manifestation. God wants us to grow in Him. Spiritual babes are cute, but especially as we mature, we should desire more than the personal edification of tongues and seek this means of edifying the body.

When my friend Robbie suddenly understood the prayer language of the woman near her, she'd never experienced this before, so she asked me about it, especially because she only received a short portion of the interpretation and the experience hadn't recurred. I believe Robbie received a taste of interpretation to encourage her that the Holy Spirit is willing to give this needed gift to her. Since that time, as Robbie has been diligent to pray, interpretation has been building, line upon line, as Robbie hears tongues being spoken (Isaiah 28:9–11). It is as if she is being apprenticed, given a little at a time, as God prepares her for more. As of this writing, she often understands the broad meaning of tongues spoken in her hearing. The fact that she initially understood word-for-word inspires her to continue to pray that she will continue to grow and serve in this gift.

There is every reason for persistence in seeking interpretation of tongues. Proverbs 22:29 says that those who are diligent will not just stand before obscure people. They will come to stand before kings. In Daniel Chapter Five, we find King Belshazzar in dire need of an interpretation. After he'd used the vessels from God's temple to serve wine, the king had watched in alarm as fingers of what looked like a man's hand began writing a foreboding message on his wall. It said: *MENE, MENE, TEKEL UPHARSIN.*

Though the king offered a substantial reward to anyone who could read and interpret the message, no one could. Finally, the queen suggested that they summon Daniel, a man known to be indwelt by the Spirit of God, enabling him to understand great enigmas. In this case, Daniel was needed for both translation and interpretation of this message. The translation itself was only: *numbered, numbered, weighed divide.* Daniel went beyond the translation to detail the fuller interpretation of God's judgment against the king through each of these few words (Daniel 5:25–30).

As with Daniel, there are times when interpretation of tongues mingles with the prophetic. Both gifts involve communicating Holy Spirit-imparted revelation of what God is saying. Edification by hearing God's counsel is what makes interpretation of tongues a greater gift than tongues alone. It's also what makes many in leadership cautious about this gift.

"My church doesn't allow interpreted tongues."

Many traditional churches outright forbid tongues. Since tongues and interpretation work in tandem, their "problem" with both gifts is neatly solved. Some who hesitate to say that these partner gifts have ceased passively quench their operation first by failing to teach us that they are part of a healthy body's ministry. Then, they disallow any interpretation that is not a direct quote from the Bible. It's an end-run around Scripture's encouragement of continuing revelation.

Yes, there may be times when verses from the Bible are quoted in an interpretation, but Scripture doesn't say it will always be that way. Be assured that all Spirit-given interpretations will be fully consistent with the Bible. But let's keep our hearts open and give the Holy Spirit the liberty to speak forth whatever God's message is for us today (Hebrews 3:15).

To be sure, as rank and file believers, we need our leaders' help with interpretation of tongues. I've seen this kind of strong leadership in action. As godly correction is administered with kindness and love, the congregation's confidence with flowing in the gifts grows.

Once, I heard a message in tongues given at a church I was visiting. A woman in the congregation spoke out an interpretation. The pastor rose and, with abundant grace, corrected that woman. He acknowledged that, while the interpretation she delivered didn't contain anything that was technically off, he was convinced in the Spirit that it had come from her heart and, though well-intentioned, it did not convey what the Spirit had been saying to the church. Further, he explained that, as the message in tongues had come forth, he had received the Spirit's interpretation himself, before she had offered hers. Finally, he brought forth the Spirit's interpretation, which was entirely different, resonating with the power of God.

Whereas I had felt uncertain as the woman spoke her comfort-oriented interpretation, the Holy Spirit's more challenging exhortation actually brought me more assurance. A wave of relief washed over the congregation, as they sensed the flock was being protectively and confidently led.

"Isn't it unfair to correct a mistaken interpreter in front of everybody?"

Sure, I felt embarrassed for the woman who was corrected; however, I do not consider application of proper judgment of an interpretation to be unfair. Especially when correction is administered with grace (as it was), I consider that correction to be both necessary and educational for the entire body, a body that should not be misled by incorrect interpretations. If we make a mistake and suffer the momentary humbling of being disciplined, let's remember that God disciplines every child He loves. Let's submit to that discipline, understanding that it is for our good.

Knowing that interpretation of tongues is subject to ordered judgment reminds us not to speak without being sure the message we bring is from God as opposed to one merely generated in our own minds (I Corinthians 14:28–29). Though God sometimes does send messages of comfort, we should resist the tendency to give into our own sympathies, lest we wrongly package the human comfort we'd like to bring as the message of God (Jeremiah 6:14). Even well intentioned, seemingly benign interpretations should not be allowed to stand as correct if they are not. Instead, leaders should only allow those interpretations that have been judged as being from God to stand (Jeremiah 23:28).

"What if I think I hear an interpretation, but I'm not sure?"

I love hearing this question. It's the quandary of a heart that truly wants to please God and rightly serve His church. It's also likely to come from a person who is following Scripture's instruction to seek interpretation of tongues. So, first, know that God adores your seeking heart.

If an interpretation comes to you and you're either unaccustomed to this gift or unsure if it is the Spirit's interpretation as opposed to your own, I would recommend holding it in your heart, at least momentarily. If you can, write the interpretation down. As you hold the message briefly, pray in the name of Jesus that the Holy Spirit will either confirm in your heart that it is from Him or let it quickly pass if it is only a human impulse. This allows time for another interpreter to speak up, possibly confirming the interpretation you've heard. Even though you may not have the privilege of presenting the interpretation this time, hearing a confirming interpretation will bolster your confidence that the Holy Spirit has indeed given you this gift. You may also serve to confirm the interpretation that was spoken.

If the message in tongues goes uninterpreted, and yet you're still unsure or timid about speaking it out, then quietly go to someone you know to have a prophetic gift and tell that person that you believe you may have received the interpretation and you'd like to submit what you've heard to judgment. You can simply show the written interpretation or tell the person what it is. If the interpretation is privately judged as incorrect, accept that judgment with humility and return to your place. If, on the other hand, the interpretation is received as from the Lord, then let the church leadership decide how it's best to proceed.

You may be asked to speak forth the interpretation yourself, or the person who judged it as correct may choose to present the interpretation to the church. Rest in humble anonymity. Resist any fleshy need to be the one heard delivering this message. That's just a trap of the enemy, trying to use spiritual pride to get you out of the Spirit. Because there shouldn't be any need to be credited or known as having heard the correct interpretation, it shouldn't matter if no attention is called to you.

Remember: in bringing any interpretation forth, your leader is taking on a sacred responsibility before the church. As you respect that leader's authority, leadership will come to respect your sensitivity in the Spirit.

"What if I hear the interpretation and I'm sure it's from God?"

I still recommend holding the interpretation in your heart briefly, especially if you're new to this gift. As you do, say a prayer that God will help you to bring forth His words only and none of your own. You can even ask for a moment to pray about the interpretation. As you do, check the interpretation for consistency with Scripture. Then, if you still sense the prompting of the Holy Spirit to speak it out, in accordance with the order prescribed in I Corinthians 14:27, you may speak out the interpretation, knowing that any interpretation that has been directly spoken to the body will be subject to judgment in the hearing of that body.

Be sure to speak clearly and loudly enough to be heard. Remember that you are only a servant-carrier of our great God's message. Resist the urge to embellish His interpretation in any way. When the interpretation is complete, wait in quiet submission to leadership. Whether the interpretation is judged as from God or not, accept the judgment that comes with grace.

After the service, you are at liberty to privately ask your leader to help you understand why your interpretation may have been judged as false. This is not an opportunity to debate the judgment or get defensive. It is a chance for you to learn. Perhaps the leader identified a conflict that your interpretation had with Scripture. Perhaps, he or she just sensed for some reason that it was not the Holy Spirit's interpretation. As humbling as it can be to have these conversations, considering where we may have gone wrong helps us avoid error in the future.

"But what if I'm misjudged?"

If you are truly misjudged, then you join the blessed ranks of countless servants of God before you. Those who bring forth the counsel of God are regularly misjudged, even by those in leadership. Like Jesus, be willing to endure the suffering of unwarranted rebukes, even ridicule. As you are being misjudged, stay at peace in the Spirit, entrusting yourself to God.

I know it's hard enough to be judged when we're wrong, but it's even harder when we're right, isn't it? Endure, content in God's love for you. Faithfully dispatch the message you have been given in the Holy Spirit, regardless of what men or women might say. Your responsibility as interpreter is merely to deliver God's message. Once you have done so, full responsibility is transferred to the hearer. No matter how wrong a person may be in judging you, like Jesus did, endure it with all the patience of the Holy Spirit. Find comfort in knowing that, as you bear up under the suffering of misjudgment, you are finding favor with God, who always judges righteously (I Peter 2:20–23).

Growth in the Holy Spirit is so completely counterintuitive to worldly achievement, isn't it? In the world, pride is encouraged, accomplishments are lauded, and achievers are celebrated. Instead, in the Spirit, we find messengers like John the Baptist, reminding us that we have nothing that hasn't been given to us by God. We are but the friend of the Bridegroom, thrilled to hear His voice (John 3:27–29). In light of John's example, as we receive and deliver interpretation of tongues, let's put John's preaching into daily practice:

"He must increase, but I must decrease."
John 3:30

Many of those who speak in tongues have rarely, if ever, prayed for interpretation. Maybe you asked once or twice, then forgot about it. Maybe you didn't realize you were supposed to pray to interpret. Maybe you're afraid to speak out in public or to risk being judged by leadership. If any of this describes you, will you say a prayer before proceeding?

In your own words, thank God for your prayer language (if you've been given one). Confess your fears, neglect, or spiritual laziness. Tell Him regularly that you actively desire interpretation of tongues if He should choose to use you in this way. Right now, no matter how humble a place you hold in the body of Christ, offer your service as an interpreter of tongues to God.

Amen?

From now on, resolve to take an active stance in the Holy Spirit each time you hear a variety of the gift of tongues in use. That means, rather than just letting tongues go by, assuming you won't hear or trusting others to hear an interpretation, become an intent listener yourself. Incline your ears to the voice of the Holy Spirit, ready, in case He would speak to you.

CHAPTER SEVENTEEN

Prophecy

What it is:

To flow forth like a fountain; to declare the Holy Spirit-imparted mind of God for edification, exhortation, consolation, guidance, or the disclosure of things to come

What it's not:

ESP, fortune-telling, psychic phenomenon, naturally deduced advice, a platform for personal theology

> *Following a brutal second round of chemotherapy, my dear friend, Hope, told me that, as she had been earnestly seeking the Lord, He had spoken the following prophetic words to her: "I am going to bring your suffering to an end." Hope didn't presume whether that meant that she would be healed of cancer or if it meant that she would die, but when doctors soon confirmed that she was in complete remission, many assumed that she had been healed. Even as others celebrated, I felt the Lord caution me. As much as I wanted to trust the doctor's report and believe that my precious friend would live, in the Spirit, what I heard was that the cancer was still there, that her suffering would end as she left this life. In a matter of months, she entered the final stages of her journey.*

Time to stop and pray, again. *Really.*

In opening up the subject of prophecy, we are treading on deeply controversial ground. It's a hotly debated arena, thick with man-made traditions and fraught with human error. If something about this scares you, you're not alone. Put that anxiety on the table. Tell God how you feel. Ask Him to speak to you clearly and to give you the courage to hear. Give the Holy Spirit permission to remove the blockages of any false doctrines that could impede your understanding what He would teach you through Scripture. Consciously open your heart to the counsel of the Holy Spirit. Persist in reading every verse along the way, building on your scriptural foundation for this important, multifaceted gift.

Finished praying? Then, take His holy hand and proceed.

"We have the Bible. What purposes does prophecy serve today?"

The purposes of prophecy are like our unchanging God—the same yesterday, today, and forever. Prophecy serves the same purposes today that prophecy has always served, which is to keep us in current communication with God. Though many connect prophecy only with foretelling, it can also serve any of a number of equally important purposes. Most of them fall under one of these five categories, set forth in I Corinthians 14:3 and John 16:13–15:

1. Edification: *undergirding, building, encouragement*
2. Exhortation: *instruction, correction, admonishment*
3. Consolation: *comfort, empathy, understanding*
4. Guidance: *counsel, direction, callings, advisories*
5. Foretelling: *annunciations, warnings, disclosure of things to come*

In Scripture, you'll find examples of these multiple purposes being served, many of which have nothing to do with foretelling. So, a message from God that edifies, exhorts, consoles, or guides can be every bit as prophetic as a message that discloses what is to come. Each of these purposes serves to advance God's redemptive objective, spreading the testimony of Jesus, which Revelation 19:10c calls *the spirit of prophecy*. Extending the kingdom of God in Christ is of the essence in all forms of prophetic utterance. This can occur in Holy Spirit-inspired sermons and teachings, as well as during corporate or private ministry.

Jesus encouraged the disciples that the Spirit of the Father would speak to them when they were delivered before the authorities to testify. He said they didn't need to worry about how or what to speak because, in that very hour, the Holy Spirit would give them the words to speak (Matthew 10:19–20). The disciples were relieved of stressing over what to say, and asked only to listen and relay. That's the voice of prophecy, communicated straight from God to the believer in the Holy Spirit, the same Spirit who is available to speak to and through us today.

Sometimes, the testimony of Jesus is supported by prophetic words that help us along God's way in Christ, as it was with Agabus in Acts 11:27–30, when a prophesied famine prompted the faithful to send relief for the brethren in Judea. As it was with Jesus' foretold passion, prophecy is not a means of avoiding the trials of life. It is a means of walking through life's hardships with God's present help.

Notice in Acts 20:23 that Paul was convinced in the Spirit that prison awaited him. Even after Agabus prophesied that Paul would be put in bonds in Jerusalem, Paul did not let that knowledge deter him from going into Jerusalem to advance the testimony of Jesus (Acts 21:10–14). That's commitment, Friends.

In the Spring of 1972, a few months after my friend, Michael, led me to the Lord, a woman prophesied over Michael that he would soon enter a season of suffering. I remember someone calling this prophecy false and the prophetess awful for having relayed such a distressing message. Within a month, Michael entered one of the most painful seasons of his life as his parents divorced and he was sent away to live under very challenging conditions. Even though the prophecy had been difficult to hear, it had prepared Michael for the wilderness ahead and assured him of God's continuing hand on his life throughout the prophesied suffering.

Like those who inquired of the Lord through the prophet in Jeremiah 46:1–6, Michael wanted to hear God's voice no matter what. Those who'd rather live in denial might spurn God's help in this way. However, those who would live like Jesus know that we are truly nourished by every word that God speaks (Deuteronomy 8:3).

"What kinds of people receive prophecy?"

It is not that these manifestations come to perfect people. In fact, to the contrary, they come to sinners like you and me—broken, contrite and unworthy souls, graced to see or hear from their forgiving Father. The Bible is clear as to the diverse distribution of this gift:

> *"But this is what was spoken of through the prophet Joel: 'And it shall be in the last days,' God says, 'that I will pour forth of My Spirit upon all mankind; and your sons and your daughters shall prophesy, and your young men shall see visions, and your old men shall dream dreams; even upon My bondslaves, both men and women, I will in those days pour forth of My Spirit and they shall prophesy.' "*
>
> *Acts 2:16–18*

When Peter preached these words, he quoted Joel's Old Testament prophecy to explain the outpouring of the Holy Spirit and the accompanying gifts at Pentecost, ushering in a renewal of communication with God in the Spirit. Many think of prophets as only leading up to Jesus' time on earth and in the first century thereafter, but clearly, even in Joel's time, God sent the message that there would be a widespread outpouring of God's Spirit in the last days. There would be an anointing on men and women, young and old alike, with the result that they would see visions, dream dreams, and prophesy, fulfilling Jesus' promise to remain in communication with them through the promised Holy Spirit.

"How do I know if it's really God speaking?"

What is your knee-jerk response when you hear someone say God told him something? We've all heard way too many stories of deranged killers and even misled believers to take such a claim lightly. Actually, this is a good thing, since the Bible directs us to discern the truth or falseness of any purported word from God, before we'd accept or act upon it.

Though it's the responsibility of prophets to judge prophecy within the church (I Corinthians 14:29), it's good for all believers to have a working knowledge about how prophecy should be evaluated. We should always prayerfully consider these questions:

- *Does the speaker confess Jesus as Lord?*
- *Is the speaker's life in keeping with the Gospel?*
- *Is the message consistent with or contradictory to the Bible?*
- *What is the witness of the Holy Spirit in me concerning this message?*
- *Is there any confirmation whether this message is true or false?*

Discerning the truly prophetic wheat from the false tares has always proved challenging. That's why I'm persuaded that all believers should also pray for distinguishing of spirits. We need the Holy Spirit to bear witness within our hearts, helping us to discern what's false and what's true. But, as important as it is to reject false prophecy, it's even more important to embrace genuine prophecy that has indeed come from God. Did Jeremiah throw out true prophecy because there were false prophets? No way! Instead, he spoke against what was false and kept prophesying what was true (Jeremiah 23:21–40, Jeremiah 28).

There are only three possible sources of any purported prophecy. It's either: 1) from the enemy; 2) from a human being's mind (Jeremiah 23:36); or it's 3) true prophecy from God. We rebuke enemy communications. If false prophecy comes through a believer, then godly correction is in order. But, if a prophecy is true, it is to be received as cherished communication from the Almighty, spoken for our good, worthy of our respect and attention.

"My church says there's no fresh revelation."

Undefined terminology of this kind can be both daunting and confusing, huh? Half the time we hear these things and don't stop to think about what they really mean, especially when it comes to gifts that scare us like prophecy. So, let's pause to clarify terms before we assume what's biblical or not. Yes—absolutely—while any prophecy that *conflicts* with Scripture should be immediately judged as false, God might choose to reveal something that isn't a direct quote, yet is still fully consistent with the Bible. *Biblically-conflicting revelation?* Throw it out for sure. *Fresh revelation?* Would you brave a closer look at the semantics with me?

Admittedly, there is widespread opposition in some churches to what is called *fresh revelation*. For many, this equates to any prophetic communication other than a direct quote of Scripture. Many defend this position by citing Revelation 22:18–19, which sternly warns against taking away from or adding to the words of that prophetic book.

Know this: when God truly speaks, it will be fully consistent with the complete authoritative counsel of Scripture, never contradictory. But sadly, in rejecting non-quoted but biblically consistent prophecy beyond the first century, human beings risk both *taking away* from God's final Word that established this gift into continuing place and *adding to* God's final Word by asserting that prophecy and/or other spiritual gifts ceased with the first century.

Some would rather omit the word *revelation* in teaching about the Holy Spirit, but I still use it because the Spirit inspired its use in Scripture. Bear in mind that the words *fresh revelation* do not appear adjacent to one another in the Bible. However, both words (and their positive, unifying concepts) are used separately to describe relative activities of the Holy Spirit.

Let's focus on the first of those two hot-button words: *fresh*. If we are flowing in the Spirit, we will find our relationship with God to be freshly vibrant, interactive, and in a state of perpetual renewal. Just as God spoke to believers in the Bible about the concerns of their day, we'll find that He will lead us in ways that are specifically relevant to our lives. He will anoint us anew, just as David exalts that God has anointed him with *fresh* oil (Psalm 92:10), typifying the Holy Spirit.

The Holy Spirit is also symbolized repeatedly in Scripture by fresh waters—as a spring, a fountain, a mighty, fresh-water river, bringing new life wherever He flows (Ezekiel 47:9). These are active, living waters, refreshing, and new. While we are warned that the stagnant marshes will not become fresh, the Spirit's current is eternally fresh (Ezekiel 47:11–12). Yes, we should definitely test what's fresh, but fresh can be very biblical and very good!

Now, consider what can be the scarier of the two words: *revelation*. This word bears the implicit meaning of newness, that is, of God showing or speaking something to someone that was, up to that moment, unseen or unheard.

Look up the following verses to find scriptural encouragement about revelatory disclosures: Jeremiah 33:3, 6-9; Daniel 2:47; John 16:13; I Corinthians 14:6, 26; Galatians 1:12, 2:2; Ephesians 1:17. Also consider John's glorious vision, revealed by the Holy Spirit, thus the title of the book: Revelation.

In Jeremiah 2:13, God noted two evils: 1) man forsaking God's fountain of living waters; and 2) man making broken cisterns that cannot hold water. We need to repent for forsaking the fresh waters of the Spirit, cast aside our broken vessels, earnestly ask God for a fresh prophetic anointing (I Corinthians 14:1), and then test what comes against the counsel of Scripture.

So, hear this good word: the Bible itself encourages us to seek revelation from God, every time we're encouraged to listen for His voice (John 10:27, Revelation 2:7). Why would He ask us to listen if He didn't want to say something to us? (We may be passive-aggressive, but God isn't.) He asks us to incline our ears toward Him because He wants to speak to us in a current, revelatory way. He may speak a quote from Scripture; He may expound upon a verse to you. Or He may speak something that's not a word-for-word quote, but is still fully consistent with the full counsel of Scripture.

"Doesn't the Bible say prophecy will cease?"

Yes, but look at when.

Read I Corinthians 13:10–13. There, we see that prophecy will not cease until the *perfect* comes. The Greek word for *perfect* is *teleios*, meaning *when things are brought to an end, finished, or completed*. To be sure, life on earth was neither perfect, finished, nor completed at the end of the first century. The disciples died out across a span of many years without a single scriptural specification that prophecy would cease at the end of the first century.

Like Paul, we still see through a glass darkly, we prophesy only in part. But when the perfect comes, when the life we know here is complete, when we have crossed over into eternity and are perfected in Jesus, there will no longer be a need for God to speak to us through prophets since, in heaven, we'll communicate with God face to face.

In I Corinthians 14, Paul gave us clear instruction for earthly life, specifically exhorting that, of all the gifts, we should most earnestly desire to prophesy (I Corinthians 14:1). Surely, if God had intended for prophecy to cease after the deaths of the first century apostles, He would have told us in Scripture. Instead, we're admonished to earnestly desire prophecy. Prophets are part of the ongoing leadership structure given by God to equip the saints for service (Ephesians 4:11–12).

Knowing there would be a need for sound judgment of prophets (I Corinthians 14:29), we are further reminded not to quench the Holy Spirit, not to despise prophetic utterances, but rather to prove all things and hold fast to what is good (I Thessalonians 5:19–21).

Yes, it can get messy.

Yes, it requires courageous, Spirit-guided leadership to judge the truth or falsehood of prophets and prophecies against the authoritative standard of Scripture.

And hallelujah, yes! Contemporary believers can still receive true prophetic revelation from our Almighty God.

As nervous about prophecy as we may be, we need to grasp that we are at war with the enemy of this world. Really. As the enemy works to derail Christ's church, one of the first things he does is try to cut off our lines of communication. Prophets are a little like phone lines. They serve to communicate God's much needed counsel to His church. We must realize that, when we succumb to fear of prophecy, we cut our own spiritual phone lines at the enemy's behest.

God is not the author of the fear of prophecy. Guess who is? Yeah. The line-cutter. Family of God, it's time to rebuke that fear and reopen ourselves to the communication God provides.

"Yeah, but wasn't prophecy just for back then?"

Way back then, God's Word promised that this gift of the Holy Spirit, that person of the Trinity pledged to counsel us, teach us, guide us, and disclose what is to come, is for all earthly generations (Acts 2:39). Roman 11:29 reinforces the continuing nature of God's gifts, saying God does not repent of having giving them. God gave prophecy to the Church. He's not sorry He did and He's not going to take it back as long as our earthly generations continue. He knows we need prophecy to stay in vital communication until we're face to face with Him in eternity.

Look at the Lord's wonderful promise of continuing prophetic communication:

> *"And as for me, this is my covenant with them," says the Lord:*
> *"My Spirit which is upon you, and My words which I have put*
> *in your mouth, shall not depart from your mouth, nor from the*
> *mouth of your offspring, nor from the mouth of your offspring's*
> *offspring," says the Lord, "from now and forever."*
>
> *Isaiah 59:21*

Yes, forever! This promise is reiterated in Joel 2:28, then fulfilled repeatedly throughout the New Testament. God knew we would always need prophecy because we will always need to hear His voice of counsel. Isn't it amazing that the God of the universe wants to speak to us, to our children, to our grandchildren, in fact, to all generations *forever*? And lest we think this gift was only meant for a few superstars, examination of the Scriptures affirms this gift as having distribution within the ranks of the body.

Remember Amos, whose prophecies are recorded in the Old Testament, was just an everyday sheepherder! Maybe his earthly job was only of common esteem, but God confided His mind to Amos, giving Amos' spiritual job exponential import and reach.

Astounding as it may seem, it's not unusual for God to speak to human beings. In fact, God told Amos that He doesn't do *anything* without revealing it to His servants, the prophets (Amos 3:7). Our unchanging God, who is still doing things today, still informs prophets today. Why would God appoint prophets in addition to ranking church leaders, such as pastors? Simple. The job is just too big. Our leaders need help, particularly in serving large congregations.

In Numbers 11:14, we find Moses overwhelmed with the burden of being the only prophet for Israel, so much so that he wanted God to kill him rather than to face his own failure to adequately lead. Then, God told Moses to gather seventy elders of Israel to stand around the tabernacle tent. God promised that He would take of the Spirit upon Moses and put Him upon the seventy elders so that Moses would no longer have to bear the burden of prophecy alone.

God kept His promise. The Spirit rested upon the elders and they prophesied that one time, but check this out: modern translations agree with the original language in saying that, after that first time, those elders never prophesied again (Numbers 11:25). Can you imagine how frustrated Moses would have been to see his heavy burden to prophesy distributed, only to have the elders use the gift that was meant for ongoing service just one time? *Seriously?!*

All was not lost for Moses. There were two men who were registered among the elders, but who had remained in the camp: Eldad and Medad. Verse twenty-six records that the Holy Spirit also came upon Eldad and Medad outside, and that they began to prophesy among the people in the camp. A young man heard them and ran to report this to Moses. Joshua, defensive of Moses' formerly unique position as prophet, attempted to quench the Holy Spirit, to restrain Eldad and Medad; however, Moses' response confirmed his hearty approval of the broadening distribution of the prophetic gift:

> *"...Are you jealous for my sake? Would that all the Lord's people were prophets, that the Lord would put His Spirit upon them!"*
>
> *Numbers 11:29*

Aren't we just like Joshua, though? Human nature leads us to focus attention on the spiritual superstars, like Moses. We put them on pedestals, even above the Spirit of God. We depend on them to hear from God instead of seeking Him directly ourselves. We quench the Holy Spirit as He moves to speak through additional prophets in our midst.

Earthly chain of command didn't stop Eldad and Medad, though. The Holy Spirit settled on them directly, sending them straight out to deliver God's counsel to the people. Though some in leadership may resist those who receive and follow direct orders from the Spirit, we can learn from the way Moses went beyond just approving of Eldad and Medad. Moses said he wished that ALL believers were prophets, encouraging responsiveness to the Spirit throughout the body.

The young man who ran to tell Moses set the right example for us. Maybe he seems like a tattler to some, but when he heard two new people prophesying, the boy realized that Moses should know about it. Moses was already their confirmed prophet, equipped to make the call about whether Eldad and Medad were prophesying by the Holy Spirit. I Corinthians 14:29 and 32 say *the spirits of prophets are subject to prophets,* and that prophets are to judge one another's prophecies. So, when we're unsure if a person is truly gifted as a prophet, we should inform other confirmed prophets within the body who can render judgment.

As we read on in Numbers, we find that God Himself gives us insight about how any believer can recognize a call into the office of prophet:

> *"He said, 'Hear now My words: if there is a prophet among you, I the Lord shall make Myself known to him in a vision. I will speak with him in a dream. Not so, with My servant Moses, he is faithful in all My household. With him I speak mouth to mouth, even openly, and not in dark sayings, and he beholds the form of the Lord.' "*
>
> *Numbers 12:6–8*

Clearly, God affirmed Moses as senior among the prophets of his day, by speaking plainly and directly, even appearing to him. But God also assures that He will induct additional prophets by means of visions and dreams. In the time of Samuel, we read that hearing from the Lord in this way was a rarity (I Samuel 3:1). So, like Moses, God gifted Samuel as a prophet by calling him directly. Unsure whose voice he was hearing, Samuel sought the counsel of Eli, who discerned that it was indeed the Lord speaking. Again, we see that God confirms His voice of prophecy through others who are sensitive to His voice.

Today, whether there is a senior prophet to consult or not, remember that God will never speak something to a true prophet that conflicts with His already established Word. It will not violate God's scripturally expressed plan or character. The minute you hear someone prophesy something that is contrary to God's Word, it should raise major red flags. Especially if the counsel is something you'd like to hear, identify it as false if it is opposed to Scripture.

I once heard about a married Christian woman who said that God had told her that it was okay to divorce her believing husband to marry another man. There was no complaint of unfaithfulness or abuse, nor had the woman's husband abandoned her. She simply felt they had grown apart, and she wanted to pursue another existing relationship with impunity. Clearly, the Bible confirms that God would not counsel her to divorce her faithful husband, though she desperately wanted that counsel, enough to be misled by false prophecy.

On a more corporate scale, I've heard more than one in church leadership resist the gift of prophecy today because of obviously false prophecy, like someone saying that God has told them that Jesus is returning at noon on Friday, even though this is in direct conflict with the Bible's counsel that no one knows the day or the hour of Christ's return. These churches are correct to reject false prophecy, but sadly, many throw out the baby (true prophets) with the dirty bath water of false prophets, inadvertently rejecting God's valuable counsel.

When we accept God's counsel of Ephesians 4:11, that He has appointed prophets to serve within the church body, we open the lines of communication between God in the church. We allow the Holy Spirit to guide, counsel, and give us judgment about the truth or falsehood of any prophecy that comes forth.

"If I receive a prophecy for the church, how should I deliver it?"

There is a balance between the bold majesty of God, and the reverent humility with which His servants should relay His messages (I Peter 4:10–11). Prophecy should be brought forth with calm authority, with His counsel center-staged, without calling undue attention to the messenger.

Prophets aren't meant to impersonate human ideas of what God sounds like; they are simply meant to relay His unadulterated counsel. That's why it's unnecessary to affect our voices or adapt His words into something we think sounds like Him. If God didn't say *my children* this or *thus saith the Lord* that, a faithful messenger will not add to or adapt it. Just speak precisely what you've heard, clearly and loudly enough to be audible within your given situation.

If you're too overcome with emotion at hearing God's words to speak understandably, ask Him to help you compose your emotions before you prophesy, or write the message down so that someone else can deliver it. Dear Believer, there is nothing wrong with a tender heart that is deeply moved when touched by God. But if a teary, choked-up voice is more your emotional response than it is part of the message itself, that weeping can become a human distraction, making it difficult to communicate God's counsel intelligibly.

As we prophesy, we should allow the church to hear the message in the way God speaks it, as much as is possible through our human instruments. Intonation can alter a message. If God wasn't wailing, shouting, or hyping it up, neither should we.

God's word is powerful and life-changing all on its own. We don't have to repackage it, dress it up, or tone it down. We simply relate the message faithfully and let His pure counsel stand.

"This could get out of hand in church. What about checkpoints and order?"

In keeping with I Corinthians 14:26, 29–32, leaders should allow two or three prophets to speak in turn, after which judgment should be passed. The subordination of prophets to other prophets can be appreciated on two levels:

First, a true prophet is able to exercise personal control over if, when, and how he or she delivers a prophecy. This makes it possible to hold a prophetic message until an appropriate time, to consider consistency with Scripture, to discern the originating source of the message, and to pray for confirmation.

Second, prophets check and balance each other, as they are jointly charged with the responsibility of discerning the originating spirit of others who prophesy. Prophecy judged as having originated from an enemy spirit or the human spirit should be rejected as false in the hearing of the congregation; whereas, prophecy that is confirmed as being from the Holy Spirit should be embraced with gratitude.

Sounds simple enough, doesn't it?

Read in combination with I Thessalonians 5:19–21, those verses in I Corinthians 14 answer the age-old question:

"How does prophecy rightly function in today's church?"

Consider the following ways we err in following God's basic instructions in church:

We err when. . .

- we disallow up to three prophecies *(I Corinthians 14:29)*.
- we allow more than three prophecies *(I Corinthians 14:29)*.
- we despise or prohibit prophecy *(I Thessalonians 5:19–20)*.
- prophets fail to wait in turn *(I Corinthians 14:31)*.
- prophecies aren't properly judged *(I Corinthians 14:29)*.
- we don't affirm what is good *(I Thessalonians 5:20–21)*.

With all this possibility of error, it's easy to see why many churches shy away from prophecy. We're reluctant to ruffle anyone who isn't used to prophecy, upsetting church politics, especially if the church has failed to comply with these passages in the past. After all, someone may be offended, even if properly corrected. Some may take their tithes elsewhere. Kooks might come out of the woodwork, spouting false prophecy. It seems too complicated to take on the burden of judgment. It's easier to either limit prophecy to preaching or rule it out altogether. The problem is, when we shy away from the expression and judgment of prophecy in church, we presume to quench the Spirit of God, putting us in direct disobedience with God's authoritative instructions of Scripture to earnestly seek and allow prophecy.

The thing is, God doesn't just want our obedience when it's easy. He wants us to submit ourselves to His Word the way Jesus did, all the way to the cross. That means dying to human control. That means we face our fears, we jettison our man-made order, and resolve to follow God's scriptural order, even when it's challenging.

Instead of looking upon prophecy as a problem within the church, let's consider it what it truly is: a gift. Let's begin to thank Him for the guidance He offers us through this amazing manifestation of His power. Think of it. The God of the universe actually wants to be in vital communication with us! That's not a hardship; that's a blessing, a truly good gift for the church.

"How long should I wait to see if a prophecy is fulfilled?"

Particularly if the prophecy speaks to our heart's desires, waiting can be brutal. Think of Abraham, waiting so many years to see his prophesied offspring. It was like that with so many Old Testament prophecies. Some were fulfilled more immediately, some came to pass after many generations had come and gone, and others speak to the end times, still awaiting fulfillment.

A friend of mine once prophesied that a childless couple would have a daughter. When years came and went without the foretold pregnancy, there were those who preemptively called my friend a false prophet. They were angry. They thought my friend had raised false hopes. Five years later, my friend heard that indeed, the woman had given birth to a baby girl.

Some might protest, wondering why God would speak to a deep desire for a child so far in advance of a pregnancy. Abraham may have wondered the same thing as the years passed between promise and fulfillment. But just as it was with Joseph, God may be giving us hope for the future to help us endure our present trials (Psalm 105:17–19). It's not easy to come down off the exhilaration of learning that you are to become a great leader in your family and to instead find yourself thrown into a pit, and then being sold into slavery by the very brothers you saw bowing down to you.

Instead of keeping the faith, we get disillusioned with prophecy and angry with God. It's tragic.

Friends, don't be surprised if you receive a promising prophetic word and the polar opposite seems to happen almost immediately. The timing might not seem right to you, but God knows what He's doing when He speaks in this way. He knew that pit was just around the corner for Joseph. He knew His prophetic counsel would help Joseph to hang on and trust Him not just during short-term difficulty, but also for a lifetime. The truth is: *a pit can be pivotal.*

Years into waiting for the fulfillment of God's word to me concerning my career, my brethren threw me into a professional pit for an extended time. I was told that my superiors were hoping that the difficulty would make me opt to quit. Everything in me wanted to believe I would be rescued immediately and set back on the path God had foretold for me years before. However, that May, God spoke a future date to me, telling me I'd be out of that pit on August sixteenth. When I heard it, I accepted His timing with relief. Even though it meant a few more months of hardship, I had God's long-term promise to hang onto as well as this date, reminding me that the end of that particular trial was in sight.

Though I told only a close friend of the date, I watched carefully as it approached. By early August, I had been reduced from a regular directing job to a busywork assignment that had me literally ironing rags, right in the sight of those I had once directed. Ironically, those rags were costumes for a production that was being shot in a huge pit! One actor mocked me to my face, giving me the opportunity to grow in character, to find contentment in my work, no matter how humble.

Funny thing, though, on August sixteenth, when I stood ironing those rags as unto the Lord, a high-ranking executive passed through that hall. I hadn't complained. I hadn't told him about the prophesied relief, but something about the sight of me ironing rags made him call me over and say, *"This shouldn't be."*

August sixteenth marked a pivotal turn in my career path. Just as it was with Joseph, that pit played a crucial role in transitioning me toward my future.

Pits can be grossly underrated, don't you think? We resist them. We whine and gripe and beg to get out of them. But look how God can use pits to grow us up and prepare us for what is to come. In my pit, I learned that it wasn't my bosses I was serving, but the Lord Jesus, motivating me to do whatever He put before me with genuine gratitude. Friend, if God has spoken to you prophetically and yet you find yourself in a pit of despair, look up! Let that pit become a well. Allow the anointing of the Holy Spirit to spring up in that place and teach you as you wait for the fulfillment of His promise (I John 2:27). Trust that God will be true to His prophetic word.

"What if I receive a message that's hard to deliver?"

Prophecy comes with a responsibility to communicate counsel that is received from God in a timely manner. There may be times when the prophet is reluctant to deliver the message. Maybe he's intimidated, like Jonah. Maybe the message is for a threatening crowd. Maybe the prophet hates to upset the apple cart of human tradition. God won't violate the free will of the prophet to whom He speaks. The prophet can opt to obey God and dispatch the message or to harden his heart and either delay or refuse, even though we are warned in Scripture not to refuse God when He fills our mouths with His words (Jeremiah 1:9).

God spoke so much through Jeremiah that he became a laughingstock, so much that Jeremiah resolved not to speak in God's name anymore. What do you think happened? God didn't stop speaking. And Jeremiah reported that God's words still burned in his heart, like fire imprisoned within his bones. Eventually, Jeremiah realized that he couldn't hold back God's counsel any longer (Jeremiah 20:7–9).

The social rejection and persecution prophets like Jeremiah experienced may partly account for why relatively few seek the gift of prophecy, even though it is so highly encouraged as being a greater gift (I Corinthians 14:1). For a season, even Jeremiah did what we are admonished never to do: he quenched the Holy Spirit and despised prophetic utterances (I Thessalonians 5:19–20). Gratefully, Jeremiah's moratorium on prophecy didn't last; however, his experience does give us insight into why many have avoided or abandoned this important gift.

It's not just about high-profile leaders dropping the prophetic call. Commonplace believers are also responsible (Numbers 11:29). Moses said that when God's people would seek God with all their hearts, they'd find Him, that distress would make them return to Him and listen to His voice (Deuteronomy 4:29-30, 36). Isaiah echoed the exhortation as a prophetic command:

"Give ear and hear My voice, listen and hear My words."
Isaiah 28:23

It doesn't seem so much a question of whether God is still speaking as it is whether we are willing to listen. Isaiah went on to revel that the Lord had awakened his ear to hear and that he had not rebelled against God's voice (Isaiah 50:4–5). In his obedience, Isaiah was entrusted with glorious counsel with which to sustain the weary, counsel straight from the heart of God.

Years ago, God revealed a guarded secret in a friend's life to me. The Holy Spirit asked me to approach my friend in love about it and showed me exactly what He wanted to say. It was a difficult message, and I am ashamed to say that I resisted the Spirit's timing. Daunted by the task, I said that I would deliver the message the next time I saw my friend face to face, knowing we lived far apart. I rationalized that a phone call wouldn't suffice. I put the Almighty on hold.

The message burned in my heart for about six months, until I finally saw this person again. I prayed fervently that God would speak through me and He did. My friend listened, and then said something I will never forget. I was told that my words would have meant much more six months prior, when my friend had been deep in the throes of dealing with the matter.

This experience taught me an invaluable lesson: when the Lord asks me to dispatch a message, I shouldn't dictate the timing of the delivery. Rather, I should look back at the timing set forth in Scripture. He says that if we hear His voice *today*, we should exhort one another *while it is still called today*. There's a reason for that. People become hardened to God's voice with every passing day. God's message can be an urgently needed lifeline to a drowning soul. So, unless God specifically directs you to wait or if you still need confirmation that God is really speaking, dispatch His message promptly. Recognize that reluctance to deliver a hard word is a tool of the enemy to delay necessary counsel from God.

"Should a prophet be able to tell me anything and everything?"

As when the soldiers goaded a blindfolded Jesus to prophesy who hit Him, Jesus was not obligated to answer (Luke 22:64). Though His eyes were covered, Jesus saw their mocking hearts. He submitted to their abuse, but not their test. Ever wonder why Jesus didn't just shock the soldiers with an accurate response? Jesus' own words give us a clue:

> *"Do not give what is holy to dogs, and do not throw your pearls before swine, lest they trample them under their feet, and turn and tear you to pieces."*
>
> *Matthew 7:6*

God's prophetic counsel is not upon human demand. It is not to be tossed to those who don't appreciate it for the sacred privilege that it is. In some cases, prophets may know more than they feel the Holy Spirit is leading them to speak, particularly when the motive for inquiry isn't pure.

That said, it's not uncommon for people to innocently approach those who are prophetically gifted with the expectation that a prophet should know everything about them or a given situation without being told. We should remember that true prophets receive and declare only the counsel God gives, as the Holy Spirit directs. They are not psychics or mind readers, searching the minds of human beings. Rather, prophets are God's servant hearers, dependent upon the Holy Spirit to communicate what God knows we need to hear.

In I Corinthians 13:9, we learn that we prophesy only in part. Until we are face to face with God in eternity, we'll only get partial glimpses into His mind. So, while there is certainly more than adequate biblical precedent for inquiring of a prophet, that prophet will not necessarily be given all the answers. Our sovereign God knows if and when it is best to communicate prophetically. He is also to be trusted to know when it's best to be silent on an issue or to speak to us solely through His already established counsel of Scripture.

"What if a believing prophet accidentally makes a mistake?"

Under the Old Testament, the standard for prophets was one hundred percent accuracy. The penalty for false prophecy was death, mirroring the penalty for all sin (Deuteronomy 18:20). Zero tolerance. However, in the New Covenant of grace, Jesus' death for our sins covers repentant believers who make an unwitting mistake in prophecy.

There is no New Testament directive that a mistaken prophet should be put to death [insert gigantic sigh of relief here]. Rather, a structure of checks and balances is set up for judgment of prophecy by other prophets within the church (I Corinthians 14:29). Correction should be handled in the same way Jesus taught us to deal with other types of sin or error (Matthew 18:15–17).

The repentant sinner receives God's mercy. The unrepentant soul steps outside the umbrella of God's grace, where we know the penalty of sin is ultimately death, separation from God, whom the rebellious have chosen to reject.

How public or private the correction needs to be depends upon the situation. Again, a recognized true prophet within the church should make the call about how to proceed, with damage control in mind. If the mistake was made privately, it is often possible to correct and resolve the error privately. However, if a believer makes a mistake in prophecy within the hearing of a group, it is advisable for ranking prophets to offer immediate loving correction within the group, especially if someone else might be misled by the false prophecy.

Rightly handled, public correction can be both appropriate and instructive to the entire body. Sure, it's uncomfortable, but the sting of embarrassment that a mistaken believer may feel when corrected will remind everyone who hears it to be more cautious about speaking for God in the future. It can encourage the mistaken person to school himself more fully in the Scriptures or to ask for judgment concerning what she thinks she's hearing before speaking it out to the body. As confirmed prophets are diligent to weed out what is false, it creates an environment where Holy Spirit-inspired prophets can grow in their gifting.

In addition to correcting the content of prophecies, elder prophets can also serve to curb fleshy add-ons that can muddy the message of God. God speaks through His prophets in the language people understand today. We don't need to whip ourselves up or speak with an ominous, booming voice to make prophecy seem more credible. We don't need to gild the Lily of the Valley by tacking on random syllables here and there. There is no need to tag prophecy with anachronistic wording such as *thus saith the Lord* instead of contemporary phrasing such as *this is what I believe the Lord is saying*. Elder prophets can advise if a person needs to speak more loudly in order to be heard, or less emotionally to be better understood. They can also assist younger prophets in discerning the best time and setting in which to bring forth a prophetic message.

"Is it okay to ask God about the future?"

Even though prophecy isn't always about the future, the tendency to wonder what's ahead crops up regularly. The words of Jesus speak to this question better than I ever could:

"Therefore do not be anxious for tomorrow; for tomorrow will care for itself. Each day has enough trouble of its own."

Matthew 6:34

Clearly, God doesn't want us wrapped up in worrying about tomorrow. We have plenty to deal with today. Yes, there are times when the Holy Spirit will disclose things to come, but following Jesus' directive, I usually let God initiate when it comes to disclosing anything about the future, especially about matters too close to my heart.

More often than not, I'll ask: *Is there anything you'd like to say to me, today?* Then, I just relax and listen. Many times He exhorts, edifies, or consoles me. He knows I love to hear His voice, and I trust that He'll guide our time together. I stay away from asking questions about anything in which I have a vested interest because I trust Him with my future, and I don't want to confuse the voice of my own hopes with His.

The *gotcha* is that we, in our humanity, normally want what seems good to us, which usually means the path of least resistance. Those personal desires of ours can be so powerful that they make us very susceptible to error. We may want that job, or that healing, or that spouse so much that we convince ourselves God said it would be given. Then, we get angry with God for not fulfilling something He never promised. In particular, time-lines we think we "hear" in the Spirit are often an expression of our own impatience, leading us into error.

Though there is plenty of Old Testament precedent for inquiring of prophets concerning what is to come, as I read the prophets themselves, I truly admire their reliance upon God to guide the conversation. So, as we explore all the forms prophecy takes, let's resolve to be much more concerned with growing in communicative relationship with Him than in inquiring about our futures. If we really need to know what's ahead for some divine purpose, let's trust that He'll tell us.

Eli advised Samuel well when he told him simply to ask the Lord to speak, then let God know that His servant was listening (I Samuel 3:9–10). Interestingly, the Lord did make a very important disclosure to

Samuel that night. It was the first of many prophetic conversations during a life given over in humble submission to God.

"What does prophecy look like for us today?"

Under the umbrella of God communicating with us, prophecy takes a number of forms. Preaching may be composed of human words, but it can also be prophetic when it crosses over into declaring what God is specifically saying to a church or person (Acts 15:32). Sound teaching can take place in the natural, but teaching can also mingle with prophecy when a teacher delivers the inspired instruction of the Holy Spirit. Prayer can give way into the prophetic when the Spirit guides our intercession.

Prophecy can come forth in a church service, in a prayer meeting, one-on-one, or individually. God can speak to us anywhere and anytime—when we're in fellowship settings, when we're out and about in the world, or when we're fast asleep in bed. Prophecy can be manifested to us visually and/or vocally. Sometimes it's literal; sometimes it's symbolic, embedded with a message. Sometimes God's voice is audible; more often He speaks to us through the inner voice of the Holy Spirit.

Though we may long for literal, audible, readily understandable communication from God, many times He draws us closer by speaking in quiet, symbolic, even mysterious ways that are equally valid and instructive. Since God is the originator, it's His choice how much to reveal of His mind and exactly how to reveal it. So, let's not despise God's prophetic messages in any form (I Thessalonians 5:20). No matter how He chooses to speak, let's open our eyes and ears to receive His counsel in the Spirit.

CHAPTER EIGHTEEN

Prophetic Visions

What they are:

Visual exhortation, edification, consolation, or disclosure of things to come, illustrating the counsel or mind of God

What they aren't:

Hallucinations, figments of our imaginations, signs of mental illness

> *After praying for a sister's deliverance from an unclean spirit that had tormented her for twenty-five years, I was asked by someone new to this type of experience if we had expelled a demon out of this believer. Not wanting to simply draw upon of my own logic or traditional thought, I asked the Holy Spirit to guide my answer. God chose to respond with a picture. Immediately, I saw our friend. I got a detailed look at the spirit of fear that had plagued her with crippling anxiety attacks. This creature was riding her, piggyback style, taunting her in her left ear. It did not possess or in any way inhabit her. The picture confirmed that it was simply on her, oppressing her, impeding her progress from the outside. It was also banished in an instant at the name of Jesus, spoken in prayer by everyday women.*

Though sometimes prophecy is only heard, we'll also take a look at how prophecy can work hand-in-hand with the visual aids of visions and dreams, or what the Bible calls *night visions* (Job 33:15–17). Whether visions are waking visions, with eyes open or closed, or whether they are visions that God gives in the night while we're sleeping, one thing all God-given visions have in common is that they serve prophetic purposes in our lives. We'll start with waking visions.

"Isn't the whole prophetic visions thing a little out there?"

Out of the traditions of man? Yes. Out of the Word of God in Scripture? Not even a little bit. When I did a quick search on my Bible software, I found just over a hundred references to vision/s in the American Standard Version of the Bible.

Over and over, God made a practice of communicating His prophetic counsel through visionary means (Hosea 12:10). As we follow the disciples' journey of faith in the book of Acts, we find numerous instances of visionary prophecy, confirming over and over that the Holy Spirit who had fallen at Pentecost continued to interact with God's people vividly, just as the prophet Joel foretold (Joel 2:28–29).

"But isn't this just for the big guns in leadership?"

We tend to think God only communicates with the superstars of the faith, but Joel's prophecy is clear that there is one unifying class of people upon whom He will pour out His Spirit in this way: His servants. Male or female, young or old, if you are His servant (even one of His everyday servants, like I am), this could happen to you. It doesn't mean you're crazy. It doesn't mean you're hallucinating. It means that God has a message that He is underscoring visually, knowing how powerfully pictures can capture our attention. Waking visions, often considered the more unusual, may come while we are in an attitude of prayer or during the course of waking life.

A friend of mine was in church when the Spirit of God spoke to her, directing her to go and pray for a specific married couple in the congregation. She didn't know their situation, but she approached them and asked if she could pray for them. They consented and my friend proceeded. She laid her hands on their shoulders and closed her eyes, expecting the Lord to speak. Suddenly, the Lord responded with a vision. She began to see this couple in the jungle. They looked so happy as she watched them play with dark-skinned children.

My friend didn't know what the vision meant at first. She opened her eyes and, overcoming a bit of trepidation, she told the couple she wasn't sure if what she'd seen would make any sense now or if it might be for the future. She described exactly what she had been shown. The man and wife smiled broadly and explained that they had been communicating with two different mission organizations about going out into the field. They'd been uncertain which field the Lord would have them to pursue. One was with a white population. The other was with a village in Africa. Through my friend's openness to the Holy Spirit, and through their own willingness to receive, this missionary couple got clear direction.

"What's it like to see a vision?"

Whether the recipient gets an internal picture with his/her eyes closed, or an open-eyed external vision in front of them, a number have confirmed my experience that it's literally like watching a movie that spontaneously begins to play. Whether it's an extended vision or a picture that plays out over just a few seconds, it's not a matter of just thinking of what a picture or scenario would look like. When God gives a prophetic vision, it is actually seen.

When I think back on a vision God has given me, I can remember what it looked like, but it's no longer a sensory experience. I don't actually see it again. Though I can imagine what a scenario would look like or reflect upon a memory, I can't drum up a literal picture in front of me, one that seems projected like a film. We don't generate visions by any human effort or imagination. We simply watch and listen as the picture unfolds.

Granted, the comparison to earthly movies falls short. We should keep in mind that though a vision may look like a movie, its purpose is not to entertain or elevate us. Rather, its purpose is to provide us with vital prophetic communication from the Almighty.

"Why does God give visions instead of just talking to us?"

Some people seem frustrated by the whole concept of visions, especially those of the symbolic variety. They wonder why God doesn't always just show them what He wants to show them in a way that requires no interpretation. God may be concealing the matter so that you'll snuggle up close to hear what He wants to explain to you in secret. He may be telling you a picture-parable that will come to resonate with meaning. Just as God wants us to hear what He's saying when He communicates with words, He sometimes chooses to engage our sense of spiritual sight, something He knows our spirits need to focus and thrive.

"Where there is no vision, the people are unrestrained."
Proverbs 29:18a

The Hebrew word for *vision* can also be translated as *sight, dream,* or *revelation.* God knows that we need to focus our attention on the bigger picture of what He's doing. He knows that there's just something about seeing that adds dimension to the spoken word. Pictures are powerfully burned on our memories. They remind us of the messages they contain. Pictures put those messages into an active context, helping us to relate to the living Word.

That part about being *unrestrained* can also be translated as *going in all directions.* Like a farmer plowing a field, human beings need a focal point to stay on track. Without that vision we make no progress, we get off course, we run around in circles, we collapse, even die inside.

Visions are healthy. Visions are good for us. Though we perish without them, with them, we thrive in the Spirit. They are like booster shots, energizing us to participate in God's work.

"Sure, in Bible days, but aren't people who hear or see things now kind of crazy?"

Undoubtedly, there is a mental illness association with hearing voices or seeing things others don't. Tumors have also been known to cause visions. There is a significant difference, however, between a physical/mental affliction and a spiritual gift.

Whereas illness-generated hallucinations prove false, random, destructive, or meaningless, the Holy Spirit's visionary manifestations prove true, pertinent, constructive, and meaningful. As the content of these manifestations is examined, the source becomes more apparent. God doesn't do random parlor tricks. Rather, when He shows us something in the Spirit, it is with prophetic purpose.

I've heard of people who have feared treatment for mental illness because they didn't want to stop hearing from God. Let me assure you that treatment won't stop you from hearing from God if the messages are indeed Holy Spirit-generated. When God truly blesses you with hearing from Him in this way, it has absolutely nothing to do with illness. The heightening of your spiritual senses is an entirely healthy pursuit, and God's communications are to be treasured by sound-minded believers.

The New Testament records numerous instances of God communicating visually with mentally sound, everyday people through messages delivered in the Spirit—through dreams, visions, and visitations, and often in combination. I suppose there were those who thought people who heard from God in these ways were crazy then, just as they might think we're crazy today.

Don't forget, the Bible says that natural people can't understand the things of God. It's to be expected that people who are walking in the power of the Holy Spirit will be misunderstood. If people mock or misjudge us because of an active relationship with God in the Spirit, it won't be the first time. It's a good opportunity to ask ourselves if we're more concerned with what people think of us than we are with growing in intimacy with God (I Peter 4:14).

Once, I was out walking when, quite spontaneously, I began to receive a vivid picture. Earlier that morning, on my way to Bible Study, I had told the Lord I would be willing to deliver any message He might give me for a member of the group, even though many of the women there were unaccustomed to such manifestations of the Spirit.

I had received nothing while I was at the study, but about an hour later, when I wasn't even thinking about it, a moving picture suddenly came to me. I saw one of the women from the group leaning over to pray for another person. I heard God's accompanying counsel that He had the gift of prophecy for this sister, and that this gift could empower her ministry if she would receive it. It was as if this gift were already purchased, wrapped, tagged, and just waiting for her to open. The Spirit confirmed to me that I was to tell her that whether or not she decided to accept this gift was up to her, but the gift was there waiting nonetheless.

As you can imagine, it can be hard to deliver such a message, not knowing how it will be received. But I had offered myself as a messenger to the Lord, so I promptly delivered it. It was well over a year before I heard that this visionary prophecy had been fulfilled.

Visions in Scripture

There are far too many biblical instances to cover in this chapter, so let's just look at a few examples and consider the application they might have for us today.

We know that God communicated visually when John baptized Jesus. John 1:32 tells us that John saw the Spirit of God descend and rest upon Jesus like a dove. This visual was confirmed with an audible voice, God the Father, speaking His mind, identifying Jesus as His beloved Son.

Strikingly, in John 5:19–20, Jesus talks about only doing things that He *sees* the Father doing. Now, Jesus did a lot of things. Extend the logic. That means Jesus saw the Father doing those things and followed suit. Jesus' purity was definitely a factor in this. Jesus was pure in heart, and He saw God.

Matthew 5:8 holds a powerful incentive when it says that the pure in heart are blessed with the promise of seeing God. Wouldn't it be amazing to actually see God? Certainly, that promise will be fulfilled in large part in eternity; however, there are ways we can see what He's doing in the Spirit now, the way Jesus did. It's another one of those natural senses we have (*sight*) that has a counterpoint sense in the Spirit (*vision*). Tuck that beatitude into your understanding. Purity of heart leads to seeing God. I want to see God and what He's doing. Don't you? That means we should want to be pure like Jesus.

"But Jesus is Jesus. How do I get to be that pure?"

It starts with admitting we can't possibly do this on our own. Though purity is the by-product of a sanctified heart, this is so not about earning communication from God through good works or years of service. It's about His power and stature, not ours.

When it comes down to it, we're all serial sinners who fall far short of the righteousness of God. But, as we humbly stand before the throne of grace, like Peter in John 13:1–8, we find the Son of God bending down with basin and towel to serve us in all our grimy humanity. Peter balked at this at first, declaring that the Lord would never wash his feet. Peter didn't feel any more worthy of grace than we do. And yet, Jesus compelled Peter to allow it, advising that Peter could have no part with Him, unless Peter let Jesus wash him.

In a very real way, we need to get past our self-sufficient pride and let Jesus wash us. As we repent and admit that we need washing, the blood of Christ cleanses us from sin, purifying our hearts so we can see God, even the lowliest of us, even in the modern age.

Decades apart, two friends of mine separately received strikingly similar visions. In each case, the purpose of the vision was to minister directly to the recipient. In both instances, these everyday women were humble before God. Neither felt in any way worthy, nor in any way sought the visionary visitation.

I remember being in a prayer meeting with the first of these women. This gathering had nothing to do with any church or organized ministry. It was just a bunch of young adults hungry for God, meeting weekly. Sometimes we fasted all day, eager to hear from Him when we gathered. That night, my friend was on her hands and knees, crying out to God. Suddenly, her cries turned to deep, heaving sobs. She looked up at a sharp angle, tears streaming, intently watching something I couldn't see. I noticed that her cries changed as she looked up, that she was mourning, in grateful agony over what she was seeing. I didn't know what was happening to her, but sensed that the Lord was ministering to her in a profound way.

Later that night, my friend told me that she had received a vision. I had never heard of God ministering through visions, but I was convinced by her testimony. I knew how deeply she loved the Lord, and that she would never lie or exaggerate. I witnessed her sincere response during this visitation. Moreover, I sensed the Holy Spirit's confirmation that what she told me was true.

My friend explained that, as she had been face down, on her knees before the Lord, she had seen blood, a lot of it, dripping down on the floor in front of her. She had looked up to see the source of the blood and found herself at the foot of the cross, watching Jesus, dying for her sins.

It had been more than thirty years since my friend received that vision, but as I was preparing to write this very chapter, my phone rang. Another devoted sister who knew nothing of my friend or her vision called to tell me what had happened to her during the past weekend after she had earnestly gone before the Lord. From their separate accounts, the two visions of Jesus on the cross, though given to two different women, decades apart, were identical.

Jesus wasn't the only one in Scripture who saw God, you know. There were others, including a disciple named Ananias. In Acts 9:10–16 we read that the Lord appeared to Ananias in a vision with very specific instructions. Ironically, God used this vision to instruct Ananias to find the newly converted Saul and pray for him to restore Saul's natural vision, after Saul's spiritual eyes had been opened to see God. This was only the beginning of Saul's prophetic journey. Transformed and renamed Paul, like Jesus, Paul continued to encounter God by visionary means.

Turn to Acts 10:9–16 for a multilevel visionary communiqué to Peter. Read how it all started with Cornelius being visited by an angel in a vision, all the way through its glorious conclusion at the end of the chapter. Ask the Lord to speak to you about this passage as you read through it, and then proceed.

Amazingly intricate account, huh? Notice the many links in this chain. God entrusted this important message to flawed human beings. They could have shaken it off. They could have disobeyed and broken any link in the chain of what God was doing, but no matter how "out there" God's message might have seemed to them, each made the choice to yield to the Holy Spirit.

Note to self:
When the Spirit of the Almighty God calls on me, yield.

Consider how specific God's counsel was about what He wanted Cornelius to do. This was a pivotal assignment in Christian history, tracking with the message of the vision Peter received, that ultimately led Peter to embrace the Gentiles into the faith for the first time.

Notice that with Cornelius, the message of the vision was specific, literal, and direct. Peter, on the other hand, got symbols. Perhaps God used symbols with Peter because Peter was already baptized with the Holy Spirit who could interpret the meaning for him. Perhaps God knew that it would be hard for Peter to get on board with embracing the Gentiles without a vividly communicated message, one that was told in mysteries, and then confirmed in numerous ways.

Confirmation is crucial when it comes to visions, especially those involving significant direction. Paul reminds us in II Corinthians 13:1 that every word should be established by two or three witnesses. Let's look back at six elements that confirmed the veracity and the counsel of Peter's vision:

1.   The Vision Came During Prayer

This momentous vision occurred while Peter was actively seeking God (Acts 10:9). Peter had gone up to a housetop, separating himself from the world and focusing His heart on God. He had stepped under the umbrella of God's protection as he submitted this time to communicate with God.

2.   The Message Was Repeated Three Times

Peter was like we are, steeped in the traditions of men. He resisted, fearful to break with what he had always considered holy. Yet, God patiently repeated Himself three times for special emphasis, searing the picture in Peter's mind, the words on his memory, even though Peter still had no idea what it meant (Acts 10:16, Genesis 41:32). It's interesting to note that after Peter denied Jesus three times, the resurrected Jesus asked Peter if he loved Him three times. Three times, when Peter affirmed his love, Jesus asked him to take care of His flock (John 21:15–17). In the vision at Joppa, also given three times, the Lord directed Peter to open up that flock he'd been urged to tend to include the Gentiles.

3.   The Arrival of the Three Men as Foretold

Look at how exquisitely the timing unfolded (Acts 10:19–21). While Peter was still reflecting on the vision, the Holy Spirit told him that three men were looking for him, men that He had sent. Peter went downstairs and found the men, confirming what the Spirit had foretold. Peter still didn't know what to make of the vision. He didn't even know why the men were there. But Peter set an example for us in that he took the steps of faith to follow the prompting of the Holy Spirit, even when he didn't fully understand where he was being led.

4. The Testimony of a Devout Man, Sent by an Angel

The message of the vision began to become clearer to Peter when the three men informed him that an angel had appeared to their master, Cornelius, instructing him to send for Peter to come to his house to bring them a message (Acts 10:22). Even though Peter knew that their tradition called it unlawful to associate with Gentiles, Peter followed the visionary counsel of God and gave them lodging, then went with them to Cornelius' house the next day. Peter knew that God had shown him through the vision not to call anything unclean that God had cleansed. Then, once Peter heard directly from Cornelius (v. 34), Peter proclaimed his certainty that all of this meant that God was no respecter of persons.

5. Confirming Manifestations of the Spirit

These Gentiles were ripe for harvest (Acts 10:44–46). As Peter preached, the Spirit fell, baptizing those who were listening with power. They hadn't been baptized in water. No one had even laid hands on them. They simply responded to the Gospel with faith and opened their hearts to the prompting of the Holy Spirit, who filled their mouths with exaltation and unknown tongues of praise. Tradition was out the window. God had taken over amongst the ranks of the newly reborn. Peter and his brethren were amazed to grasp that the Holy Spirit had confirmed His presence in the Gentiles with tongues, just as He had in them.

6. Recalling of God's Previously Spoken Word

When Peter returned to Jerusalem, circumcised believers took issue with him. To be fair, they hadn't seen or heard what Peter had. So, Peter walked them through it step by step (Acts 11:16). He reminded them of Jesus' words of Acts 1:5, a crucial point of confirmation that we should all consider today. It's not that the inclusion of the Gentiles wasn't in God's previously spoken Word of Scripture (Isaiah 49:6, 56:6–8). It's just that they'd become so steeped in the traditions of man that it took a significant event to get them back on track with the prophesies of God's Word. Indeed, the time had come to fulfill Isaiah's prophecy that foreigners would join themselves to the Lord, and that God's house would be a house of prayer, not just for the Jews, but for *all* people.

Over the centuries and still to the present day, there remain those pure-hearted souls who long to see God. They eschew man-made tradition and cling to the promise of Scripture, that the Holy Spirit continues to pour out on all flesh, even the commonplace among us, communicating God's counsel through visions today.

"Aren't visions just about the big stuff?"

Visions are about whatever God wants to show us. Some visions are quite simple, even tender. While other visions may seem more momentous on a spiritual level, God really is in the details of our lives—edifying, exhorting, and consoling us prophetically through visionary means. Great or small, visions are prophetic gifts from God's River, designed to draw us deeper into the mind of God as we, like Jesus, see what the Father is doing.

Just knowing God sees us as we struggle and cares enough to give us a glimpse of His heart toward us helps us to hold on and keep growing in grace. Sometimes, a vision can be like receiving a divine sympathy card, a reminder that God stands with us, a very present help in our times of trouble (Psalm 46:1).

My friend, Buzz, lost his beloved wife in a tragic accident years ago. He was beside himself with grief. It was a heart-rending reunion as many of our dear college friends traveled great distances to be a part of her memorial service.

While in prayer for Buzz, the Lord gave me a simple picture: I was shown parched earth in front of me. Land that was once well watered now had a dry, caked layer of cracked mud on top. There was no vegetation anywhere except in the very center, where a pale long-stemmed rosebud stood straight up, without even a bush to support it, between the cracks in the hard earth.

As I looked to the Lord about this picture, I sensed immediately that He was saying that, after the desert of this devastating loss, Buzz would find love again. Still, I sensed the Spirit instruct me to only comfort Buzz by describing the unexplained picture. I was to leave it to the Spirit to help Buzz realize the vision's meaning at a later time when he was ready to receive it.

Indeed, Buzz was visibly moved to hear that God had sent him this picture while he was in the throes of grief. He was consoled that his heavenly Father saw his pain and he accepted it gratefully, without interpretation.

Years later, I received an e-mail from Buzz with a photo of the fair-skinned woman he went on to marry. In his note, he gratefully acknowledged that he had found his rose.

The Bottom Line with Visions

Remember: Every vision from God serves a prophetic purpose, consistent with Scripture. Like an aurally received prophecy, it communicates the counsel or mind of God by edification, exhortation, consolation, or disclosure of things to come. Especially as we begin to encounter these gifts, it's instructive to consider what specific purpose a particular vision serves.

For example, the vision for Buzz served two prophetic purposes: First, it ministered tender divine consolation. Second, it was embedded with a symbolic message, disclosing what was to come, that something lovely that was not yet open, would come to bloom in time.

While the Bible encourages us to earnestly seek prophetic communication with God, it is always geared toward getting to know Him better. We shouldn't ask God for visions because we're curious, or because we want Him to prove Himself to us by setting off some kind of holy pyrotechnics. Those are the kinds of signs the Bible instructs us not to seek. Rather, as we follow Scripture in seeking God's prophetic counsel in a visionary way, our motivations should be pure. It should be all about loving God, wanting to serve Him and to partner with Him as we get a glimpse of His divine direction. Like the Greeks who came, purposed to worship in John 12:20-21, let the honest desire of our hearts simply be: *"...we wish to see Jesus."*

CHAPTER NINETEEN

Prophetic Dreams

I was outdoors, having a casual conversation with a small gathering of people. Suddenly sensing the presence of God, I turned back to my right. There, high above the mountains, was Jesus, arms outstretched against a golden sky. I simply thought: Oh. Okay. It must be time. Without hesitation, I left my companions and began to fly toward my Lord. Glancing around, I saw many others nearby, soaring toward Jesus. I was mildly surprised to recognize someone I hadn't been sure would be there. I looked back to Jesus, confident that He knew exactly those who were His. I awoke, the dream indelibly engraved on my memory.

By day or by night. Waking or sleeping. Not only does the Bible say that God will minister to us in waking visions, He also gives us dreams that the Scriptures sometimes call *night visions*.

> *"Indeed God speaks once, or twice, yet no one notices it. In a dream, a vision of the night, when sound sleep falls on men, while they slumber in their beds, then He opens the ears of men, and seals their instruction, that He may turn man aside from his conduct, and keep man from pride."*
>
> *Job 33:14–17*

Why does God speak through dreams? Elihu's counsel to Job tells us that God speaks to us, even repeats Himself when we're awake, but sometimes we just don't hear Him. However, when we're at rest, when the competitive din of the world dies down, it is then that God opens our ears.

This passage from Job cites three purposes for God speaking to us via night visions:

1. To Seal our Instruction

That's right. God actually instructs us through dreams. How many times have you cried out to God, asking what you're supposed to do about a situation? Your personal desires and agendas may deafen you by day, making it hard for you to hear His prophetic voice while awake, but He may offer instruction through night visions if you are willing to receive in this way. He may also instruct you concerning things you're not otherwise aware that He's asking you to do.

2. To Turn Us Aside from Our Conduct

When we're asleep, since we're not distracted by the world around us, we can be more open to hearing from God. You know it's true. We schedule our days. We carry out our purposes, leaving little or no time to listen for God's counsel. But if we yield to the Holy Spirit, God can use dreams to turn us from our worldly intents and into His purposes, not the least of which is to communicate with us and to give us the opportunity to respond to His instruction.

In Matthew 1:18–25, consider how Joseph's conduct was impacted by the dream God sent. By day, when he discovered that Mary was with child, Joseph determined to put her away. Yet by night, the Holy Spirit withdrew Joseph from his human purposes and instructed Joseph to fulfill God's purposes. The personal stakes were high for Joseph, no doubt. But Joseph not only heard God's direction through this dream, he acted upon it.

3. To Keep Us from Pride

When we're asleep, our defenses are down. The prideful facade we often maintain is beyond our reach, back in the waking world. Our insecurities surface. We are naked before the Almighty with no fig leaf of pride to mask our vulnerability. And yet, we are right where He wants us—completely safe—in the care of our loving, all-knowing God.

By day, Joseph's pride may have led him to put Mary away. The shame of pregnancy prior to marriage should not be underestimated in that culture. Women were stoned to death for less. On top of that, Joseph knew that the child his betrothed was carrying was not his. How this must have bruised his manly ego.

One can imagine that when Mary told Joseph of her pregnancy, she must have explained that she had not betrayed him, that rather, the Holy Spirit had come upon her. (*Indeed God speaks once...*) Perhaps Joseph doubted Mary, and she went on to relate how Gabriel himself had appeared to her with God's message. (*...or twice, yet no one notices it.*)

In his waking hours, Joseph may not have been able to hear God's message, even though it came through an angel to Mary. But in Joseph's sleep, God also sent an angel to minister to Joseph in a dream. In so doing, God opened Joseph's ears. He sealed Joseph's instruction. He turned aside Joseph's earthly conduct, and kept Joseph from pride.

When Joseph woke, he followed God's instructions and took Mary as his wife. What's more, Joseph denied himself the earthly pleasures of a husband by keeping Mary a virgin until after Jesus was born. Clearly, Joseph didn't want there to be any question about Jesus' paternity. As Joseph let go of his own plans and followed God's directions, God blessed Joseph in a special way, very much in keeping with the sacrifice of pride required by Joseph's obedience.

Think of it! In exchange for the shame God knew Joseph would endure, He gave Joseph a position of great esteem in the kingdom: as the adoptive father of the King of Kings.

"I'm nervous about this.
Isn't listening to dreams kind of New Age?"

There is plenty of false teaching about dreams associated with the New Age movement as well as the occult. No one ever accused Satan of being original. Indeed, he's big on counterfeiting, even the gifts of God. But, tell me—would you throw away all your real money just because somebody tried to pass off a fake bill on you? No. You'd educate yourself to discern the sometimes-subtle differences between what's fake and what's real. You'd reject the counterfeit and continue to use what's genuine and valuable.

When it comes to dreams, the enemy derails us on a couple of fronts. Offensively, he floods the market with fakes. Covertly, he derails the body of Christ by convincing us that God doesn't speak through dreams anymore, effectively disabling one of God's biblically verifiable prophetic communication systems.

Friends, don't be fooled by Satan's trickery. Study the Scriptures. Sift the nourishing wheat of God from the tares sown by the enemy. Discard what is worthless; cling to what is good. Recognize the gift night visions can be to your relationship with God. Rebuke the enemy in the name of Jesus; then, welcome the Holy Spirit to speak to you in this way.

If you're still respectfully nervous about whether a dream message is truly from God, take comfort. You're not alone. In Daniel Chapter Two, King Nebuchadnezzar's courts were crawling with counterfeit dream interpreters, so much so that Nebuchadnezzar refused to even relate the contents of the dream that troubled him to the point of insomnia. The charlatans defended themselves, saying no one could tell the king what his dream was, no one (their words) *except the gods*. Enter Daniel, a young man who lived with the one true God. You see, the king was royally cranky over this enigmatic dream and ordered all his wise men, including Daniel to be executed. When he heard this, Daniel personally petitioned the king for time, and then went home.

We can learn something from Daniel's wisdom. Daniel left the king's courts, courts that were ringing with the voices of liars and doubters. Daniel went to his own house, where he enlisted the prayer support of trusted companions. Then, Daniel did something that might seem completely counterintuitive, considering the lives of so many were on the line. He went to sleep! Daniel turned off every waking voice and made himself available to hear the voice of the One who never sleeps or slumbers.

> *"Then the mystery was revealed to Daniel in a night vision..."*
> *Daniel 2:19*

With Daniel's own life in the balance, the stakes couldn't have been higher. Still, Daniel trusted what God revealed to him in a dream. What's more, Daniel launched into a flurry of praise to God, even before going back to Nebudchadnezzar, knowing both the king's secret dream and its interpretation. That's how sure Daniel was of what God had shown him. Read how confidently Daniel presented this complex, symbolic night vision and its meaning to the king who would have executed Daniel had he been wrong. Instead, the king was so struck with Daniel's accuracy that he fell on his face before him and recognized Daniel's God as Lord of Lords, a revealer of secrets.

This wouldn't be the last time God revealed His prophetic counsel to Daniel through a dream. Read Daniel Chapter Seven. This time, Daniel sought the counsel of another man to interpret his detailed night vision. Again, the stakes were high. Kings and kingdoms were in the balance. We learn in verses fifteen and twenty-eight that Daniel was grieved after the night vision itself, and still troubled over it after hearing its interpretation. But what did Daniel do?

First, notice that though the dream alarmed Daniel, Daniel did not reject it as a message from God. There is a tendency to think that if a dream is disturbing we should know that it couldn't be from God. Daniel, however, accepted this disquieting night vision as God's message. He may not have understood it yet, but he knew that God had entrusted him with a sobering secret, foretelling ominous times to come. Also, though Daniel was known as having the ability to interpret dreams himself (Daniel 1:17), Daniel wisely sought out a godly interpreter to detail the dream's meaning.

Despite the fact that the interpretation left Daniel pale with alarm, observe Daniel's discretion. Though the message was catastrophic in its implications, Daniel kept the matter to himself. He quietly recorded the vision and its interpretation, sealing God's apocalyptic counsel into Scripture.

Indeed, God speaks to His people in dreams throughout the Bible. When I searched for references to dream/s (and night vision/s) in the American Standard Version, I found over a hundred references, many of them relating powerful first-hand accounts of vital communication.

No wonder King David sang out in praise (Psalms 16:7): *"I will bless the Lord who has counseled me; indeed, my mind instructs me in the night."* David knew that the Lord was the source of his counsel and that— even as he slept—he could receive valuable instruction.

Many others, like Paul, relied on God's dream counsel. Check out Acts 16:9–10 and Acts 18:9–10. Paul wasn't just freewheeling. He was submitting himself to the marching orders of the Holy Spirit. Receiving prophetic counsel through dreams couldn't be more biblical.

"Not that I'm comfy with either,
but isn't it easier to accept a waking vision?"

Maybe so. Dreaming is a natural state. All of us dream many dreams, even if we don't remember them. So, we're left to wonder if God sent the dream, or if our subconscious minds, or even the enemy produced it. We'd rather that God would take the mystery out of His mysterious ways. We'd much prefer a jaw-dropping, waking visionary experience—straightforward and literal—something we can't possibly doubt or misinterpret. I hear you.

Interpreting dreams requires faith and discernment. After all, there is a lot of error. But don't you think that God would appreciate it if we truly believed what His Word says about Him speaking to us through dreams? What if we didn't demand more spectacular waking visions in order to recognize that He is speaking to us? Wouldn't you like to be so responsive to the Holy Spirit that it didn't require a wide-awake bolt from the blue for you to discern that a message is from God? Oh, to have that kind of faith, that sweet sensitivity to the flow of God's River!

Five Kinds of Dreams

Clearly, not all dreams are from God. But how do we tell them apart? How do we know which dreams to heed and which ones to disregard or even rebuke? It helps me to evaluate individual dreams if I categorize different types of dreams. In the "not from God" category, there are what I call *Spam Dreams, Navel-Gazing Dreams,* and *Enemy Virus Dreams.* Then, there are two types that come from the Holy Spirit: *Message Dreams* and *Visitation Dreams.*

1.   Spam Dreams

Just the way you sort out spam from personal mail and trash it, recognize these dreams as the random ramblings of your resting mind.

They may be wacky, even entertaining, but don't try to read anything into them. God's dreams have His special stamp on them, individually addressed to you. Listen to the Holy Spirit's voice of discernment and delete any "spam dreams" you receive.

2.   Navel-Gazing Dreams

These are normal expressions of the relaxed subconscious working on personal issues. Performance anxiety dreams fall into this category. You may be able to suppress your fears and conflicts by day, but by night they surface. The mind works on them as you sleep. These dreams may be an expression of your desires. They can help you get in touch with your psychological issues or maybe to clean out a bit of suppressed lint now and then, but they're not messages from God. These are messages you send to yourself, so exercise caution if a dream speaks to the desires of your heart.

3.   Enemy Virus Dreams

Just like Satan, these dreams are meant to steal your confidence, kill your joy, and destroy your relationship with God. These dark dreams are designed to draw you into fearsome bondage and away from our liberating Savior. They glamorize sin. The memory of them entices us to follow through with their suggestions of disobedience in our waking hours. They attack, infect, and accuse. They lie, just like their deceitful sender.

If, while dreaming, you find yourself aware that the enemy is at work, rebuke him in the name of Jesus, and Satan—like the inferior that he is—will have to vacate your mind (Zechariah 3:2, James 4:7). There have been times I've done this within a dream, and I was awakened immediately, released from the grip of Satan's pernicious propaganda.

If you wake up and recognize the enemy's stamp on a dream, do not entertain it. We might be quick to rebuke an enemy dream that's frightening or blasphemous, but watch out for those dreams that give sin a pleasant allure. They are just as diabolical (Micah 2:1). No matter how beautiful or enticing, this type of dream is a virus to your system. Discern its devious sender. Resist him. Stand with your all-powerful Savior and rebuke the devil.

"What about recurring nightmares?"

Remember, as it was with Daniel (Chapter Seven), sometimes God sends disquieting messages to His servants through dreams. For this reason, we shouldn't automatically think a dream is from the enemy if it disturbs us. However, if you prayerfully evaluate a dream (or series of dreams) and discern that they're from the enemy, there are some things you can do:

A. Pray

In your waking hours, submit the matter to prayer. Enlist the help of a prayer partner to agree with you in this (Matthew 18:19).

B. Clean House

Examine your heart as well as your physical dwelling. Ask the Lord to help you identify anything you may have done or may possess to leave yourself open to such an attack. Rid your home of books, games, movies, amulets, decor, and trinkets related to occult practices and false gods (Acts 19:19). Whether these items are of monetary or sentimental value, they have no place in a believer's home (Deuteronomy 7:5). If you have consulted a medium, astrologer, horoscope, or psychic reader, renounce those practices in the name of Jesus (Deuteronomy 18:10–13). Resolve to stop thinking of these practices as innocent fun, and see them for the enemy openings that they are.

Consider the nature of the enemy attack. If you are being plagued by dreams of an ungodly sexual nature, consider any doors you've left open through pornography in your home via printed materials, television, or your computer. It's not that there's anything inherently wrong with watching TV or surfing the Internet. But there are sites, shows, print materials, and movies that provide footholds to the enemy. No matter how harmless they may seem on the outside, they can become open invitations to the enemy to invade your dreams. Continuing to host the suggestions of the enemy is like putting a ladder up to your unlocked bedroom window when burglars are in the neighborhood (John 10:10). Instead, evict the enemy and all his trappings.

C. Pray Some More

Once all the enemy's footholds are out, bind him against re-entry in the name of Jesus (Matthew 16:19). Repent. Ask Jesus to wash you and invite the Holy Spirit to occupy all those places that the enemy had infiltrated. Pray specifically for protection against any further enemy onslaughts through dreams (Matthew 12:43–45).

"This scares me. I don't want to open myself to a world the devil inhabits."

Friends, we're already in that world. This battle with the enemy wages in our lives whether we want to face it or not (Ephesians 6:12). I Peter 5:8 exhorts us to be watchful, because our adversary prowls like a roaring lion, intent to devour us. We are to resist the devil, knowing that we do not stand alone. Evil forces do battle daily. They mock us, like young David was mocked, as we pick up that smooth stone, our cornerstone rock of defense: Jesus. Like Goliath, they taunt that we'll fail, that we're in way over our heads. But when we stand in faith— resisting every force of darkness—that fearsome giant falls, pathetic and powerless, at our feet.

4. Message Dreams from God

Ah, finally. We're getting to the truly good stuff. These prophetic dreams exhort, console, edify, and/or declare things that are to come (I Corinthians 14:3, John 16:13). Sometimes they're literal, interpreting themselves. Sometimes they're symbolic. Sometimes they're a mix. Elements that may seem literal may actually be representative or have dual meaning. Read Genesis 37:1–11 for an example of a symbolic message dream.

Even Joseph's ungodly brothers knew that Joseph's dream wasn't just about sheaves. They were threatened because they recognized that the sheaves represented each one of them, bowing down to their father's favored son. While it's interesting that, in the end, sheaves are harvested as food supply, infusing that symbol with additional significance, what rankled Joseph's brothers was the idea that they would one day submit to the brother they resented. Then, think how they felt when Joseph spoke of a second confirming dream, one in which the sun, moon, and eleven stars were bowing down before Joseph. This time even Jacob rebuked Joseph, recognizing that the sun, moon, and stars represented Joseph's father, mother, and eleven brothers.

Now, we know the end of this story, that Joseph's dreams were not generated out of personal pride or aspirations of dominance. But put yourself in Joseph's sandals when he was just a youth, believing that these unfulfilled night visions had meaning, despite the jealous reactions of his brothers and the rebuke of his father. Remember: all Joseph got was a symbolic picture. There was no voice of explanation, no reassuring heavenly emissary.

Ask yourself: *Am I willing to receive a symbolic message from God and trust Him to show me the meaning?*

"What's it like to get a dream from God today?"

It's still like it was for Joseph or for Paul. When we awaken from a God-sent dream, there is a powerful sense of God's presence, along with a prompting to reflect on the dream. Unlike meaningless dreams that quickly slip away, these dreams vividly burn in our memories as we wake, giving us the chance to consider them. Like Daniel, we should write these dreams down in detail immediately and seek God to reveal His meaning. No matter how odd a symbol might seem, record it and examine it prayerfully, considering the context of the message.

"How do I figure out what the symbols mean?"

You don't. You don't deduce, decode, or apply human logic. Understanding symbols is in no way an intellectual exercise. It is a spiritual gift, a form that interpretation of tongues can take when the Holy Spirit gives a believer the meaning of the unknown language of a symbolic dream.

This is why I don't advocate dream dictionaries. They put us on a deductive track, rather than listening for that still, small voice of God. Like Jeremiah, when God shows us a symbol, we listen for Him to explain it (Jeremiah 1:11–14). Instead of working on it in the flesh, we pray. We open our ears to what the Holy Spirit wants to teach us about how each symbol fits into God's message. As you wait prayerfully, listen for spontaneous answers that arrive in your mind, not reasoned, but delivered.

You may feel led by the Spirit into Scripture for understanding of a symbol God has used in His Word before. Still, listen intently for any accompanying direction, since there are certain biblical words and symbols that have multiple, even opposite meanings. So, even as you search in your Bible, stay open to the Holy Spirit and allow Him to take the lead in refining your search.

Keep in mind that, in the same way that God used symbols pertinent to biblical times with biblical figures, He may also use contemporary symbols, pertinent to today's world, with you. He knows you are not only familiar with things like sheaves, statues, or cattle, you're even more familiar with modern devices that were unknown to people like Joseph or Daniel.

Whether through ancient or modern symbols or through a combination of both, God sovereignly chooses the language of the dreams He sends. Symbolic dreams require us to quiet our human minds and press in for understanding. They draw us to listen for the interpreting voice of His Spirit. Think of the Holy Spirit as your divine Guide, leading you down His path to reveal God's message. Stay close, tracking His steps, listening for His voice of instruction, watching as He points out what He'd like you to see. It may be tempting to run ahead and take the lead, but discipline your mind to follow, every step of the way.

When I was preparing to teach a small group of women about the Holy Spirit, I asked God to anoint me for this service, especially because many of these believers were unschooled about His modern-day flow in the lives of everyday believers. When I went to bed, I welcomed the Lord to speak to me as I slept. Before dawn, God gave me a symbolic night vision:

> *I was on my back in bed. Though I remained physically asleep, I was spiritually awakened by the strong, unmistakable presence of God, like a soft stirring, as if to say, "I'm here and I'm about to do something." Suddenly, a refreshing shower of water started falling directly on me from the ceiling. It was spraying from a*

smoke detector above me, soaking my face, upper torso and sheets. Fascinated, I turned to examine the drops on my right upper arm. The drops were large and luminous. They felt like something between water and fresh oil. I turned to my left and gazed at what was normally a flat, off-white wall on the westernmost side of the room. The wall looked like a deep blue river, actively running to the right. The flat wall was now made of immersed blocks, pumping up and down, in concert with the river's flow. Then, I noticed a number of small harvested bundles of wheat, floating on the surface of the wall/ river, moving with the current. I looked closer at the sheaves. Resting in the center of each bundle, there were—of all things—pistachio nuts.

I awakened, cool and dry, knowing that I had received a message from the Almighty. I recorded the dream and submitted it to prayer. I set aside any tendency to figure it out for myself and asked for the Holy Spirit's counsel about its meaning.

First, it was clearly impressed upon me that I had received the anointing of the Holy Spirit that I had requested to help me teach my small group. I was reminded that the falling action of the water and fresh oil both typify this anointing (Acts 10:44; Leviticus 8:12). That shower from above felt like standing with the fishermen at Engedi, being refreshed by the spray as the river of the Holy Spirit cascades off the cliffs onto the fertile land below (Ezekiel 47:10).

I had to ask God about the smoke detector, especially since it didn't exist on my actual ceiling. It was one of those strange symbols we sometimes write off as bizarre, but I felt the Spirit draw me into the Scriptures for understanding. I was led to read about how the glory of God filled the temple like smoke in Revelation 15:8. I was reminded that smoke detectors are very sensitive to smoke, even smoke we can't yet see. God was going to increase my sensitivity to His powerful presence as His glory rained over my body, the temple of the Holy Spirit.

I wondered: *why was my plain, inanimate western wall suddenly a flowing river?* The Spirit helped me see. In Jerusalem, people stand as close as they can to what Jews call the Western Wall. Built with blocks of stone, it's a remnant of the ancient Jewish Temple. Countless pilgrims of faith approach this wall, stuffing written prayers into the cracks, longing to be heard by the one true God believed to dwell in that holy place.

Do you see the connection?

God was showing me that He had heard my cries as I'd grieved at the wall of human tradition, longing for a fresh outpouring of His presence. He counseled me that as I stayed close to Him, others around me would be transformed by the mighty river of His Spirit (John 7:38–39). Inanimate building blocks that had remained wedged into place for years would become truly living stones (I Peter 2:5). They would begin to move freely, contributing to the growing current of grace, flowing in the right direction.

Next, there were those sheaves bobbing along on the river, symbolizing that, indeed, there would be a harvest yielded from the service into which I'd been called. Suddenly, the Spirit reminded me. God had used sheaves as a symbol before, in Joseph's dream. I enjoyed that common ground for a moment before it hit me to ask:

What about those pistachio nuts?

I was compelled to use my Bible software. It felt a little silly, searching on the word *pistachio*. I had no idea if that word was in the Bible. The ASV mentioned *nuts*, but didn't specify pistachios. Then, surprise! In the original Hebrew and the NASB, I found that one reference to *nuts* translates specifically as *pistachios*. Guess where? They show up many years after the sheaves dream in Joseph's story, after he'd been made ruler over Egypt, in charge of selling stored grain during the dream-foretold famine. This picture was coming together.

In Genesis 43:11, I read how Joseph's father Jacob (Israel), sent *pistachio nuts* with Joseph's brothers as part of a package of gifts. In verse twenty-six, we see that the brothers presented these gifts and bowed down, seeking undeserved grace from Joseph, unwittingly fulfilling the prophetic dream of the bowing sheaves.

The Holy Spirit confirmed to me that the pistachios on the sheaves in my dream meant that the Father would send grace gifts to accompany the harvest that would come to my small group. Each woman who submitted herself to the flow of His River would be equipped with gifts for service. Indeed, that is exactly what happened.

"How do I know if the dream is prophetic if it discloses something I want?"

It really can be hard to tell the difference between a dream that is a subconscious expression of our personal hopes and a dream in which God lets us know He will give us that desire of our hearts. If you receive such a dream and you're not sure, just record it and trust that if it is a message from God, it will come to pass. As you wait, pray about it. Look for confirmation and check the dream's consistency with the message of Scripture.

God has ministered to my friend, Jessie, many times through night visions, some symbolic and some quite literal. She was given symbolic dreams disclosing that the apartment in which she lived would become unsafe. Still, the last thing she wanted to do was move, especially because the dreams, while foreboding, were not specific as to the type of danger or the timing.

Soon, a heavy rainy season came, soaking in through exterior walls. Suddenly, Jessie was forced to vacate her apartment when toxic mold was discovered growing in the drywall and carpet. Tests showed that toxic mold spores were at dangerous levels in the air, penetrating all her wood, paper, books, fabric and mattresses. She lost almost everything she owned.

Though her insurers wouldn't cover mold-related losses, Jessie hung onto the promise of Joel 2:25 and trusted that God would restore everything. Checks and gifts started to arrive. Jessie held it in her heart when she received the following dream:

> *A co-worker approaches Jessie and gives her a large envelope. There is a substantial check inside, totaling the exact amount she had already received. Behind the check is a stack of twenty-dollar bills. There are also cards from others that include additional monetary gifts. Jessie senses that this envelope contains more than what she'd lost on the insurance claim, and that God is using His people to help restore all her losses.*

When Jessie woke up, she recorded and dated her dream, then told me about it. The dream was specific and literal. It didn't require interpretation, only the faith to believe that God would fulfill it. The things in the dream that had already transpired encouraged her to look forward to the things that hadn't, as well as the full restoration yet to be.

Two days passed. Jessie was at work when a co-worker, who knew nothing of the dream, handed her a thick envelope. Can you imagine how stunned she was to find that the envelope contained two hundred dollars in twenties? Not only did she experience the blessing of her colleague's generosity, she also received confirmation (via the twenties) that her dream had been prophetic, that God would restore all that the toxic mold had taken. By year's end, not only was there full restoration, there was also substantial career growth, qualifying Jessie for a pension and health insurance. What started with disaster turned out to be her most lucrative year to date.

Whether literal or symbolic, when God sends a message through a night vision, it is with holy purpose. It may be a call to intercede. It may be imbedded with counsel (Psalm 16:7). It may be the Holy Spirit's way of manifesting Himself to you as your Comforter, Helper, or Teacher.

Think of it this way: if you had a much missed loved one overseas and that loved one had the capacity and desire to send you a video message, wouldn't you want your loved one to send it? Wouldn't you watch for its delivery? Wouldn't you excitedly open and play the message, probably repeatedly, to appreciate every nuance of what your beloved wanted to communicate? Can you imagine knowingly leaving the message unopened on your stoop, where it could deteriorate or be stolen away? Of course, not.

How much more should we earnestly desire to hear messages from God through dreams? Sure, we'll weed out and discard the spam that comes in dreams. We'll deal with our personal mail. We'll discern enemy hoaxes. But we'll treasure the visions God gives us by night, as He ministers to us, His beloved, even as we sleep (Psalm 127:2).

5. Visitation Dreams from God

This category of dreams is distinct in that the message from God is personally delivered. We see or hear directly from the messenger.

In visitation dreams, we are actually visited by the Lord Himself or an angel who has been divinely appointed by Him to appear to us (Psalm 17:3).

Think how high the stakes were for Joseph after Jesus was born. Herod was a deadly threat to the newborn Savior, and Joseph could not afford to make a mistake. So, an angel of the Lord was sent to Joseph in a dream (Matthew 2:13). Notice that the angel not only told Joseph where to take the family to escape Herod's slaughter, the angel also said that Joseph should stay there until Joseph heard from that angel again. Joseph was obedient to the message of the Lord. He kept the family in Egypt until the angel appeared again, after Herod's death, with instructions to take the Child and His mother into the land of Israel.

"Do people still get visitation dreams today?"

These dreams are not commonplace. That's one reason they're so striking when we receive them. But yes, just as it was with Joseph, our all-powerful God may choose to visit us in a night vision today. Why do I think so? Two reasons: First, God doesn't change—yesterday, today, or forever. His character and modes of communication stand unaltered throughout Scripture. The Lord directly instructed Joseph and Paul in visitation dreams *yesterday*. He visits us in night visions *today*, and He will continue to reveal Himself to His people *forever*.

Though that first reason is foremost, another reason I believe God still visits us in dreams today is because He has visited me. I find plenty of biblical precedent for this, lots of scriptural support that this prophetic work of the Holy Spirit is meant to continue, and no indication whatsoever that this outpouring was to cease (except as wrongly quenched by men) until we are face to face, at home with Him forever in eternity.

Can you imagine the thrill of seeing Jesus face to face?

Though I saw Jesus at a distance when I dreamed of His second coming, I didn't get a close look at His face, a face I had longed to see. Then, one night, suddenly He was there, in a night vision. The dream was short and sweet. I recognized Jesus immediately as He stood, wearing white, in the center of a room. The walls, ceiling, and floor were blood red. Jesus was greeting people as they made their way beyond Him to the back right corner door. I stepped up close and looked into His compassionate eyes. He smiled softly at me. I knew immediately that the others were going through that door into eternity and that it was not yet my time.

"Why should I believe you when you say you've been visited in a dream?"

Though I know before the Lord that I am telling the truth, it's not really important to me that you believe me. I'm more concerned that you apply what the Bible says to your working belief system today. If you believe the Bible, you believe that the Lord Himself instructed Ananias in a vision. If you believe the Bible, you believe that the Lord sent an angel to visit Joseph in multiple dreams. If you believe the Bible, you believe Joel's prophecy, reiterated by Peter, about God pouring out His Holy Spirit in the last days, manifesting Himself to His servants in dreams and visions.

I believe the Bible, not *because* I've seen miracles or been visited in dreams. It's just that those manifestations followed after I believed. Yes, this happened in the modern age, to an everyday servant-girl like me. I'm no superstar of the faith. I'm just a flawed, forgiven, follower of Jesus. I've done nothing to deserve the grace I've received. I haven't earned so much as a glance from God and yet, quite unexpectedly, He has come to me in night visions that are so tender and sacred that I can scarcely find words to describe them. Isn't that just like God, though, to be wonderful beyond human expression? Suffice it to say that His presence is unforgettable.

Balance about Dreams

Keep in mind that we dream many dreams every night, the majority of which we don't even remember. Balance is important. Chasing after the leads of Spam Dreams is a waste of time. Putting too much stock in Navel-Gazing Dreams wrongly enthrones the self as an authority for living. Attacks by Enemy Virus Dreams should be curtailed through prayer.

As we sort out our dreams, let's do so with the understanding that most of our dreams probably are not Messages from God. Those who seek the Lord for this prophetic gift should keep a few basic parameters in mind when sifting the wheat from the tares. Remember:

- *Not all dreams are Spam.*
- *Not all dreams are Navel-Gazing.*
- *Not all disturbing dreams are Enemy Viruses.*
- *Not all pleasant and inviting dreams are from God.*

In light of this, let's always be sure to pray for discernment to know the difference.

"What can I do as I seek to hear from God through prophetic dreams?"

Though all the gifts of the Holy Spirit are unearned, there are things you can do to prepare yourself to hear from God in this way. As you follow I Corinthians 14:1, you are on firm ground to earnestly seek any form of the gift of prophecy, including prophetic dreams. Just as Paul encouraged Timothy in I Timothy 4:15, give yourself wholly to seeking your spiritual gifts. Anything less wouldn't be considered *earnestly seeking*, would it?

Earnest seekers don't just ask once, and then give up. No, they are everyday believers who persist in prayer. They ask and keep on asking. They allow Jesus full access, to keep their spiritual houses clean. They pore over the Scriptures, not out of obligation, but out of the holy hunger that comes from wanting to know the God who still speaks to us. That understood, the following disciplines can be helpful as we seek to hear from God through dreams:

BEFORE YOU GO TO SLEEP:

1. Be set to record what you receive.

Unrecorded dreams can be fleeting. Have what you need to record your dreams ready. That might mean putting a journal or tape recorder in your bathroom or on your nightstand.

2. Pray when you go to bed.

Invite God to speak to you through dreams (Jeremiah 33:3). Lamentations 2:19 directs us to pour out our hearts to the Lord at the beginning of the night watches. So, pray that the Lord will give you eyes to see and ears to hear anything He would show you during the night. Bind the enemy from interference and loose the Holy Spirit to anoint you afresh (Matthew 16:19).

WHEN YOU WAKE:

1. Be still.

Before you get up, lie quietly and reflect. See if you remember a dream you had that seems striking, symbolic, or of spiritual import. Ask the Holy Spirit to confirm if this dream is from God.

2. Record and date the dream.

If the dream seems as if it could be from God, write everything down in detail, no matter how odd a detail might seem (Dan 7:1).

3. Ask God to give you His interpretation.

Resist any fleshy desire to figure it out logically. Instead, incline your ears to the voice of the Holy Spirit, as He spontaneously delivers thoughts into your mind. Follow His lead, step-by-step. If you don't understand something, ask a specific question and then wait for an explanation.

4. Check for consistency with Scripture.

Make sure any counsel you believe you've received through a dream is consistent with God's Word. Reject any messages that conflict with the full authoritative counsel of Scripture.

5. Consult an elder counselor.

If you sense that the dream is important, submit it to someone who has a confirmed prophetic gifting (Daniel 7:16). Even if you believe you know the interpretation, ask your counselor to pray, then tell your counselor the dream. Allow the Holy Spirit to speak any confirming interpretation before you share what you have received.

Seriously consider any interpretation your counselor receives, especially if it conflicts with yours (Proverbs 11:14). Your counselor may help you differentiate the voice of your own spirit from the voice of the Holy Spirit.

6.   Seek independent confirmation.

Ask the Lord to confirm His message, particularly if it involves direction. If you have a significant decision to make, resist the urge to make that move based on one unconfirmed dream message. Wait for independent confirmation before you act.

7.   Follow God's instructions.

Obey the confirmed direction you receive in the Spirit, even if it's not what you want to hear or do. At the same time, be sensitive to the Spirit about when to hold the message of a God-given dream in your heart (Luke 2:19).

"Why aren't I hearing from God through dreams?"

While the Spirit distributes gifts to every believer, He distributes them as He wills (I Corinthians 12:11). We need to make peace with His divine wisdom in choosing which gifts to give to which people and when. Receiving prophetic dreams may not be among your gifts. It's also possible that it's a gift God has for you, but you just have yet to receive it. Ask yourself these questions:

- *Have I earnestly asked God to receive this kind of communication?*
- *Has God tried to speak to me in this way, but I haven't had ears to hear?*
- *Have I willfully ignored a message God has tried to get through to me?*
- *Is God is waiting for me to obey previously imparted instruction?*
- *Am I willing to hear from God, no matter what He says?*

Friends, examine your hearts prayerfully about this. Do you really want to hear from God through night visions? Then, be ready to receive and respond. When we listen and obey, the lines of communication stay open. We enter into that pure place where we may actually see God.

"Does the Spirit help believers
to interpret God-given dreams for others?"

Yes. As with all forms of prophecy, this gift is largely purposed to edify others. Just like Daniel, you might be called upon by God to serve as an interpreter, sometimes when the stakes are quite high. It happened to me when the Lord was reaching out to my friend, Diana.

Beautiful, energetic, and keenly intelligent, Diana was a seeker. Raised half Jewish and half Lutheran, she believed in God in general, but though she admired the teachings of Jesus, she struggled to accept Jesus specifically, especially the resurrection and the need to be born again.

Nobody ever loved beautiful clothes or getting them at a bargain more than my friend, Diana. In January of 2007, she was delighted to find a brown cashmere sweater at a sidewalk sale for just a few dollars. In a hurry to get on with her day, she decided that, rather than go through the door and up the stairs of her condo building, she would toss the sweater up to her housekeeper on the second floor balcony. To shorten the throw a bit, she gamely began to scale the wall of the building. Diana didn't remember falling, but when she regained consciousness, rescue workers surrounded her. Having fallen off the building from only a short height, she had broken her foot in four places. Little did she know how profoundly this incident would speak to the next year of her life.

Accepting the immobilizing broken foot as God's way of getting her attention, Diana called me regularly, asking many questions about the Christian faith. She wanted me to be like a sponsor in the Lord to her as she committed herself to diligently seek answers.

Ten months later, despite our regular talks, Diana was still having serious intellectual doubts. I encouraged her to put those doubts onto the table with God and to ask Him to help her to believe.

Soon, Diana shared with me that she'd had an arresting dream, so stunning that she felt that it might have been from God. She didn't know about the power of the Holy Spirit, that God indeed speaks to people through night visions. All she knew is that she could not escape the powerful imagery of the following dream:

Diana saw herself going around an upwardly spiraling, perilous ledge of a very tall, cylindrical building, so tall that the top of it reached up into the clouds. The higher she got, the more frightened she became that she would fall to her death. Everything in her wanted to get up to the top of the building, to safety. The ledge seemed progressively narrower as she climbed. Suddenly, on the ledge ahead of her, she came upon a door. She didn't want to go back, but the door stood between her and forward progress. In fact, she reasoned that the only way to get up to safety at the top would be to take hold of this door and swing out, off the ledge and around to the other side where the ledge continued toward the top. She felt terribly afraid of grasping the knob, of blindly trusting that the door would support her weight and help her proceed to safety, yet somehow she felt encouraged that it would. As she reached out to grasp the knob, large, strong hands secured hers. She awoke, the dream burning on her memory.

Diana called me to ask what the dream could mean. She honestly wondered if it meant that she was going to die.

I prayed for guidance in interpretation, and then related what came to me in the Spirit. I told her that we're all going to die sometime, and that the important thing was not how or when we'd die, but rather to live in a state of readiness. I assured her that God had answered her prayer and was trying to help her to believe through this dream. I shared with her that the dream was a picture of her life, lived on the edge, pushing the limits in her desire to fill the hole that had gnawed at her all her life. I explained that Jesus was the Door, then read John 10:9 to her where He identifies Himself as such. I also read Revelation 3:20, where Jesus stands at the door and knocks, waiting for us to invite Him in to sup with us and we with Him.

I shared with Diana about the real step of faith it is to take hold of Jesus, to let go of the natural footing we've depended on all our lives before Him. I assured her that Jesus was there, knocking, waiting for her to trust Him and open the door of her heart to Him. Even as much as it looked dangerous to take hold of that Door in complete dependence upon His saving grace, it was actually the safest thing she could possibly do. It was the only way to eternal security. When, in waking life, she had tried to climb her building, avoiding safe passage through the door, she had met with disaster. However, if she would just reach out and trust Jesus, He would take her hands and be her salvation.

Early the next Sunday morning, Diana went into a crumpet shop with her Bible. As she sat there, eating a crumpet, she began to pray. She looked at the door of the shop and envisioned that door as the door of her life, a door at which Jesus stood knocking. She repented of her sins. With everything in her, she looked at that door and took Jesus at His word. She asked Jesus to come through that door, into that shop, and into her life to sup with her. As soon as she did this, she felt the amazingly palpable presence of Jesus enter that door, and most importantly, her heart. Like a woman accepting a proposal of marriage, she received Jesus as her Savior and Lord, setting off a whirlwind romance.

In a moment, Diana's doubts disappeared as the Holy Spirit filled her with faith to believe. For the next two months I watched her flourish in His love. She eagerly enthused to anyone who would listen to her about what the Lord had done in her life, that she was sure of her eternal security, that she was ready to meet her Maker. She enjoyed the best Christmas of her life, her first as a believer. Never more at peace, never so full of joy, Diana visited her family with gifts, exuding to them about her newfound love for the Lord.

The day after my dear friend returned from this trip, she fell ill with pneumonia. A week later, Diana suddenly passed from this life, into the arms of the Lord she had so recently trusted for salvation.

You see, for my beloved friend, the stakes couldn't have possibly been higher. And in her eleventh hour redemption lies a sobering reminder of the crucial need for every believer to move in the power of the Holy Spirit. After decades of searching, Diana was one of those who simply had not been able to believe. God knew she needed that prophetic dream to help her. He knew she needed a Spirit-imparted interpretation and a powerful waking visitation of the presence of Jesus. He also knew her days were numbered, that there was no time to waste.

Family of God, know that as we seek God's counsel through dreams, as fascinating as it can be, it is not to be toyed with and not to be taken lightly. Rather, it can literally prove to be a matter of life and death. Eternal security for those we know and love really can rest in the balance. For Diana, the counsel of her dream to trust Jesus, coming when she was drowning in a sea of doubt, proved to be a lifeline for all of eternity.

CHAPTER TWENTY

Hearing Aids for All of God's Sheep

Fresh out of college, I took my first full-time job at a Health Club. I had no career aspirations other than to work hard at whatever job God provided. One day, while in my home shower of all places, I suddenly heard a kind male voice from behind me, over my right shoulder. It was so distinct that I turned and looked to see if anyone was there. I saw no one, but I had recognized the Lord's voice immediately. He had simply said, "You're going to make movies for Me." Like Sarah, eavesdropping as God spoke to Abraham about their coming son, I laughed.

You must understand. I was just a regular, low-profile person. I'd never had so much as a thought about a career in television or film. I hadn't even seen that much of either. It would be years before I would discover Isaiah's prophecy that tracked so closely with this experience:

> *"And your ears will hear a word behind you saying, 'This is the way, walk in it,' whenever you turn to the right or to the left."*
> *Isaiah 30:21*

Though amused at first, I knew God had spoken, sovereignly directing my career path. On my own, I was grossly unqualified. In fact, I hadn't even been interested. But from the moment I heard His voice, I followed, convinced He would make what seemed impossible happen. His words rang in my ears through training, trials, temptations, and rejection, encouraging me onward until the first fruits of fulfillment came years later.

Jesus said that His sheep know His voice, that they won't follow a stranger's voice, but that they will follow His voice (John 10:4–5, 27). He spoke of His sheep collectively. It wasn't just leader sheep who would recognize His voice, but all His sheep, even everyday sheep like me. Ask yourself: *Do I really know the voice of Jesus? Would I follow Him by voice alone?*

"Does God really still direct us specifically?"

Years ago, when we moved cross-country, I had sensed that we should look for a place to live in a particular neighborhood, but in checking over rental listings, it seemed prohibitively expensive. Days before we were to begin what seemed an impossible apartment search, I received a call from one of my prayer partners. Allie told me she'd been praying about our move, that we'd be led to the right place at the right price, and then she said, *"…and I really feel that you're going to end up on 4th Street, near Montana, where the steps go down to the beach."* Had I not known that Allie has ears to hear God's prophetic voice, I might have brushed this off, but because this specific intersection came to Allie in prayer, I held it in my heart.

Within a few days, we were tromping around a few square miles of housing, following rental leads and finding nothing workable within our budget. En route to a new lead, we randomly stopped at the previous corner to call about a rental sign we saw.

Just then, I noticed a nice sedan go through the adjacent traffic light, then U-turn back and pull up to the curb beside us. An older man got out and said, "This might sound crazy, but I just said as we were driving by, *'That young couple looks like they need an apartment. Do you need an apartment?'"* When I answered that we did, he pointed across the intersection to an apartment building nearby. As I followed his eye-line, I saw the crossed street signs and it suddenly dawned on me where we were, right at 4th and Montana! The man said he owned that building, and he had a two bedroom with a two-car garage available if we were interested. The apartment was everything we needed, for well under half what we'd budgeted, right there at a prophetically revealed address. Can anybody say *God is amazing?*

"I want to hear God's voice. But how?"

It's not like I get that kind of specific direction all the time. The two prophetic messages I've just cited came more than twenty years apart. But after hearing the first one, I realized that God does, indeed, speak to us in this way. Having had a taste of what that's like made me hungry for more. That hunger grew into earnest desire, which is exactly how the Bible says we should seek prophecy (I Corinthians 14:1). *Earnest* means more than just being open, reading a book on the subject, or asking a time or two. *Earnest* means *to hotly pursue*. That kind of desire isn't just a fleeting fancy. It's a lifestyle, a deep craving we satisfy by consistently pressing into Him.

Years ago, I began to follow Scripture by earnestly seeking His voice—not for the sake of the gift itself—but the natural by-product of my love for Him was that I persisted in telling Him how much I longed for His presence, how much I wanted to hear His voice. *(I still do!)*

"Yeah, but exactly how does this work?"

There are two equally biblical ways for us to hear God's voice: *audibly* (as in John 12:28) or through *the inner, still small voice of the Holy Spirit* (I Kings 19:12). Let's consider the prophet Samuel's first encounter of the aural kind, which is chock full of applications for us today. Remember, Samuel was just a boy, at a time when words from the Lord were as rare as they may seem to you now. Pray and ask the Holy Spirit to speak to you as you read I Samuel Chapter Three.

Finished? Now, ask yourself each of the following questions. Make note of any verse that shows you the answer, and jot down any answers that come to you in the Spirit:

- *What was young Samuel doing prior to hearing God's voice?*
- *Where was Samuel when God first spoke?*
- *What was Samuel's posture each time the Lord spoke?*
- *Why was word from the Lord rare in those days?*
- *Why didn't Samuel recognize God's voice?*
- *How did Eli instruct Samuel to answer the Lord?*
- *Why was Samuel afraid to tell Eli what God said?*

Now, as you apply what you've learned from Samuel's experience, ask yourself:

- *Do I spend time, ministering to God? (I Samuel 3:1)*
- *Do I go to a quiet place to listen for God's voice? (Acts 10:9)*
- *Am I fully at rest before Him? (I Samuel 3:3)*
- *Has hearing His voice been rare because of sin? (I John 1:6–10)*
- *What should I do to invite God to speak to me? (I Samuel 3:9–10)*
- *What responsibilities go with hearing from God? (Ezekiel 2:7, 3:17–21)*

Yes, even though God can speak to us anytime and under any conditions, there's a lot we can learn from the prophets, like Samuel, who grew to converse with God regularly. No doubt, hearing God's audible voice commands attention, but it seems that more often He speaks in gentler ways. Though Elijah might have expected the Lord to be in the dramatic wind, earthquake, or fire (I Kings 19:9–12), the Lord came to meet with Elijah after those noisy elements had passed, speaking with His still, small voice—a voice all God's sheep should learn to recognize.

Add Habakkuk's experience to Samuel's, noticing the elements that are in common.

> *"I will stand on my guard post, and station myself on the rampart, and I will keep watch to see what He will speak to me, and how I may reply when I am reproved."*
>
> Habakkuk 2:1

Like Samuel, who reclined in the temple, and Peter, who found a quiet housetop, Habakkuk resolved to set himself apart from the world and go to a tower (rampart) where he could focus his attention upon God. Habakkuk demonstrated that prayer wasn't just about petitioning God. It was also about watching and listening intently, expecting a response. Habakkuk wasn't perfect. It's clear that he was mindful of falling short, in that he approached the Lord humbly, ready for a reproof. Instead, the Lord spoke these words of instruction:

"...Record the vision, and inscribe it on tablets, that the one who reads it may run."

Habakkuk 2:2

Tell the truth. When you tune out the din of the world and go to that quiet place, when you confess your sins, still your heart and minister to the Lord, do you *really* expect a reply? And, if the Lord were to speak to you, would you be prepared to write down what He says?

Notice that God gave Habakkuk a reason to write down what He showed him. God wanted to equip those who read the prophetic message to run with it, to respond to what they heard. Further, God wanted His words recorded because He was showing Habakkuk things that were yet to come. The inscribed message served as a record, so when that prophecy was fulfilled, others would be persuaded that God had indeed spoken.

"Should I write down what God speaks to me?"

Whenever you can, I'd recommend it. A dated log can help you to remember what might otherwise be forgotten. Recording what we hear also helps us judge what we've recorded against the authority of Scripture, to which all such messages should be subordinated. We can show messages to our elders in the Lord. We can weed out error. We can track confirmations and fulfillment. We can begin to distinguish words that truly came from God, from seemingly promising words that returned void because they came from the voice of human desire.

Habakkuk's directive to write prophecy down is far from isolated in Scripture (Isaiah 8:1, 30:8–10; Jeremiah 30:2, 36:4–8, 18; Revelation 1:11). Though the ancients used tablets and scrolls, you can use whatever works for you. You can write on a legal pad, in a journal, or type directly into your computer. I have a friend who uses a voice recording device, then transcribes later.

Know that you can test what you've written down, and then learn from your mistakes. You can also reflect on those wonderful moments when you've truly heard from God.

"How do I tell His voice from other voices?"

If you're in good mental health, when you're alone and hear an inner or audible voice, there are three possible sources: 1) it's the enemy; 2) it's your human spirit; or 3) it's the Spirit of God.

1. The Voice of the Enemy

Satan is the accuser of the brethren (Revelation 12:10). John 8:44 calls him a murderer and a liar, who speaks from his own nature. If the voice accuses, kills your spirit, or lies, that's the enemy, not God. Satan will tell you you're crazy to think you could hear from God. He'll tear you down, saying that God doesn't care about you. Satan has even been known to use Scripture out of context (Luke 4:1–13). If the voice you hear tempts, demeans, or discourages you from pursuing God, that's not the Holy Spirit. Rebuke that devourer in the name of Jesus.

2. The Voice of the Human Spirit

When we think we hear things concerning ourselves, we're most likely to mistake our own inner voices for God's. This happens most often when an inner voice seems to speak to our own heart's deepest desires for healing, provision, and especially human love.

If we hear a voice, promising something that we want or think we need, we should immediately flag it, and then seek independent confirmation and/or judgment, knowing that it could just be our own desires talking. It's not that God doesn't ever speak to us about what we desire, as He spoke to Abraham about his desire for a son. We should just be all the more vigilant to avoid error when the voice says something we'd like to hear.

The same principle applies when hearing God for others. Let's not allow our sympathies to direct us. No matter how much it seems like it would be good if God were to say it, we shouldn't put words in His mouth, telling others what we know they long to hear. Let's take the cautions of Jeremiah 23:16 into account.

Listening to the voice of human imagination is a heavily trodden path to futility. This includes amplifying something that God actually said in keeping with our longings, like attaching a particular person God hasn't promised onto a nonspecific prophecy about a spouse to come. God may speak to our desires; however, we should carefully delineate what God actually said as opposed to fusing God's message with a human heart's cry.

Here's a quick exercise: Right now, pause and think about the things you deeply want. Jot them down before you proceed. Label that list: My Heart's Desires.

Got it? Let a prayer partner know that you want to be particularly watchful about keeping these specific longings in perspective. Not only can each item on your list become an idol before God, it can also become the predominant voice of your human spirit.

Pray down your list. Ask God to help you distinguish your voice from the Holy Spirit's, especially concerning every yearning you've cited. Each time you believe you hear a voice speaking to anything on your "desires" list, consider the distinct possibility that you may have heard the voice of your own spirit.

It's okay to keep praying about your desires, but as you do, set your affections upon your loving Father, trusting that He understands what you truly need. Whereas our own expressed desires can easily disappoint, God's word never returns void. Earnest desire to hear God's voice means that we must consistently quiet our own desires, making Him our every consolation, our every ambition, the genuine and enduring passion of our souls.

3. The Voice of the Holy Spirit

This is that gently powerful voice that brings us into closer communion with God in Christ. This voice exhorts, edifies, consoles, guides, or discloses things to come. This voice is always completely consistent with God's already spoken Word of Scripture, and always speaks the truth, even if that truth is difficult or contrary to our own desires.

God's voice draws us into holiness and enlists us in the work of His kingdom. His voice is not generated in our minds. Rather, He puts words directly into our mouths (Jeremiah 1:9). We don't think up what we suppose He might be saying. Instead, His words bubble up, fresh and unplanned within us. His voice reaches us with complete spontaneity, every word a surprise to our ears. When it's God speaking, there is no striving. There's no struggle to choose words. They simply flow, without human composition, like that crystal clear river of His Spirit (Revelation 22:1).

Gratefully, we are not left alone to distinguish between all of these voices. We can consult with our elders, and pray for discernment from the Holy Spirit. We can stand with Jesus to rebuke and banish the enemy. We can humbly admit the error of listening to our own desires. We can use God's already spoken Word of Scripture to examine any voice we hear.

"How do I get ears to hear God's voice?"

Are you getting the idea that there's nothing passive about hotly pursuing prophecy? For something that's best done in stillness of heart, it's a very active process. It's not that we earn this gift through works, but let's consider some things we can do to prepare our ears to hear.

Resist the Flesh

Nothing stops up our ears to the Holy Spirit like the flesh. The flesh builds up like earwax, dulling our hearing to the voice of the Spirit.

Think of the sheer volume of fleshy voices you hear. The flesh may chatter to you via dysfunctional family, gossipy friends, or that disgruntled co-worker at lunch. The flesh prattles on through the Internet, television, radio, music, reading materials, and movies. That's a lot of yakking, competing for your attention.

Consider active things you might do to eject the flesh and make way for the Spirit's voice within you. Sometimes, we need to repent and let Jesus purify our hearts. Many times, we can quiet the voices of this world by simply turning off the television or secular music, tuning out the voices of the flesh, preferring the company of the Holy Spirit.

Praise, Pray, and Listen

Enter His gates with praise. Ask God to speak to you by His Spirit. Bind the enemy in the name of Jesus, and ask the Father to silence your own inner voice so you can hear His. If you have a prayer language, use it. The Holy Spirit may go from interceding for you to speaking to you. Pray with your mind, too. Tell God you want to know Him in deeper ways. Tell Him you're listening, then do. When our prayers are monologues, we don't exactly provide opportunity for a response, do we? So, make listening time a regular part of your dates with God. *Did I say dates?* Yes, dates. Set aside special time to be with the Lover of your soul.

Study the Scriptures

The more time we spend in the Bible, the better we get to know His voice. If we want to be equipped to judge what is spoken, it really helps to have a working knowledge of God's Word (II Timothy 2:15). Studying is more than breezing through a daily quota. When we pore over the Scriptures, asking the Holy Spirit to teach us each time we read the Word, we practice listening for His still, small voice of instruction.

As you read, if you don't understand something or if you suspect there may be more there than you're getting on the surface, linger on that verse or passage. Tell Him you don't understand; ask Him to help you see what you're missing or how it might apply to you.

Listen for His voice of explanation. He may speak to you in that moment, but keep your ears open as you go from the "classroom" into the "lab" of your day. That answer might come hours or even days later, so keep those ears open.

Walk in the Spirit Continually

Practice sensitivity to His abiding presence. No matter where you go or what you do, invite Him along. Think of Him as refilling you with every breath, walking with you every step you take. Invite Him into in every encounter, every conversation. Ask Him to let you know if there is anyone He'd like you to minister to in any way, even if you're shopping for groceries or going to a meeting you dread.

Reach out when He prompts you.

Yield when He subdues you.

Withdraw yourself when you sense that your participation in a particular situation or conversation grieves Him. Acknowledge Him as your very present helper and guide (Psalm 46:1).

"What if God speaks to me about something I want?"

Especially if it involves making a decision, ask God to confirm His word to you and/or submit it to your elders in the Lord for judgment. Even if you must act on short notice, God is capable of providing the confirmation you need.

I have a friend, Brad, whose home was in the path of a huge wildfire. Forecasted northeast wind gusts of up to 60 miles per hour threatened to drive the fire into his neighborhood. Many prayed that God would calm the winds and protect them, none more fervently than Brad, as he was faced with deciding whether to quickly pack up his family and leave or stay.

As Brad stood outside, watching the approaching blaze on the crest of the mountain near his home, he asked God to help him make this high stakes decision. Brad listened, and heard that still, small voice instruct him to stay. Though staying was what Brad naturally wanted to do, God quickly confirmed His answer by giving Brad an internal vision of how He was protecting him. As Brad looked toward the fire, he saw a very large angel standing at the end of his driveway, blowing the fire away from them. Soon, the news verified a sudden, unpredicted shift in the winds, pushing the fire into the opposite direction, away from their home.

So, yes, God does sometimes intervene about things we want, like Brad wanted protection. But as we seek to hear God's voice, remember this: though there is biblical precedent for God speaking to us about personal matters, when the Bible exhorts us to earnestly seek prophecy in I Corinthians 14:3, we are especially encouraged to seek prophecy that will edify, exhort, and console *others* within the body. Even though we should remain open to anything the Holy Spirit would speak to us individually, our greater enthusiasm should be directed at wanting to serve through this gift, actively listening for others more than for ourselves.

"What if God repeats Himself?"

God called out to Samuel four times in I Samuel 3. Sometimes He repeats Himself to get our attention, often as way of convincing us that it really is His voice. He may repeat Himself for emphasis, or to alert us to an urgent matter requiring our response (Genesis 41:32).

My friend, Sandy, was sitting on the beach, having her quiet time while her daughter, Holly, was out surfing. When Sandy started reading her Bible, she heard the Lord say, "*Watch the water.*" She looked at the ocean briefly, then went back to reading. Again, the Lord said, "*Watch the water.*" Sandy gazed at the Atlantic again, wondering why God would interrupt her time with Him, and then resumed her reading. A third time, the Lord said, "*Watch the water.*"

Sandy knew that if God spoke to her three times, she'd better pay attention. Sandy closed her Bible, stood, and watched the sea. To her shock, a large shark's fin rose almost completely out of the water, directly behind Holly, confirming the need for the alert.

Sandy calmly shouted to Holly to come in immediately, all the while asking, "*What now, Lord?*" He replied clearly, "*By the time she gets in [to the shore], he [the shark] will have moved off.*" God went on to explain that Holly had gotten in the way while the shark was eating, but that it would be safe for her to go back to surfing right away.

Now, I don't know how many mothers would have the faith to send a beloved daughter back into waters a shark had just vacated, but once Holly reached the shore, Sandy explained and assured her daughter that she could go back to surfing. Though Holly has a healthy respect for the dangers sharks pose, she trusted the confirmed word God had spoken to her mother and returned to the breakers.

When Sandy sat down, fighting that mental image a mother never wants to see regarding her child, the Lord spoke once again, underscoring the point of this high stakes object lesson. He distinctly said, "*I just wanted you to see that I can be trusted with those who have been entrusted to me.*" This settled what had been a growing concern in Sandy's heart, persuading her that though she could never expect to adequately protect her daughter as she ventured out into the world, her Father God would do so.

"I'm so hungry to hear from God. Why isn't He speaking?"

Since we live by every word that proceeds from God's mouth, it stands to reason that we can become starved of hearing His prophetic voice. You might wonder why God isn't feeding you in this way. Consider these possibilities as you diagnose the cause of your spiritual hunger:

The Holy Spirit Has Been Grieved

From the moment Adam and Eve satisfied themselves with that forbidden fruit, sin separated us from our holy God. As the flesh displaces the Holy Spirit in our lives, we distance ourselves from the prophetic sustenance we crave.

In Ephesians 4:30, we're admonished not to grieve the Holy Spirit. Grief follows when someone has been bereaved. When we sin, we bereave God of our fellowship, thereby grieving the Holy Spirit.

When sin and rebellion abounded with Israel, God's bereaved response was to show Amos a delicious basket of summer fruit (Amos 8:1), and then He foretold a sin-induced period of withdrawal of His nourishing words:

> *"Behold days are coming," declares the Lord God, "when I will send a famine on the land, not a famine for bread or a thirst for water, but rather for hearing the words of the Lord. And people will stagger from sea to sea, and from the north even to the east; they will go to and fro to seek the word of the Lord, but they will not find it."*
>
> *Amos 8:11–12*

Micah prophesied against false prophets who were leading God's people astray, saying that their seers would be ashamed and embarrassed when God withheld answers. But, while many suffered the pangs of spiritual hunger, Micah was filled with the Spirit's power, enabling him to pinpoint sin that kept the religious from hearing God's voice (Micah 3:7–8).

If you're hungry for God to speak to you, and yet you're not hearing anything, you might ask yourself if some sort of rebellion is blocking access to His table. Examine your heart. Even if others are sinning around you, just like Amos and Micah, you can still feast on the Lord's voice, even in the presence of your enemies, if you are walking in repentant obedience to the Shepherd of your soul (Psalm 23:5).

Still famished to hear from God? If you aren't aware of any active sin, ask yourself if you've obeyed what God has already spoken to you, first through the Bible and, in subjection to that, through past prophetic instruction. God may be waiting to serve up the next course until you've faithfully ingested what He's already put on your plate.

When supply is available, hunger and thirst are very good things. They remind us that we need to eat and drink. If we never felt these God-given sensations, we might neglect what is necessary to our physical survival. Nourishment is no less necessary in the Holy Spirit. In fact, God may be using the very hunger and thirst you feel to draw you into repentance and closer to His table. He welcomes the repentant to feast on the abundant sustenance available in the River of His delights (Psalm 36:8).

The Holy Spirit Has Been Quenched

Quenching the Spirit is all about usurping His control, something we are all very prone to do (I Thessalonians 5:19–20). If you have control issues, be especially watchful or you could find yourself on a self-restricted diet, nibbling on crumbs when you could be sated with the main course of God's prophetic counsel.

Some say that they stay healthy by just munching on the tasty fruits of the Spirit. After all, fruits like love are stressed above prophecy. But here's the thing: We don't get to cherry-pick the aspects of the Holy Spirit we find easiest to accept. The Holy Spirit flows with the full complement of fruits and gifts, distributed as He wills. We either let the whole River flow through us, or we don't.

When we quench His prophetic voice, we're tacitly building a dam that can restrict the flow of the fruits, since they all run in that same River. For a while, we might not notice how malnourished we are. We become like spiritual anorexics. We look in the mirror and don't see how we're wasting away as we purge what little we ingest. We exercise like crazy in the natural, trying to maintain an appearance of fitness; however, in our spirits, we are slowly starving.

It's not just the shepherds who starve the flock by corporate quenching. As ordinary believers privately live out the day to day of our lives, we all tend to push the plate away from ourselves, quenching the Holy Spirit in more passive ways. (I know I do.) Ask yourself:

- *When I pray, do I allow time for the Holy Spirit to respond or do I quickly detail my order then rush off, abandoning the meal before it's even served?*

- *Am I trying to feed my flesh, or is my appetite truly for God?*

- *Do I see God as a waiter who is obligated to serve me instead of desiring His prophetic words as a means of serving Him?*

- *Are my queries all about me and rarely about seeking sustenance for others?*

- *Am I trying to coax God into telling me what's on future courses instead of trusting that He'll distribute prophetic nourishment as He wills?*

- *Am I trying to manipulate the Lord into serving up things that aren't good for me?*

- *Am I turning my nose up at the manna He has already put before me through godly counselors?*

The Meal is Still in Preparation

As much as I may think it's all about the growl of my empty stomach, it's important to realize that God is managing comprehensive provisions for all of creation. Sometimes that means waiting for God's prophetic counsel as Daniel once did. In Daniel 10, we read how Daniel amplified his hunger to hear from God by adding physical fasting. Like Job, Daniel valued the words from God's mouth even more than his necessary food (Job 23:12). Daniel wasn't experiencing a sin-induced famine from God's prophetic counsel. Rather, as he waited on God for three weeks, he voluntarily denied his desire for tasty food and drink, refusing to be satisfied by anything but God's words. That's how desperately Daniel hungered for God's counsel.

Just because it took twenty-one days to receive a response doesn't mean God was ignoring Daniel. Daniel was assured that God saw

Daniel's humility and came in response to prayers that Daniel had prayed from the very first day! Not only did Daniel receive an explanation, that God had been occupied on other fronts, but he was also given understanding regarding the vision he had seen, that it pertained to the future. It was something God knew could wait as He took care of a more present crisis. Further, Daniel's hunger-magnified weakness was immediately strengthened as soon as he received the Lord's nourishing prophetic counsel.

My friend, Cheryl McKay, had been waiting a long time for her prophesied husband. (You can read her compelling story in her book, *Finally the Bride*.) Some time ago, God gave Cheryl a dream in which a pie was baking. The accompanying counsel was that her husband-to-be was like that pie, on the way, but not yet ready. As much as she felt ready to be married, God showed her that her husband was still in the fires of preparation. The Holy Spirit asked her if she wanted this man before he was ready or if she'd be willing to trust Him and wait for His timing. As much as Cheryl looked forward to when that pie would be ready to come out, she opted to give God time to prepare her husband as He knew best. Years passed before God fulfilled this prophetic word, but remembering it helped to sustain Cheryl as she waited.

Maybe you're holding onto a prophetic word. Maybe you haven't grieved or quenched the Holy Spirit. Maybe it's just about waiting for God's sovereign timing. Perhaps you'll think of that pie and how much more delicious it will be when baked to golden brown perfection.

"I'm confused. I obeyed God's voice, but it didn't turn out how I expected."

After his wife's parked car was hit, Jeremy felt that God was prompting him to forgive the damages and not ask for repayment. Though new to hearing God's voice in this way, Jeremy obeyed, telling the man that he'd been forgiven of much in his life and that God had told him to forgive this debt. Surprisingly, the man refused to accept and insisted upon paying for repairs.

Soon, Jeremy heard new instructions from God: that he was to offer to clean another family's house. Again, Jeremy made the offer. Again, Jeremy was refused. So what could this have been all about?

Isaiah 55:11 assures us that God's word doesn't return void, that it will accomplish whatever God desires and prosper in what He intends. So, if God truly did speak to Jeremy, surely His voice was sent to serve some divine purpose. It's also conceivable that, in God's economy, His word was intended to multitask, serving holy purpose on a variety of levels. Here are some possibilities you might apply in your own life:

Voice Recognition Training

Sometimes, early instances of hearing God's voice can help us begin to recognize that it really is His voice, like Samuel when he first heard from God in his youth (I Samuel 3). Especially as we're learning to differentiate God's voice from the voice of our own natural desires, we should consider whether what we're hearing is something we'd like to hear.

For Jeremy, these instructions were counterintuitive to what a person would want to do in the natural (like someone else's housework), or even have the right to expect (like repairs on a car someone damaged). Further, in both instances, Jeremy was being encouraged to demonstrate scriptural principles of forgiveness and selfless service, which sounds like God.

Obedience Schooling

When it comes to counterintuitive instructions, it's hard to top God telling Abraham to offer his beloved son, Isaac, as a sacrifice (Genesis 22:1–2). It's an extreme case of obedience, but remember that Abraham and God had been conversant for decades. Abraham was sure it was God and set out to obey, trusting the nature of the God he knew.

The degree of difficulty was certainly lower for Jeremy than for Abraham, but both men were ultimately relieved of their assignments after they had moved forward in obedience to God's voice. Neither lost a thing. Jeremy didn't have to bear the financial burden of fixing the car, even though he willingly sacrificed his right to be restored. And, I believe, Jeremy's obedience delighted God's heart much more than any sacrifice could have (I Samuel 15:22). So, sometimes, it can be about teaching us to obey His voice (Exodus 19:5, Jeremiah 7:23).

Let Go of Expectations

Confused about why things didn't go the way you thought they would after you obeyed God's voice? Sit under a shady plant with Jonah for a while (Jonah 4:6). While you're at it, read Jonah's whole story.

Remember that God's word is sent out to fulfill *His* purposes, not ours. When God speaks, our job is to obey, then leave the results up to God, trusting that He will maximize the use of His word for His divine purposes, purposes that may be completely different from what we, in our finite human minds, expect. Just because a person refuses help or forgiveness doesn't mean it shouldn't have been obediently offered. God may be working on that other person in ways you don't even know. So, let's let go of our natural notions, jump in God's car, let Him drive, and trust that He'll choose His desired destinations.

Getting to Know God's Heart

As we hear God's voice, we get to know Him better. We get a sense of the things He feels on a broader scale. Consider when God spoke to Hosea, instructing him to marry a harlot, knowing how devastated Hosea would be when she became unfaithful. This helped Hosea to understand how God feels when His people are unfaithful to Him. In my friend Jeremy's case, God may have allowed a glimpse into His own divine heart, the same heart that lamented to Isaiah saying:

"I have spread out My hands all the day unto a rebellious people, that walk in a way that is not good, after their own thoughts."
Isaiah 65:2 ASV

God has suffered rejection on a scale none of us will ever even approach. When God asked Jeremy to extend grace and that grace was refused, it may have served to acquaint Jeremy with how God feels when we refuse the grace He freely offers us. Further, it might prompt each of us to consider ways we may be refusing God's forgiveness or help ourselves.

As we grow in relationship to God, let's acknowledge that there's a difference between being acquainted with Him and truly knowing Him.

Even when it comes to human relationships, the truth is, we don't begin to really get to know a person until we understand what makes him truly happy and what breaks his heart. So, each time something about what pleases or grieves God hits home for us on a personal level, we get to know Him better. Ironically, as we bond with God in His rejection, we become a source of great joy to Him, and our relationship deepens on both fronts, all through hearing and obeying His voice.

"What does God's voice sound like?"

Ever tried to describe a color to a blind person, or what a sound is like to a person who has never heard? When there's no frame of experiential reference, we are left to search for words that convey the sensation of how hearing God's voice makes us feel.

Elijah heard the sound of a *still, small voice* as God drew near the cave where he was hiding (I Kings 19:12). The disciples heard a *rushing mighty wind* as the Holy Spirit fell upon them at Pentecost (Acts 2:2). The volume and force varied, but both instances are consistent with scriptural references to the Spirit as the breath of God, both gentle and powerful in turns.

In Genesis 1:2, we read that the Spirit of God moved over the face of the waters (Psalm 29:3). Take a moment and picture the impact the breath of God had on the deeps. Whether He comes as a soft breeze or a mighty wind, water responds. Ripples form; the surface moves.

Ezekiel and John compared God's voice to the sound of *many waters* (Ezekiel 43:2, Revelation 1:15). In keeping with Ezekiel's vision of the Holy Spirit as the River of God, there are discernable differences in what could be heard at various sites along the way, from the faint bubbling of the fountain, springing up in the temple, to the steady lapping of the waters of baptism, leading to the crescendo of those same waters, cascading off the cliffs at Engedi. Imagine the sound of that waterfall. Hear the consistent crash of water, pelting the riverbed below. Listen for the softly effervescent resulting spray as it showers the trees along the underlying banks (Ezekiel 47:12).

John adds another descriptor in Revelation 14:2, saying God's voice is like the sound of *thunder*, alluding to the unmistakable authority and grandeur with which God speaks (Job 37:4; II Samuel 22:14).

Now, I don't know about you, but when a human being speaks to me, I don't get the accompanying sensations that these sounds evoke. So, when words come to me like a breeze, when a message bubbles up in me like a fountain, I try to still myself and listen. I wait prayerfully to see if that inner stirring of the waters within me continues—that simultaneous, effervescent flooding of my spirit that helps me to recognize His voice—very much like a cool wind gently blowing, propelling me to move in the Holy Spirit's desired direction.

Sometimes, as in Scripture, the Lord speaks in more dramatic ways. I have a friend who reported hearing God's audible exhortation to stop smoking, which came thundering into her surprised ears. He knew that's what it would take to get her attention, and did He ever! Another friend said she literally heard angelic singing, accompanying the announcement that God was bringing her husband to her, a prophecy that was soon beautifully fulfilled.

So, as we listen for God's prophetic voice, let's let go of our natural experiences. He doesn't sound like your grandfather. He doesn't sound like any actor who has ever attempted to impersonate Him. Rather, He has an altogether distinct, discernable voice of His own, a voice that His sheep learn to recognize (John 10:4).

"How can I invite God to speak to me?"

Maybe you've never asked to hear God's voice. Maybe you've been afraid of what He'd say. Maybe you've asked, but your desire hasn't been exactly earnest. Take heart. Today, you can begin to follow Scripture by asking God to speak to you. If you don't think you'd recognize His voice, ask Him to help you. Invite the Holy Spirit to give you voice lessons. Put aside your fears and controls, push away the doctrines of man, and ask the Almighty to speak to you—not to hear God's voice as a sign, but as the natural result of your love for Him.

You may have always thought of these things as happening to super-heroes of the faith, like Elijah. But in James 5:17, we're reminded that Elijah was a man, an everyday person, just as we all are until we receive the amazing power God wants to give us.

Do you really want to hear God's voice? Readiness can be a factor. Consider Isaiah's readiness when the Lord asked who would be willing

259

to carry His prophetic message to the people (Isaiah 6:8). Isaiah didn't hesitate. With a servant's heart we'd all do well to emulate, Isaiah simply answered, *"Here am I, send me."*

If you're ready to stand with Isaiah, whoever you are, great or small within the body of Christ, I invite you to pray with me. Maybe you're not ready for this kind of commitment, but if you are, sincerely speak these words aloud:

> *Loving Father,*
>
> *With all my heart, I long for Your wonderful presence. I want to see whatever You choose to show me. I want to hear every message You send to me. No subject is taboo. No task is off-limits. No matter how painful the correction, I want to hear it. I give You full access to every aspect of my life.*
>
> *I sit at Your feet gratefully, redeemed by the blood of Your precious Son, Jesus, and I bind any enemy influence in His name. Fill me to overflowing with the power of Your Holy Spirit. Anoint me in a fresh way, even in this moment as I pray.*
>
> *Open my eyes to see what You would show me, Lord. Open my ears to hear every word You would speak. Waking or sleeping, I welcome You to visit me with visions. I invite Your prophetic counsel, whatever You would say, by day or by night. I make myself wholly available to hear and serve You in every way You see fit. I submit myself completely to Your divine guidance.*
>
> *Speak, Lord. Your servant is listening.*

Afterword

"But to each one is given the manifestation of the Spirit for the common good. For to one is given the word of wisdom through the Spirit, and to another the word of knowledge according to the same Spirit; to another faith by the same Spirit, to another gifts of healing by the one Spirit; and to another the effecting of miracles, and to another prophecy, and to another distinguishing of spirits, to another various kinds of tongues, and to another the interpretation of tongues."

I Corinthians 12:7–10

In the Holy Spirit, it's like Christmas afternoon, Family of God. Esteemed leaders and humble followers, elders and youth, sons and daughters alike—we've all come to celebrate. We've savored time spent with our triune heavenly Host. We've eagerly opened up a wide array of power gifts and examined them with interest, and now it's time to go home—back to the routine of everyday living. Our Father has informed us that there's a power gift for everyone who passes through His Door, to be given to each individual as the Spirit wills. But as He rises to distribute these gifts to His children, questions still hang in the air:

- *Do we really want to receive?*
- *Do we really want to serve in power?*
- *Will we choose to slip out empty-handed?*

Never forget, Believer. Those fish out there—they're not for our consumption. Every fish that goes uncaptured represents a living, breathing soul, a soul desperately in need of being caught up in God's redeeming love. Despite our fears, despite the sacrifices that we must make to live out this empowered way of fishing, it is our spiritual service of worship. If we can't find the courage to use these power gifts for our own sakes, okay. Let's do it for them. The reality is that humanity is drowning in a desperately dead sea. The manifestations of the Holy Spirit provide us with a lifeline, powerfully equipping us to rescue the perishing.

Friends, hear the invitation of God to every believer: set aside the limitations of everyday life and step into the amazing calling that awaits you. The Spirit and the Bride really do say, *"Come!"* Drink freely of the kingdom's crystal clear, life-giving River, flowing straight from the throne of God and of the Lamb. Gratefully accept whatever gift He offers, and then use it to serve Him in power.

> *"Now unto Him who is able to do exceedingly abundantly above all that we ask or think, according to the power that works within us, to Him be glory in the church and in Christ Jesus to all generations forever and ever. Amen."*
>
> *Ephesians 3:20–21*

About the Author

Susan Rohrer is an honor graduate of James Madison University where she studied Art and Communications, and thereafter married in her native state of Virginia. A professional writer, producer, and director specializing in redemptive entertainment, Rohrer's credits in one or more of these capacities include: an adaptation of *God's Trombones;* 100 episodes of drama series *Another Life;* Humanitas Prize finalist & Emmy winner *Never Say Goodbye;* Emmy nominees *Terrible Things My Mother Told Me* and *The Emancipation of Lizzie Stern;* anthology *No Earthly Reason;* NAACP Image Award nominee *Mother's Day;* comedy series *Sweet Valley High;* telefilms *Book of Days* and *Another Pretty Face;* Emmy nominee & Humanitas Prize finalist *If I Die Before I Wake;* as well as Film Advisory Board & Christopher Award winner *About Sarah.* Rohrer is also the author of *IS GOD SAYING HE'S THE ONE?: Hearing from Heaven about That Man in Your Life.*

> *"But whatever things were gain to me, those things I have counted as loss for the sake of Christ. More than that, I count all things to be loss for the surpassing value of knowing Christ Jesus my Lord...that I may know Him, and the power of His resurrection."*
>
> *Philippians 3:7–8a, 10a*

IS GOD SAYING HE'S THE ONE?

Hearing from Heaven about That Man in Your Life

Does God really speak about the choice of a husband?
Will that best guy friend of mine ever see me "that way?"
Is there really such a thing as a match made in heaven?

Maybe you find yourself asking these questions. They might even predominate your thoughts and prayers. You may be wondering if the answers you're hearing really are from heaven and, if so, what to do about it.

If you find yourself single and hopeful about a particular man's potential in your life, then this might be the book for you. If you counsel single women, this book could serve as an effective guide for one-on-one conversation as well as group discussion and study.

Bible-based, candid, and accessible, Rohrer illustrates this book with true-life stories as she explores commonly asked questions about what may be one of the most important decisions in a woman's life.

Made in the USA
Lexington, KY
14 December 2012